Multinational Corporations and Climate Change

How do global firms confront the defining challenge of our era? Drawing from international business, political economy, and environmental policy, Jonas Gamso offers an integrated framework for understanding how multinational corporations manage physical, transition, liability, and reputational climate risks through strategies of adaptation, avoidance, transfer, diversification, and acceptance. Blending rigorous empirical analysis with detailed case studies of Ørsted, ExxonMobil, and Saudi Aramco, among others, he reveals how companies make strategic decisions amid accelerating climate impacts and shifting policy landscapes, while also illuminating the effects of public policy and international relations. The book provides essential insights for scholars of international relations, business, and development, as well as for policymakers and practitioners seeking to align economic competitiveness with global sustainability.

JONAS GAMSO is Associate Professor and Deputy Dean of Knowledge Enterprise in the Thunderbird School of Global Management at Arizona State University. His research has appeared in *International Studies Quarterly*, the *Journal of World Business*, *World Development*, and other journals. His commentary has been featured in *The Conversation*, the *Stanford Social Innovation Review*, and *The World Today*. He also directs the UN Global Compact's SDG Innovation Accelerator at ASU.

Multinational Corporations and Climate Change

Risks, Responsibilities, and Resilience

JONAS GAMSO
Arizona State University

CAMBRIDGE
UNIVERSITY PRESS

CAMBRIDGE
UNIVERSITY PRESS

Shaftesbury Road, Cambridge CB2 8EA, United Kingdom

One Liberty Plaza, 20th Floor, New York, NY 10006, USA

477 Williamstown Road, Port Melbourne, VIC 3207, Australia

314–321, 3rd Floor, Plot 3, Splendor Forum, Jasola District Centre,
New Delhi – 110025, India

Cambridge University Press is part of Cambridge University Press & Assessment,
a department of the University of Cambridge.

We share the University's mission to contribute to society through the pursuit of
education, learning and research at the highest international levels of excellence.

www.cambridge.org
Information on this title: www.cambridge.org/9781009610902

DOI: 10.1017/9781009610919

When citing this work, please include a reference to the DOI 10.1017/9781009610919

First published 2026

Cover image: © sorbetto / DigitalVision Vectors via Getty Images.

A catalogue record for this publication is available from the British Library

Library of Congress Cataloging-in-Publication Data

Names: Gamso, Jonas author
Title: Multinational corporations and climate change : risks, responsibilities, and resilience / Jonas Gamso.
Description: Cambridge ; New York, NY : Cambridge University Press, 2026. | Includes bibliographical references and index.
Identifiers: LCCN 2026013997 (print) | LCCN 2026013998 (ebook) | ISBN 9781009610902 hardback | ISBN 9781009610940 paperback | ISBN 9781009610919 epub
Subjects: LCSH: International business enterprises–Environmental aspects | Climate change mitigation | Social responsibility of business
Classification: LCC HD2755.5 .G361 2026 (print) | LCC HD2755.5 (ebook)
LC record available at https://lccn.loc.gov/2026013997
LC ebook record available at https://lccn.loc.gov/2026013998

ISBN 978-1-009-61090-2 Hardback
ISBN 978-1-009-61094-0 Paperback

Contents

Tables

Figures

Preface

I began thinking seriously about climate risks to multinational corporations (MNCs) in 2022, after unusually severe monsoon rains caused catastrophic flooding in Pakistan. The floods killed more than 1,500 people and affected over 30 million. They destroyed thousands of schools, hundreds of clinics, more than 8,000 miles of roads and railways, and over 400 bridges. Altogether, nearly one-third of the country was submerged, resulting in damages of approximately $40 billion. While media coverage rightly focused on the humanitarian crisis, it occurred to me that storms like this, which have been happening more and more frequently, could prove devastating not only to human health and well-being, but also to companies.

I had been studying political risks to MNCs for several years, and in 2022 I was working on a study about the World Bank's provision of political risk insurance to foreign investors. As I read about Pakistan, I began to consider whether the Bank should expand its insurance offerings to cover natural disasters linked to climate change. I drafted an editorial on this idea, which eventually appeared in the *LSE Business Review*. That could have been the end of it, but I kept thinking about climate risk.

Soon I discovered that other scholars had been exploring this topic as well. A wave of studies showed that MNCs were concerned enough about climate risk to systematically avoid the world's most climate-vulnerable countries. This led me to launch my own study, which focused on whether climate-focused foreign aid might mitigate investors' concerns. This piece was eventually published in *Climate and Development*, but I quickly realized that giving proper attention to the climate-related challenges facing global business would not be possible in one article.

That realization set me on a journey that culminated in this book – an attempt to understand how climate change is reshaping the global business environment and how firms, governments, and the international community are responding. What began as a question about extreme weather events stemming from rising global temperatures soon became a broader inquiry into how climate change is reshaping the conditions under which international business operates. I became concerned not only about the physical threats posed by a warming world, such as floods, storms, and droughts, but also about the ripple effects that these events have on policy and global economic structures. It is now clear that climate change is more than a niche issue for business studies or international relations. It is a cross-cutting challenge that demands new conceptual tools and empirical insights, and that raises urgent questions about how firms and governments interact in an increasingly uncertain global environment.

This book is an effort to map that terrain. It examines how climate change generates both risks and opportunities for MNCs, how firms adapt (or fail to adapt) to changing conditions, and how national and international policy efforts shape the business landscape in climate-vulnerable regions. The chapters that follow weave together statistical analysis, interviews, and case studies to explore key dynamics at play, from investor flight in the face of climate vulnerability, to the uneven distribution of climate finance, to the emergence of new green business models. Throughout, I draw on insights from business administration, political science, and development studies to understand what is happening, why, and what might come next.

I have been fortunate to receive thoughtful feedback on this research from numerous colleagues. I am especially grateful to Senior Commissioning Editor Valerie Appleby at Cambridge University Press, who helped me develop my initial proposal into a book project, as well as Senior Editorial Assistant Carrie Parkinson. My gratitude also goes to two anonymous readers whose comments improved the structure and content of the book tremendously. I also thank colleagues who provided feedback on segments of the manuscript at the American Political Science Association, the International Studies Association, and the Academy of International Business annual conferences, as well as at a faculty research seminar at the Thunderbird School of Global Management. Special thanks to Quan Li and Stephanie J. Rickard, who provided detailed comments as conference discussants, as well as RyuGyung Park, who offered comments via email. I am also grateful to Ivan Dubinin and Sakshi Bhangale for excellent research assistance. This book benefited from a sabbatical granted by my academic department, the Thunderbird School of Global Management at Arizona State University, which allowed me to focus my attention in a way that would not otherwise have been possible.

My collaborators on other initiatives and projects also deserve gratitude for shaping my thinking on international business, global political economy, and sustainable development. They include Josh Ault, Shirley-Ann Behravesh, Lena Booth, Charla Griffy-Brown, Anna Dimitrova, Pedro Gorozpe Aguilar, Robert Grosse, Andrew Inkpen, Kellie Kreiser, Allen Morrison, Michael Moffett, Euvin Naidoo, Roy Nelson, Evgeny Postnikov, Kannan Ramaswamy, Landry Signé, Valerie Sy, Hossain Ahmed Taufiq, Mary Teagarden, and Farhod Yuldashev. I am also grateful to friends and family for their support and belief in this project: John and Maureen Brown, Phyllis Kaye, Kate and Mark Morrissey, Stephen, Matthew, and Mi-Ang Tom, Sasan Behravesh, Erin Chou, Mark Davis, Tim Effler, Lauri Gilfoy, Chris Graver, Nick McMann, Mike Miller, Bris Mueller, Ben Petree, Andrew Rosenberg, Preethika Sainam, Mary Sully de Luque, Joe Wingenfeld, and many more. Special thanks to Marietta Morrissey, Jeff Gamso, and Nicholas Gamso, for their constant support, and to Nutmeg for steady companionship. Finally, my greatest debt is to my wife and partner, Michelle Tom, who provided unwavering support through the entire process – and taught me a thing or two about sustainability along the way.

Before concluding, it is worth briefly reflecting on how the world looked in 2022, when I first began working on this book. At that time, the conventional wisdom in the business and policy communities was that climate change was a serious and growing crisis. The world was not doing enough, momentum was building. Policymakers were prioritizing decarbonization through initiatives like the EU's Green Deal and the US' Inflation Reduction Act. Market enthusiasm was also growing, fueled by the accelerating electric vehicle (EV) revolution and the rapid global expansion of solar and wind energy. After years of delay, developed countries finally met their $100 billion climate finance pledge to poor and middle-income nations, and new investment vehicles were emerging to mobilize private capital for climate resilience and clean energy projects.

Several years later, the picture looks more complicated, offering both reasons for hope and renewed cause for concern. On the positive side, electric vehicules (EVs) and EV infrastructure have become far more ubiquitous. China's BYD company has surged in global EV sales, expanding rapidly across Asian, European, and Latin American markets. Tesla's cars and trucks are now commonplace on American roadways, and charging infrastructure in both urban and rural areas has improved considerably. Global investment in renewable energy hit record highs in 2023 and 2024, and battery prices have continued to fall, making energy storage more affordable and scalable.

But there are troubling trends as well. Global greenhouse gas (GHG) emissions reached an all-time high in 2024 and showed no sign of peaking in 2025. One emerging contributor to this trend is the rapid growth of energy-intensive artificial intelligence applications and the data centers that support them, which require vast amounts of electricity that is often drawn from fossil fuel-based grids. At the same time, political momentum has faltered. In the US, a change in presidential leadership in 2025 has brought renewed skepticism toward climate science and rollbacks of key climate provisions enacted under the previous administration. European countries have also slowed or reversed climate policy implementation in response to political pressures and energy cost concerns. Around the world, the tension between long-term climate goals and short-term political and economic pressures has become more acute.

This context makes the contents of this book all the more urgent. If anything has become clearer since 2022, it is that the climate crisis is not going away. For business leaders, policymakers, and international institutions, the need to address climate risks and harness climate-related opportunities is more pressing than ever. This book is offered in the spirit of confronting that challenge, with clarity, data, and a recognition that how we respond today will shape our world for better or for worse.

1 *The Climate Challenge*

"Welcome to the climate apocalypse."
"The climate disaster is here."
"Beyond catastrophe: A new climate reality is coming into view."

These headlines in *The Boston Globe* (Shankman 2021), *The Guardian* (Milman et al. 2021), and *The New York Times Magazine* (Wallace-Wells 2022) speak to the degree to which climate change and its impacts are permeating public consciousness, driven by the extreme storms, mega droughts, and unprecedented heatwaves that are occurring across the globe. Temperatures have risen dramatically over the last thirty years (see Figure 1.1), and extreme weather events stemming from climate change are now impacting every region of the world and hitting the poorest countries hardest (Eckstein et al. 2021; Lindsey and Dahlman 2024). Weather and climate disasters have been growing in frequency and severity, generating billions of dollars in costs.[1] It is estimated that by 2100, climate change could lead to 83 million excess deaths (Bressler 2021), displace two billion people (Geisler and Currens 2017), and cost the global economy over $100 trillion dollars (Deloitte 2022).[2]

Long a concern to activists and members of the scientific community, climate concerns are now commanding attention from policy and business elites. The 2024–2025 Global Risk Perception Survey from the World Economic Forum (WEF) found that the three most severe perceived risks over the next ten years are (1) extreme weather events, (2) biodiversity loss and ecosystem collapse, and (3) critical change to

[1] One study found that climate change is responsible for approximately $143 billion of the costs associated with extreme weather events each year (Newman and Noy 2023). See a full list of extreme weather events linked to climate change from the World Meteorological Organization here: https://experience.arcgis.com/experience/5cb119c71c6c4f8a89b837bf5cf353b8.

[2] See Kahn (2022) on the challenges to making accurate cost forecasts.

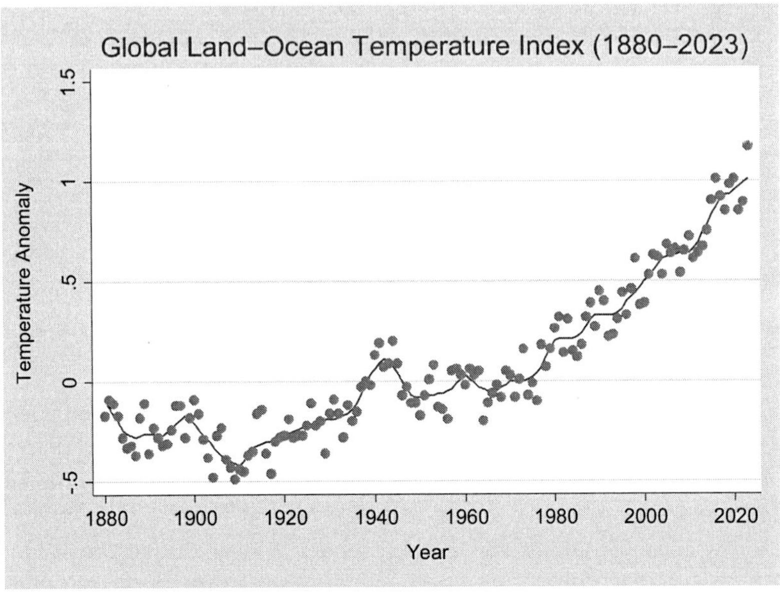

Figure 1.1 Yearly global temperatures.
Global surface temperature relative to the long-term average from 1951 to 1980. The dots are annual averages. The line is lowess smoothed. Data is drawn from NASA's Goddard Institute for Space Studies (GISS).

Earth systems.[3] In 2021, more than seventy CEOs from many of the world's largest companies published an open letter urging governments to prioritize climate change, even through strict restrictions on the private sector.[4] The general public is also increasingly aware of, and concerned about, climate change and its impacts (Lee et al. 2015).

Despite the increasingly urgent tone of world leaders, as well as ongoing efforts by policymakers and companies to reduce global emissions, the United Nations Environment Programme's (UNEP) 2024 report estimates that the Earth will warm by well over the Paris Climate Agreement target of 1.5 degrees Celsius by 2100, barring significant and rapid reductions in greenhouse gas (GHG) emissions (Lamboll et al. 2023; UNEP 2024). Consequently, we should expect

[3] Survey results are available here: www.weforum.org/publications/global-risks-report-2025.
[4] See details here: www.weforum.org/agenda/2021/06/supercharging-public-private-efforts-in-the-race-to-net-zero-and-climate-resilience.

extreme weather events to continue increasing in the years and decades to come.[5]

The research community has devoted great attention to evaluating the threats posed by climate change, including the economic, political, and social impacts that are likely to stem from a warming world. Among other topics, scholars have investigated the implications for economic growth (Abidoye and Odusola 2015; Akram 2012; Alagidede et al. 2016), political violence (Salehyan and Hendrix 2014), food security (Nébié et al. 2021), and migration flows (Garcia 2022; Scott 2020; Wennersten and Robbins 2017). Additionally, reporters and analysts have investigated the effects that climate change is having on national security (Hill and Turner 2023) and occupational health and safety (Gelles and Andreoni 2023). This scholarship and analysis has contributed greatly to our collective knowledge, yet there has been surprisingly little attention devoted to the challenges that climate change is bringing to MNCs.[6]

By their very nature, MNCs have a complex and multifaceted relationship with the climate. They have subsidiaries and suppliers around the globe, including in the countries that are most vulnerable to changing temperatures, which puts their operations in harm's way. Yet they are not just victims. Many are contributors to global warming through their carbon-intensive activities, while others are providers of innovative solutions that can help to avert climate catastrophe.

While these points are broadly understood, there is much we do not know, particularly about how MNCs are adjusting their strategies to account for climate change and its impacts. To fill this void in our understanding, the chapters that follow explore several research questions:

- To what extent is climate change attributable to the activities of MNCs?

[5] The intensity of extreme weather events could grow further still if climate change causes the Earth to reach certain tipping points. For example, the collapse of the Atlantic Meridional Overturning Circulation, the ocean currents known as the Gulf Stream, which is in its weakest state in centuries (Caesar et al. 2021), could be on the horizon (Ditlevsen and Ditlevsen 2023). This would likely lead to dramatically cooler temperatures in Western Europe, reductions in rainfall in the Amazon rainforest, and rising sea levels on the eastern coast of North America.

[6] Notable exceptions include Arnell (2015), Rivera et al. (2022), and Wright and Nyberg (2015).

- How severe are climate risks to MNCs and what tools are MNCs using to manage them?
- What opportunities is climate change creating for innovative and forward-thinking firms?
- What role are national governments and members of the international community playing in addressing climate change and to what extent do these efforts intersect with the activities of MNCs?

Before explaining this book's strategies for answering these questions, it is appropriate to briefly review what we already know about climate change, international business (IB), and the intersections between them.

1.1 What We Know about Climate Change and Multinational Corporations (MNCs)

While scholars of climate change have devoted relatively little attention to its impacts on MNCs, it would be inaccurate to say that IB has been ignored altogether. There is a sizable literature on the positive and negative effects that MNCs have had on the global environment. Additionally, a small but important series of studies have provided evidence that climate risks are a growing concern for MNCs, and there have been some reflections on the sorts of market opportunities that global firms may seize in the context of climate-related disruptions. While these topics are explored in depth in the chapters that follow, I will briefly address each with reference to the existing scholarship before identifying the knowledge gaps that will be filled in the remainder of the book.

First, we know that many MNCs have contributed to rising temperatures through their extraction of natural resources (Griffin 2017), their manufacturing processes (Gutowski et al. 2013), and their transportation of goods across the world (Zhang et al. 2020). Contributions to global warming from the fossil fuel industry are particularly significant, accounting for the majority of GHG emissions in the late twentieth and early twenty-first centuries (Griffin 2017). That having been said, this evidence is balanced by a series of findings that show MNCs to be drivers of climate improvement, owing to their use of relatively green technologies and practices (Dardati and Saygili 2012), and the adoption of eco-friendly practices and policies in the countries that host them (Perkins and Neumayer 2012; Wu et al. 2016). Thus, MNCs have played dual roles, with some contributing to climate change and others helping to reign it in.

Second, it is increasingly evident that climate change constitutes a significant threat to the infrastructure that MNCs rely on. Companies require buildings, vehicles, roadways, and employees to develop, manufacture, store, and transport goods and services. These needs are all the more acute for companies that operate across national borders, as these MNCs may require air and sea ports, transcontinental railroads, and sprawling communication networks, as well as a wider array of staff that might be affected by extreme weather. Many MNCs are, therefore, quite vulnerable to extreme weather that damages key infrastructure or makes it inaccessible.

Beyond the intensification of extreme weather and natural disasters, companies must also contend with new policies, legal rules, and social norms being brought about by changing temperatures. These new standards are putting pressure on many MNCs to adjust their business models, lest they run afoul of policies, face heightened legal exposure, or become pariahs to consumers or investors.

These risks are not lost on MNCs, which are highly sensitive to risks and often quite risk-averse (see Giambona et al. 2017). In a recent risk management survey from Deloitte, 47 percent of respondents marked improving environmental, social, and governance (ESG) management, including climate risk, as a very or extremely high priority (Caldwell 2021). Additionally, evidence suggests that MNCs are avoiding the emerging market nations that are most vulnerable to the impacts of climate change (Chen et al. 2022; Gu and Hale 2023; Shear et al. 2023), especially those nations that lack the capacity to make their infrastructure resilient to extreme weather (An et al. 2022).

Third, we know that global challenges, be they political, social, economic, or, in this case, environmental, can lead to the establishment of competitive advantages for innovative and forward-thinking companies. Firms have demonstrated as much in the context of world wars (Klein 2013), global recessions (Habibi and Kohli 2022), and large-scale pandemics (Bortoló et al. 2023). Climate change, too, offers significant opportunities for companies to bolster their green reputations (Su et al. 2015), cut costs (Link and Naveh 2006), and move into new and emerging markets (Li et al. 2018). Companies like Patagonia have demonstrated the reputational benefits that can come from green practices, while EV producers such as Tesla have reaped significant market rewards as demand for EVs and adjacent products has boomed. These examples show that some companies can cultivate a competitive advantage by adopting green practices or by entering and innovating in green markets and that, in doing so, they can help to develop and advance solutions to the climate crisis.

1.2 Remaining Knowledge Gaps

We have established some key information about MNCs and climate change. Yet there is much that we do not know. First, while it is evident that some MNCs have been contributing to climate change while others have brought eco-friendly practices to the nations that host them, we do not have well-developed frameworks for identifying the firm- or country-level factors that determine whether companies are likely to contribute to global warming or to climate solutions. Chapter 2 offers such a framework, clarifying internal factors that make companies more or less likely to align their operations with environmental sustainability, as well as external factors that shape firms' business practices.

Second, while it is evident that climate change poses significant risks to MNCs, it is not entirely clear if, or to what extent, these companies are adjusting their business models. Chapters 3 and 4 investigate this matter, offering a detailed layout of the sorts of climate risks that MNCs face and the strategies that they can use to manage them. One such strategy is avoidance, and Chapter 4 offers empirical analysis to assess whether companies are avoiding climate-vulnerable nations, going beyond previous studies by disaggregating foreign direct investment (FDI) by sector and climate vulnerability by type. After a detour to explore opportunities for MNCs in Chapter 5 and the unique factors facing energy companies in Chapter 6, I return to the issue of risk in Chapter 7, with an eye to the roles that national governments are playing in alleviating MNCs' climate risks. This chapter offers another set of empirical tests to determine whether proactive national governments can assuage climate risk concerns in a manner that prevents MNCs from avoiding their countries. I carry out a similar analysis in Chapter 9, this time looking at how engagement with the international policy community affects MNCs' climate risk perceptions and their consequent business activities.

The argument that guides Chapters 7 and 9 centers on the idea that MNCs are primarily being deterred from investing in climate-vulnerable countries by concerns that they will incur the costs of making the infrastructure that they rely on resilient to extreme weather. These concerns pertain to the private infrastructure that MNCs own and manage as well as the public infrastructure that they routinely use. However, if those costs are instead assumed by host states, then investors, unburdened by adaptation costs, will be more inclined to follow through on investments in climate-vulnerable settings. This presents a solution to governments concerned that they will be unable to attract FDI or stimulate exports due to rising exposure to climate change, as shoring up their nations' climate resilience can assure risk-averse foreign firms. However, it also presents a challenge, as many states, particularly those representing the poor- and middle-income countries that are most vulnerable to climate change (Mendelsohn et al. 2006), struggle to secure sufficient resources to cover these costs (Besley and Persson 2014). For these countries, financial support from the international community can help to fill the funding void.

Engaging in the international economy is an important ingredient in securing economic growth and development (see Adegboye et al. 2020), and so attracting international commerce – and preventing avoidance – is often a priority for policymakers (see Katitas and Pandya 2024). For this reason, shoring up infrastructure in hopes of reducing MNCs' climate risk concerns makes a lot of sense. However, this also raises significant ethical issues, including concerns about moral hazard, socializing costs while privatizing gains, and leaving the costs of climate management to the developing countries that are most affected by climate change – even as Western companies and rich countries have been the primary drivers of global warming. Within this context, equitable policy solutions that take the burden off cash-strapped developing countries are explored in these chapters as well.

Third, while it is clear that there is a significant opportunity for companies in green markets, we lack a systematic assessment of the range of market opportunities available to firms. To fill this void, Chapter 5 provides a comprehensive framework that identifies three interconnected and, at times, overlapping pillars of sustainable business opportunity that are emerging due to the climate transition: (1) early adopters can establish advantages relative to competitors,

(2) new green markets for carbon-neutral goods and services are being generated, and (3) companies that develop climate management technologies and techniques will capitalize on growing demand for climate solutions.[7] Chapters 8 and 10 add additional layers to the analysis by exploring the roles that domestic- and international-level public policy play in fostering sustainable business opportunities. These chapters also explore the potential for collaborations between governments and MNCs to produce solutions that can help put the world on a more sustainable path.

A combination of qualitative and quantitative research methods has been used to carry out the analysis in this book. To understand the strategies that MNCs and policymakers are utilizing, I conducted semi-structured interviews with individuals representing the private, public, and nonprofit sectors.[8] This qualitative data informs my analysis throughout the manuscript and references to interviews are sprinkled throughout the text. Additionally, to assess the ways that MNCs are adjusting their business operations in light of climate risks, I carry out statistical analysis using data from over 100 countries spanning two decades.[9] This quantitative work, which is presented in Chapters 4, 7, and 9, investigates how MNCs in various sectors are reacting to climate change, as well as whether policy efforts are affecting those reactions. Using mixed methods in this manner allows me to assess empirical relationships and underlying processes, while offering internal and external validity. Additionally, most chapters include simple descriptive statistics and data visualizations to show key trends.

1.3 Theoretical Framework

Throughout the book, resource dependence theory (RDT) serves as the foundation for understanding how MNCs adjust their operations in response to climate change. RDT holds that no organization is self-sufficient. Instead, organizations must engage with their external environments to obtain the essential resources that they depend on, which

[7] This framework is drawn in part from Richard and Lambert (2023).

[8] Interview participants were identified using convenience sampling. Interviews were carried out in person or via Zoom, with most lasting around one hour. See Table A.1 in the Appendix for additional details.

[9] Countries included in the quantitative analysis are listed in Table A.2 in the Appendix, while descriptive statistics for all variables are provided in Table A.3.

can range from raw materials to information to financial capital. To manage and mitigate their dependencies, organizations adopt various strategies, such as forming alliances, diversifying their resource bases, and vertically integrating (Pfeffer and Salancik 1978).[10] Firms can attempt to negotiate their environments in order to create more favorable institutional contexts in the settings where they have dependencies (see Shu and Lewin 2017).

While not initially developed with an IB orientation, RDT has become a mainstay in IB scholarship (Jiang et al. 2023). MNCs face a complex array of dependencies, relying on resources from home countries and also from beyond their national borders (Buckley 2002). The nation- and hemisphere-spanning dependencies that characterize MNCs – dependencies that become still more complex over time as MNCs expand their reach into new markets in the process of managing their dependencies (Pfeffer and Salancik 2003) – make RDT an apt tool for understanding their location choices, inter-organizational relationships, and intra-organizational dynamics (Jiang et al. 2023). RDT can further help us to understand how MNCs manage their dependencies in an international context that requires them to navigate diverse political institutions, economic structures, and social norms (Buckley and Lessard 2005), while also attending to a complicated portfolio of stakeholder relationships (Ghemawat 2003).

RDT has been suggested for understanding changing dependencies brought about by major global trends such as climate change (Jiang et al. 2023). Indeed, as companies face heightened climate risks, they will be increasingly dependent on the institutions and structures of their home and host markets, including safeguards against extreme weather and regulatory regimes. They will also become dependent on a different array of products, services, and innovations that help them to adapt their operations to a warmer world. Perhaps most saliently, companies depend on the natural environment itself, which is changing with the climate (see Bergmann et al. 2016).

MNCs will also need to adopt dependence management strategies to ensure that they have access to critical resources as the climate changes. For example, MNCs may shift their dependencies to less climate-vulnerable markets in response to growing concerns about extreme

[10] See Hillman et al. (2009) for a detailed overview of RDT, including its theoretical foundations.

weather events. Likewise, heightened regulatory pressures in home or host countries may force companies to adopt more sustainable business models (Gustafsson et al. 2022).

By the same token, RDT provides insights into the processes by which MNCs can gain competitive advantages through the early adoption of green practices. As firms recognize the interconnected pillars of sustainable business opportunity in a climate transition, such as establishing an early adopter advantage, tapping into new markets for carbon-neutral goods and services, and contributing to global sustainability, they must navigate dependencies on technology, expertise, and regulatory support. By strategically managing these dependencies, MNCs can position themselves favorably in the evolving market landscape.

1.4 The Significance of This Book

This book contributes to the scholarly literatures in IB, international political economy (IPE), and sustainable development, while also providing substantive insights for business managers and policymakers seeking to understand and foster sustainable business practices in a global context. It thus bridges gaps between different disciplines and perspectives, and between theory and practice, in exploring business management in a changing world.

The most significant contribution is to the IB scholarship. As discussed earlier, there is a large and growing academic literature about the impacts of climate change, yet surprisingly little work has been done on its implications for MNCs, despite the various ways in which they are likely to be affected. Notably, a vast body of literature has investigated noncommercial risks to global companies, emphasizing political, social, and cultural risk factors,[11] but there have been only a few studies dedicated to climate risk (An et al. 2022; Chen et al. 2022; Gu and Hale 2023; Shear et al. 2023; Weinhofer and Busch 2013), with none (to my knowledge) offering a comprehensive analysis of the climate risks facing MNCs and the business and policy strategies that can be used to manage them. This book will fill the void by offering the first large-scale, holistic, data-driven analysis of climate risks and their implications for global business.

[11] For example, see Sottilotta (2016) on political risks.

There is also a significant need to better understand the opportunities that exist for MNCs in the context of changing temperatures. To this end, this book provides frameworks for identifying the factors that lead global companies to advance environmental betterment, as well as strategies that they can use to foster competitive advantages in the emerging green economy.

This book also contributes to the literature in IPE, particularly to the segment of the field dedicated to the political enablers of global trade and investment.[12] This scholarship has traditionally focused on domestic-level policies, such as property rights protections (e.g., Nunnenkamp and Spatz 2004), political openness (e.g., Nieman and Thies 2019), and labor regulations (e.g., Olney 2013), as well as the roles of intergovernmental organizations (IGOs), such as the World Bank (Gamso and Nelson 2019), and regional trade and investment agreements (e.g., Büthe and Milner 2008, 2014; Frenkel and Walter 2019; Gamso and Grosse 2021; Jandhyala and Weiner 2014; Tobin and Rose-Ackerman 2011). Yet policy efforts to reduce environmental risks to global companies have gone largely, if not entirely, unstudied. By identifying domestic- and international-level policy factors that reduce investors' aversions to entering climate-vulnerable countries, Chapters 7 and 9, in particular, offer important contributions to the scholarship in this area. Additionally, Chapters 8 and 10 advance IPE research by exploring partnerships between governmental bodies and businesses that support sustainable development and green innovation – a topic that has received surprisingly little attention from analysts.[13]

Additionally, this book offers contributions to the field of sustainable development. Scholars of development have often highlighted the direct and indirect roles that MNCs play in supporting economic development (Ram and Zhang 2002; Wang 2009, Xu et al. 2020), while simultaneously lamenting that MNCs contribute to environmental damage (Zhang et al. 2020) and that states may weaken environmental standards in an effort to maximize their attractiveness to global companies (Aisbett and Silberberger 2021; Santos and Forte 2021). This book offers insights on these matters by clarifying the contexts in

[12] See Milner (1999) and Pandya (2016) for reviews that cover much of this literature.

[13] See Lehmann (2006) and Lin (2019) for notable exceptions.

which such concerns are realized, as well as those in which the presence of MNCs leads to environmental betterment.

Finally, this book will add a new dimension to the ongoing discussion about deglobalization and the retreat of global companies. Numerous books and articles have been written about the apparent phenomenon of deglobalization in recent years (e.g., Balsa-Barreiro et al. 2020; Madhok 2021; Moyo 2019; Witt 2019; Zeihan 2022). Some authors attribute this trend[14] to protectionist policies brought about by the movement of manufacturing jobs to China (Witt et al. 2021), while others highlight the policy impacts of income inequality (Kornprobst and Paul 2021), a psychological reaction to global integration (James 2018), and the COVID-19 pandemic (Lee and Park 2020). This book offers another explanation: climate risks are leading many global companies to withdraw from countries that they perceive to be too dangerous to operate in. In the absence of risk management solutions, this trend will continue, harming companies and countries in the process. Yet, new modes of global business are emerging due to changing global temperatures, potentially paving the way for a more sustainable era of globalization.

In addition to its contributions to academic scholarship, this book offers key insights to businesspeople and policymakers. Members of the business community have been highly attentive to global disruptions and to the implications for their companies. Concerns about noncommercial risks have caused many companies to avoid investment opportunities that they otherwise would have made (Giambona et al. 2017), while giving rise to a robust industry of risk management consultants (Thompson 2014). At the same time, forward-thinking companies have often seized business opportunities brought about by major disruptions (Wenzel et al. 2021), at times developing important innovations in the process (Lien and Timmermans 2024).[15]

Yet business practitioners have often neglected to give climate change the same sort of attention as other challenges and crises, such as political upheavals and social unrest, even as extreme weather stemming from changing temperatures is creating comparably severe disruptions. This likely reflects the limited personal experience that

[14] This idea that the world is deglobalizing is, it should be noted, a contested one (e.g., Ghemawat 2017; Grosse et al. 2022).

[15] Firms that invest in innovation in the context of crises tend to enjoy superior financial returns as well (Am et al. 2020).

many business executives have with such climate-driven events, which leaves them insufficiently worried about their potential impacts (Weber 2006). However, climate change can no longer be thought of as a distant threat, as its impacts are becoming more visible to businesspeople, policymakers, and the public. The time has thus come for global companies to take climate change seriously. This book will help put climate change on the agenda of the business community, offering best practices for global companies to protect themselves from climate-related threats as well as strategies for developing and advancing climate solutions.

This book also offers important guidance for national governments and IGOs that wish to foster a global environment that encourages environmental sustainability as well as global trade and investment. These parties often make efforts to support global companies by shielding them from social and political risks in the foreign countries that host them (see Gamso and Dimitrova 2024). They have also taken steps to enhance resilience to climate change through, for example, legislative processes (Dubash et al. 2013), the provision of foreign aid (Kono and Montinola 2019), and debt relief mechanisms (Thomas and Theokritoff 2021). Yet there has been little recognition in the policy world of climate change as a form of noncommercial risk to MNCs. Nor have the resources and interests of MNCs been sufficiently leveraged to advance climate solutions. This book addresses these oversights by providing policy strategies, informed by data analysis, that governments and IGOs can use to support a new era of sustainable, resilient, and innovative global business.

As a final note, I hope that this book will encourage analysts, members of the business community, and policymakers to see that promoting environmental sustainability is not at odds with ensuring a robust global economy that is rich with business opportunities. To the contrary, the chapters to come will show that managing the impacts of global warming is crucial to ensuring business stability and that forward-thinking MNCs can play fundamental roles in fostering a sustainable future for all.

2 *MNCs as Contributors to Climate Change and Innovators for Climate Solutions*

While the chapters to come focus on the impacts that climate change is having on global companies, this relationship is not unidirectional. To the contrary, companies have often been accused of contributing to global warming, whether by activists,[1] policymakers,[2] or even their own executives.[3] Polling data suggests that many people share this perspective, believing companies to be among the main culprits responsible for rising temperatures. For example, 64 percent of respondents to an AP-NORC poll conducted in 2022 said that corporations and industry have "a great deal or a lot" of responsibility for climate change,[4] while a similar percentage of Americans polled by *The Guardian* blamed oil and gas companies specifically (McGreal 2021). Likewise, majorities in thirteen countries polled by Politico/Morning Consult in 2021 agreed that fossil fuel companies should be held responsible for their impacts on the environment (Heath 2022).

The widespread belief that corporations carry responsibility for global warming is not unfounded. Extracting fossil fuels, manufacturing goods, and transporting products across long distances emit large amounts of carbon dioxide (CO_2) and other GHGs into the atmosphere, which in turn traps heat and raises the global temperature. According to one study, approximately 20 percent of global CO_2 emissions come from MNCs' global supply chains (Zhang et al. 2020). Another study

1 For example, climate activists protested large oil firms in Davos, Switzerland, ahead of the 2023 WEF meeting (El Dahan 2023).

2 For example, Alexandria Ocasio-Cortez, of the US House of Representatives, has criticized oil companies for contributing to global warming (Tabuchi and Friedman 2021) and large tech companies for failing to counter climate change denialism on their platforms (Stampler 2019).

3 For example, in 2006 ExxonMobil acknowledged that burning fossil fuels had contributed to climate change (Matthews and Eaton 2023).

4 Details are available here: https://apnorc.org/projects/more-americans-are-pessimistic-about-the-impact-they-can-have-on-climate-change-compared-to-three-years-ago.

identifies US-based MNCs as the 12th largest carbon emitter in the world (Lopéz et al. 2019). Fossil fuel companies have made particularly significant contributions, with one study finding that 100 fossil fuel producers – some private and others state owned – are the source of 71 percent of GHG emissions since 1988 (Griffin 2017) and another finding fifty-seven oil, gas, coal, and cement producers responsible for 80 percent of GHG emissions from 2016 to 2024 (Watts 2024).

Beyond their own carbon-intensive activities, firms and industry associations spend billions of dollars attempting to persuade governments to soften or delay environmental regulations (Brulle and Downie 2022; Cory et al. 2021).[5] In the context of RDT, these companies are negotiating their environments by engaging in political activities to shape the policies and practices of governments that they depend on (see Hillman et al. 2004). For example, companies such as ExxonMobil and business associations such as the Global Climate Coalition lobbied against US ratification of the Kyoto Protocol in the early 2000s (Brulle 2023; Grasso 2019). More recently, various automobile manufacturers, including Volvo, Daimler Truck, and Volkswagen, as well as the Truck and Engine Manufacturers Association, lobbied to prevent the US from strengthening emission standards on heavy-duty trucks,[6] while Toyota pushed back against policies in various countries that would mandate or incentive a rapid shift to EVs (Tabuchi 2021).[7] Firms have also sought to shape public opinion through campaigns to downplay their contributions to climate change or deny that global warming is occurring at all (Dunlap and Brulle 2020).[8] They often employ credentialed experts to legitimize these claims and give them a veneer of scientific backing (Franta 2022).

[5] There is evidence that these efforts are effective. Goldberg et al. (2020) find that US congresspeople that vote against environmental policies receive more campaign contributions from oil and gas companies than those that vote for them. Likewise, a 2024 report from the Center for American Progress found that the 123 members of the 118th Congress that had made statements denying human-caused climate change had received a lifetime total of $52 million in campaign donations from fossil fuel firms (So 2024).

[6] Details are available here: https://influencemap.org/report/US-Heavy-Duty-Transport-Climate-Change-20434.

[7] Ironically, Toyota was an early mover in environmentally friendly cars, with its Prius hybrid being a turning point for the industry, but failure to invest in EVs has led it to trail competitors.

[8] These efforts can be quite successful, even persuading those who believe that human activities contribute to climate change (Jiang et al. 2024).

Such efforts have been carried out by members of the oil and gas, coal-rail-steel, and electric utility industries, even as the companies in these industries were well aware that global warming was underway (Brulle 2021; Stokes 2020).[9]

While any sort of company can contribute to global warming through business operations and influence campaigns, the multinational-spanning nature of MNCs can supercharge their impacts. In particular, MNCs can engage in a manner of forum shopping, carrying out pollution-intensive production in nations with weak environmental regulations – often referred to as pollution havens (Cole 2004). Within this context, an MNC surveying locations for the establishment of a manufacturing plant may logically select a country that has lax environmental regulations over one with a stricter regulatory regime. In line with RDT, this company is reducing its dependence on countries with unfavorable regulations to minimize operational constraints and costs (see Cuervo-Cazurra et al. 2018). The point is illustrated by Apple Inc., which has relocated a significant portion of its production to China (Davidson et al. 2023), a country that has weak environmental regulations compared to the US, where Apple is headquartered (Marks 2010). Perhaps it should come as no surprise that Apple's Chinese suppliers have been accused of routinely polluting the air and water around their facilities while Apple turns a blind eye (Barboza 2011).[10]

This forum shopping can also incentivize national governments to systematically weaken environmental regulations in order to attract foreign investment or position their nations as suppliers to global companies. This is illustrated by Indonesia's 2020 omnibus law, which aimed to attract FDI during the COVID-19 pandemic. Among other things, the law simplified and streamlined environmental regulations to reduce burdens on foreign firms (Simatupang et al. 2023). While Indonesia has enjoyed a subsequent uptick in FDI inflows,[11] it has also experienced heightened deforestation and habitat loss (Regan 2020).

9 In recent years, messaging has focused more on delaying climate action, as opposed to denying that climate change is occurring (Si et al. 2023).

10 One interview participant – a sustainability manager from an MNC specializing in the distribution of consumer packaged goods – explained that their company had been able to shift away from countries with strict regulations into other markets with weaker standards.

11 According to a World Bank report, FDI inflows to Indonesia grew by 29.4 percent following the ratification of the omnibus law (International Bank for Reconstruction and Development/The World Bank 2022).

Such deregulation might be further encouraged by MNCs that use the same sorts of lobbying tactics described earlier to influence policies and public opinions in foreign countries. US-based Exxon, for instance, spent approximately €37.2 million lobbying the EU during the 2010s in an effort to delay or prevent EV-friendly policies (Ambrose 2020). This included a lobbying push in December of 2019, just weeks before the EU's announcement of its European Green Deal, during which Exxon unsuccessfully pushed for the removal of strict vehicle tailpipe standards.[12] Likewise, US airlines lobbied the European Commission in 2024 against plans to monitor certain pollutants being emitted by their aircraft (Niranjan 2024a). MNCs have also taken steps to weaken multinational agreements. As noted earlier, industry lobbyists sought to prevent the US from joining the Kyoto Protocol in the 2000s. More recently, record numbers of representatives from the fossil fuel and industrial agriculture sectors attended the UN's COP29 climate change talks in Azerbaijan to advocate for their interests (Noor 2024; Sherrington 2024).

Through these mechanisms, MNCs are widely believed to foster a race to the bottom, particularly in less developed countries with weak regulatory systems (Drezner 2000). Indeed, some studies support the notions that companies purposely seek weak environmental regulations when engaging in trade and investment (Akbostancı et al. 2007; Ascani et al. 2023; Cole 2004; Copeland and Taylor 2004; Duan and Jiang 2021) and pollute more intensively in these settings than in their relatively well-regulated home countries (Ben-David et al. 2021). Likewise, some research suggests that governments weaken environmental standards (Konisky 2008; Woods 2006) or maintain low standards (Porter 1999) in a competitive fashion to attract trade and investment.

Yet various other studies fail to find support for the race to the bottom argument (e.g., Frankel and Rose 2005). Moreover, as is discussed in the next section, quite a few studies find that economic globalization is strengthening environmental standards around the world, suggesting that MNCs may be contributing to better climate outcomes through their transnational activities.

[12] Details are available here: https://influencemap.org/report/An-InfluenceMap-Note-ExxonMobil-Lobbies-the-EU-Commission-add01200dc694b00e9ac4bebf660227b.

2.1 Are the Critics of MNCs Wrong?

Contrary to the pollution haven and race to the bottom hypotheses, some analysts argue that MNCs are a force for environmental improvement, rather than degradation, and that their activities around the world are spurring a race to the top. According to this perspective, MNCs operating in foreign countries bring environmentally responsible approaches with them, and their presence supports the adoption of green practices and technologies by local companies, as well as stricter environmental policies by host governments. MNCs can also be innovators that develop new products, technologies, and techniques to reduce or offset the environmental impacts of their operations. These MNCs are negotiating their environments much like the companies that seek to soften regulations or move away from strict regulatory regimes, but in this case they are leveraging their access to critical resources and favorable conditions in a manner that strengthens environmental standards and fosters innovations that reduce carbon emissions.

Proponents of the race to the top hypothesis highlight that MNCs tend to have greener technologies and practices than local companies in host countries (Dardati and Saygili 2012). There are several reasons why this is often the case. First, MNCs have more resources and capabilities to invest in the development of cleaner and more efficient technologies (Gonenc and Poleska 2023). Second, MNCs often face higher environmental expectations and pressures from their home governments, customers, and shareholders, which can motivate them to adopt stronger environmental standards and practices across their operations (Christmann 2004; Kim et al. 2016). Third, MNCs may see environmentalism as a means of reducing their liability of foreignness and establishing a social license to operate in host countries (Hunter and Bansal 2007), particularly when this is a priority for local stakeholders (Kawai et al. 2018).[13]

The green technologies and practices that MNCs bring with them to foreign nations may then diffuse to local suppliers, subsidiaries, and

[13] As a former director of a company-facing division of an IGO emphasized in an interview, firms can build trust with stakeholders, reduce opposition to their operations, and maintain long-term access to key markets and resources by demonstrating environmental responsibility and contributing to sustainable development locally. This often motivates green business efforts in host countries.

competitors (Wu et al. 2023), creating a pollution halo effect (Duan and Jiang 2021). Some MNCs go so far as to mandate strict standards for their foreign suppliers or subsidiaries (Curkovic and Sroufe 2011). Yet even if MNCs do not impose standards or purposefully share their technology or know-how, the mere presence of relatively green MNCs can have a positive spillover effect, as local companies adopt better environmental standards in order to cooperate or compete with their multinational counterparts (Kim et al. 2022).

Furthermore, the presence of MNCs in foreign markets can lead to stricter government regulations (Perkins and Neumayer 2012; Saikawa 2013). This may occur because governments wish to attract or retain MNCs by providing a regulatory environment that matches those of MNCs' home countries (Rivera and Oh 2013). Local firms can also play a role, lobbying their governments to strengthen standards in order to attract or compete with foreign companies that prioritize environmental sustainability (Saikawa 2013). In keeping with RDT, these local companies are reacting to the demands of the foreign companies that they depend on, thereby negotiating an institutional environment that favors their interests (see Shu and Lewin 2017).

Additionally, environmental awareness generated through the activities of MNCs may activate or galvanize public opinion or civil society actors in a manner that prompts environmental policy changes (Eang et al. 2023). For example, in 2019, ahead of Climate Week, Patagonia launched a campaign to raise awareness of climate change, in which teen activists called for stricter climate regulations from policymakers (Beer 2019). The effectiveness of these efforts in terms of activating the public are uncertain, but the potential is there for second order effects that ultimately advance climate policy action.

2.2 Racing to the Top or to the Bottom?

As we can see, there are arguments and evidence supporting both the race to the bottom and the race to the top hypotheses. Studies have sought to reconcile these conflicting narratives by identifying conditioning factors that determine which sorts of environmental impacts are being generated by MNCs. This literature can be used to develop a simple framework for clarifying the conditions under which the cross-national activities of MNCs support better or worse environmental policies, practices, and outcomes. See Table 2.1.

Table 2.1 *Determinants of climate-friendliness.*

	Facilitate Climate-Friendly Outcomes	Facilitate Climate-Unfriendly Outcomes
Internal Factors	MNCs' company characteristics such as industry type (e.g., professional services, technology), environmental capabilities, and customer base (environmentally conscious).	MNCs' company characteristics such as industry type (e.g., resource-intensive), lack of environmental capabilities, and customer base (less environmentally conscious).
External Factors	Home country's institutions such as strict environmental norms and standards, strong stakeholder pressures, and international agreements.	Host country's institutions such as weak political and legal systems, corrupt bureaucracies, and absorptive capacity.

Framework for identifying the factors that determine whether MNCs' activities in foreign countries produce climate-friendly or climate-unfriendly outcomes.

This framework categorizes conditioning factors according to whether they are internal or external to the company and whether they encourage either climate-friendly or climate-unfriendly outcomes. Internal factors are institutional characteristics of MNCs, which can either align with sustainability or be at odds with it. External factors encompass the characteristics of MNCs' home and host countries, which can mandate or incentivize different sorts of environmental practices.

2.2.1 Internal Factors

We can begin with internal factors. These include the company's industry type, its environmental capabilities, and its customer base, among other things.

With regards to industry, firms operating in certain sectors, such as fossil fuel extraction, electricity and heat production, manufacturing and construction, and agriculture are likely to have significant carbon footprints by virtue of their reliance on energy-intensive processes, extensive use of nonrenewable resources, high emissions inherent to production methods, and the substantial land-use or environmental degradation associated with their operations. In contrast, MNCs in industries like information technology or professional services that focus on intellectual capital, rather than physical or natural resources, are likely to have less carbon-intensive operations. The same is true of industries such as logistics or energy storage that inherently prioritize efficiencies because their cost structure or revenue models depend on optimizing resources.[14]

A company's capabilities are also likely to be significant determinants of its climate impact. Studies have found that firms with greater environmental capabilities are more likely to invest in countries with stricter environmental regulations, while those with weaker capabilities tend to target pollution havens (Bu and Wagner 2016; Madsen 2009). This is probably because highly capable firms can more readily manage their environmental impacts to comply with regulatory standards. This relationship between company-level capacity and investment location becomes amplified as MNCs grow larger (Bu and Wagner 2016), which likely reflects the even greater availability of resources that large firms can deploy to meet strict standards and, to the extent that larger MNCs are more geographically diversified, their experience meeting standards in various locations.

A third internal factor is the MNC's customer base. Firms that cater to more environmentally conscientious customers often signal their own commitments to sustainability (Wu and Ma 2016). To give just one example, The North Face has invested in building sustainable supply chains in order to maintain its appeal to customers that it believes are prioritizing sustainability in their purchasing decisions (Overfelt 2020). Evidence suggests that customers with high incomes (Aertsens et al. 2011; Eze and Ndubisi 2013; Lea and Worsley 2008) and educations (Chan and Lau 2000; Bartkus et al. 1999; Eze and Ndubisi 2013) are particularly likely to engage in environmentally sustainable consumption, as those with higher incomes can afford to buy sustainable products (Mortimer 2020) and those with higher education levels are more knowledgeable about environmental issues and the ways in which their

[14] As one interviewee explained, companies such as these often equate environmental waste with financial waste.

consumption decisions can affect the environment (Czarnek et al. 2021; Geng et al. 2017). In contrast, companies are less likely to prioritize sustainability if their customers do not demand it.

2.2.2 *External Factors*

External factors center on MNCs' home and host country characteristics. Studies show that MNCs based in countries with stronger environmental standards are more likely to establish supplier and investment relationships in countries with similarly high standards (Prakash and Potoski 2006, 2007; Zeng and Eastin 2012). This may reflect a preference for similar home–host country regulations (Cezar and Escobar 2015) or it may stem from pressures firms face from their home governments, consumers, or activists (Kawai et al. 2018). MNCs based in well-regulated countries with strong market power are especially likely to bring good standards abroad with them (Gamso 2017), likely reflecting the degree to which these countries shape global business norms. Additionally, MNCs from countries that have committed to international climate rules tend to bring pro-environmental norms with them when they trade or invest internationally (Christmann 2004).

In contrast, MNCs from countries that have weak environmental regulations tend to target host countries with weak standards. For example, studies find that forming trade and investment relationships with China can lead to worse environmental outcomes (Ali et al. 2022; Gamso 2018). More generally, MNCs based in major emerging market nations tend to direct their investments toward countries with weak regulatory regimes that match their own (Duanmu 2014).

The host country's political and legal systems are also important. Governments with strong institutions tend to be better at providing public goods (Arora and Chong 2018), including environmental protections (Deacon 2009). There is evidence that democracies are better at protecting their environments than nondemocracies (Arvin and Lew 2011; Farzin and Bond 2006; Li and Reuveny 2006), as voters' wishes for clean air and water are prioritized by their elected officials.[15]

[15] On the other hand, representative political institutions create avenues for corporations to voice their desires for weak environmental provisions, and democratic governments often have limited coercive power to police the activities of companies and individuals (Dryzek 1987). This has led some to posit that authoritarians have the advantage when it comes to protecting the

Likewise, countries with high levels of bureaucratic capacity are more readily able to promote environmental protection (Povitkina 2015), including by monitoring private sector actors and enforcing strict environmental regulations (Adams and Klobodu 2017; Weiss and Jacobson 1999). These benefits are amplified where corruption is low, such that bureaucrats cannot be readily bribed (Desai 1998) or otherwise prevented from enforcing environmental laws (Damania 2002; López and Mitra 2000; Sundström 2015).

In addition to domestic political institutions, nations that are characterized by greater innovation and marketization tend to enjoy higher levels of green spillover from FDI inflows (Wang et al. 2021). This is probably because they have higher absorptive capacity to utilize the advanced technologies and management practices brought by foreign investors. Likewise, countries that house a more diverse array of industries experience reduced emissions from trade and FDI, relative to countries with a less diverse industrial landscape (Ma and Wang 2021; Ning and Wang 2018). These countries have lower dependencies on carbon-intensive sectors, such as mining, manufacturing, and agriculture, as well as a greater capacity to absorb and adopt the advanced technologies and environmental standards brought by foreign investors, which can enhance their energy efficiency and reduce their carbon footprints.

2.3 Encouraging a Race to the Top

We can draw several takeaways from the race to the bottom vs. race to the top debate. First, some companies are contributing a great deal to global warming via their emission-intensive activities in areas such as extraction, manufacturing, and transportation. The emissions of fossil fuel companies are particularly significant. MNCs, by virtue of their size and geography-spanning operations, can have particularly large

environment (Buitenzorgy and Mol 2011; Midlarsky 1998). China, in particular, has been cited as an autocratic country capable of implementing strict environmental standards in a way that would be challenging for democracies with numerous veto players (Gilley 2012). Yet some scholars express skepticism, arguing that the effectiveness of China's authoritarian approach to environmental protection is overstated, or even that its environmental efforts are effective despite its autocratic regime (e.g., Eaton and Kostka 2014; Li and Shapiro 2020).

effects on climate change and on environmental degradation more generally. Thus, a segment of MNCs foster a race to the bottom by conducting their dirtiest activities in pollution havens with weak environmental standards, often while making efforts to soften or delay the regulatory efforts of governments.

Another set of MNCs are having the opposite effect. These companies are creating a race to the top via their embrace of high environmental standards, the technologies and managerial techniques that they use and diffuse to other companies in their orbit, and the impacts that their very presence has on governments, local partners, and civil societies in host countries. These companies are often compelled by the preferences of their customers, their home and host governments, and various other stakeholders that have encouraged them to commit to sustainable business practices.

From an environmental perspective, the priority should be to elevate those companies that are contributing to the race to the top, while seeking either to marginalize other firms or improve their environmental performance. Yet it is important to recognize that there are many challenges and barriers that hinder the adoption of more sustainable practices and technologies by MNCs. Some are internal, such as lack of awareness, knowledge, skills, motivation, or resources, while others are external, related to institutional dynamics or stakeholder demands. Therefore, there is a need for effective and innovative strategies and solutions that can overcome these challenges and barriers. Governments have a role to play by providing support for research and development (R&D), education and training, infrastructure and services, and international cooperation. Governments can also use policy instruments, such as regulations, standards, taxes, subsidies, incentives, information disclosure, public procurement, and public–private partnerships (PPPs), to encourage or compel MNCs to act more sustainably. These sorts of efforts will be discussed in greater detail in Chapter 8.

Additionally, as we will see, MNCs are not only affecting climate outcomes, but also are themselves being affected by changing temperatures. Ironically, some of the same companies that have been contributing most intensively to climate change face the greatest risk from its impacts.

3 *Climate Risks to MNCs*

The rise in global temperatures over the last half century has been accompanied by unprecedented changes to the natural world, including rising sea levels (Mengel et al. 2016), mega droughts (Williams et al. 2022), and biodiversity loss (Malcolm et al. 2006). Likewise, in the social world, climate change may be contributing to civil wars (Burke et al. 2009; Devitt and Tol 2012), interpersonal crimes (Mares 2013; Mares and Moffett 2016), and household violence (Zhu et al. 2023), as well as to a greater prioritization of environmental conservation by individuals, organizations, and policymakers (e.g., see Venghaus et al. 2022). These changes to the ways that humans live and work carry significant risks for companies – particularly for global companies whose operations span multiple countries that each face distinct environmental challenges. But what are climate risks, exactly, and in what ways do they threaten the operations of MNCs? This chapter addresses these questions, providing a detailed breakdown of the climate risks facing multinationals.

3.1 Noncommercial Risks

Before delving into climate risks, it is useful to situate them within the wider array of international business risks that MNCs routinely encounter. These include commercial risks related to poor planning or execution by companies themselves, but so too do they include various external, noncommercial risks that are out of a given company's control, such as economic volatility, hostility from political actors, and social unrest in host countries. Companies undertaking foreign investments or seeking offshore suppliers routinely survey the landscape for noncommercial risks as a component of their due diligence efforts. When risks are evident, firms utilize a host of strategies to manage them (Korbin 2022), such as diversifying their investments across countries and regions to reduce their exposure to a single market (Giambona et al. 2017), building relationships with local stakeholders, such as governments, communities, or NGOs, to gain legitimacy, trust, and support for their operations (Dang et al. 2020; Iankova and Katz 2003), and engaging in corporate social responsibility (CSR) to generate goodwill (Richert et al. 2015).

Policymakers have also taken steps to protect MNCs from noncommercial risks. Home country governments, which have an interest in supporting and protecting companies headquartered within their borders, may offer risk management services directly to companies, such as political risk insurance,[1] or build ties to host countries by forming trade and investment agreements (Gamso and Grosse 2021; Neumayer and Spess 2005) or establishing financial linkages (Shapiro et al. 2018). Host states also make efforts to protect foreign companies that do business in their nations, in an effort to maintain commercial ties and to demonstrate a welcoming business climate to other foreign firms. They do so by establishing trade and investment agreements with home countries (Jandhyala et al. 2011), allowing MNCs to bring claims to international arbitrators instead of national courts (Berge and St. John 2021), and engaging in dialogue and coordination directly with foreign investors to understand and address their concerns (Sattorova 2019).

Among regional and international organizations, the World Bank has been particularly active in its efforts to shield MNCs from noncommercial risks, in hopes that this will prompt these companies to invest in countries that they might otherwise avoid (see Gamso and Nelson 2019). Other international bodies serve similar functions, such as the United Nations Commission on International Trade Law. These efforts reflect the liberal orientation of these organizations, which were founded, in large part, to support global economic integration (Ikenberry 2018).

3.2 A Typology of Climate Risks

While a typical typology of international business risks prioritizes economic, political, and social factors, climate risks have emerged as

[1] For example, the US International Development Finance Corporation offers political risk insurance, among other services, to US-based firms investing abroad. Details can be found here: https://dfc.gov/what-we-offer/our-products/political-risk-insurance.

a comparable threat to the operations of MNCs.[2] To quote Jim Yong Kim, then-president of the World Bank, "every company, investor, and bank that screens new and existing investments for climate risk is simply being pragmatic."[3] Indeed, Fitch Ratings estimates that climate vulnerabilities could lead 20 percent of global corporations to see their ratings downgraded by 2035, absent mitigation efforts.[4]

When one thinks of climate risk, extreme storms exacerbated by global warming are probably top of mind. Indeed, such physical risks pose significant threats to MNCs. Yet they are just one of the four risk types that companies should be considering, with the others being transition risk, liability risk, and reputation risk (see Table 3.1).

3.2.1 Physical Risk

Physical risks stem from the impacts of climate change on extreme weather and natural disasters.[5] While it was once thought impossible to determine whether any given natural disaster or extreme weather event was related to climate change, attribution studies now allow us to identify climate as a causal factor.[6] Such studies have found that climate change contributed to the European heatwave of 2003 (Stott et al. 2004), severe drought in the Amazon in 2010 (Shiogama et al. 2013), flooding that submerged approximately one third of Pakistan in 2022 (Otto et al. 2022), and extreme heat across North America, Europe, and China in 2023 (Zachariah et al. 2023).

Events such as these can damage the physical infrastructure that companies rely on, including their own buildings and vehicles, as well

[2] Vulnerability to climate risk varies, with some companies being at greater risk than others. For example, El Ghoul et al. (2024) find that those with high levels of debt face an especially high degree of risk. Likewise, several interview participants highlighted agricultural producers as being especially susceptible because their output depends directly on weather patterns, water availability, and temperature stability – all of which are being disrupted by climate change.

[3] Kim's full comments can be found here: https://worldbank.org/en/news/speech/2014/01/23/world-bank-group-president-jim-yong-kim-remarks-at-davos-press-conference.

[4] Details are available here: https://fitchratings.com/research/corporate-finance/climate-risk-related-downgrade-may-affect-20-of-global-corporates-by-2035-08-03-2023.

[5] See Horton et al. (2024) for a series of visuals of global heating and extreme weather trends. See Arnell et al. (2021) and Dawson et al. (2018) for country-specific assessments of physical climate risk and for modeling strategies.

[6] See Otto (2023) for a discussion and review of attribution studies.

Table 3.1 *Four types of climate risks to Multinational Corporations (MNCs).*

Type of Climate Risk	Description
Physical Risk	The risk of direct or indirect impacts from extreme weather events or long-term shifts in climate patterns that affect the availability and quality of natural resources, infrastructure, and human health.
Transition Risk	The risk of financial losses or stranded assets due to political, economic, and societal changes that aim to mitigate or adapt to climate change.
Liability Risk	The risk of compensation claims or litigation against companies that are held responsible for causing, contributing to, or failing to prevent climate change damages.
Reputation Risk	The risk of profitability loss or damage to brand value due to negative public perception of a company's activities or positions on climate change.

as public roads, bridges, and ports. This damage can impose a host of expenses on firms, whether in terms of rebuilding damaged infrastructure, shoring up their operations preemptively, or enduring work and production stoppages. Extreme weather can also affect the ability of firms to hire new employees or to protect the health and well-being of existing staff. Extreme heat already kills millions of people each year (Zhao et al. 2021), and rising temperatures will make it all but impossible for humans to live in various parts of the world (Powis et al. 2023; Vecellio et al. 2023). Likewise, geographic regions experiencing extreme storms or droughts will not be hospitable places for people to live and work, nor will the coastal regions or small island nations that face partial or total submergence.

According to S&P Global, 66 percent of major global companies will have at least one asset facing a high degree of physical risk by 2050, assuming a high-impact climate change scenario.[7] The physical risks threatening these companies include:

[7] See the full report here: www.spglobal.com/esg/education/essential-sustainability/climate/physical-risks.

- Heatwaves, which can reduce labor productivity, disrupt transportation and energy systems, increase cooling costs, affect crop yields, and compromise infrastructure.[8] The Earth has recently reached its highest temperatures in thousands of years,[9] and the situation is likely to worsen, with heatwaves projected to occur twelve times more frequently by 2040 according to one study (Román-Palacios and Wiens 2020). Another study finds that dangerous heat levels will increase by 50 to 100 percent in many tropical areas and by a factor of three to ten in much of the midlatitudes (Zeppetello et al. 2022). As noted earlier, extreme heatwaves carry significant impacts for companies, not least of all by immobilizing workers.[10] Indeed, labor hours lost to heat exceeded 2.5 billion in 2021 in the US alone, costing the economy billions of dollars in lost productivity (Davenport 2023).
- Wildfires, which can damage infrastructure, disrupt power supplies, increase insurance costs, and harm human health and well-being. Wildfire seasons broke records in recent years in nearly every corner of the world, due primarily to hotter, drier temperatures and stronger winds. This is exemplified by Australia's "Black Summer" in 2019–2020, the 2020 Arctic fires, and the 2020 and 2021 California wildfire seasons, which caused the highest and second-highest areas of burned acreage on record (United Nations Environment Programme and GRID-Arendal 2022). Therefore, it should come as no surprise that the number of firms in the S&P 500 that mentioned "wildfire" as a possible risk factor in their annual reports increased fourfold between 2010 and 2019 (Reed 2019). Extreme fires are projected to increase 30 percent by 2050 and 50 percent by 2100 (United Nations Environment Programme and GRID-Arendal 2022), suggesting that firms' exposure levels will only grow in the years to come.

[8] For example, in 2024 extreme heat in New York City caused the metal in the Third Avenue Bridge to expand, leaving it in the swung open position for several hours (Ham 2024).

[9] Exactly how many thousand years is a matter of considerable debate, but some scientists argue that it has been over 100,000 (see Dance 2023).

[10] According to the International Labour Organization (ILO), over 70 percent of workers worldwide can expect to be exposed to extreme heat (Flouris et al. 2024).

- Extreme water stress, which is affecting twenty-five countries and approximately 25 percent of the global population each year, according to the World Resources Institute (Kuzma et al. 2023). Exposure is likely to grow, with one study projecting a twofold increase in suffering from extreme drought due to low terrestrial water storage by 2100 (Pokhrel et al. 2021). Water stress can reduce water availability and quality for industrial processes, agriculture, energy production, and human consumption. It poses a particular threat to consumer staples, such as household goods, food and beverages, and hygiene and personal care products, but other water-intensive sectors will be affected as well, including agriculture, mining, and manufacturing. For example, a 2015 drought in Brazil caused General Motors' water and electricity bills to increase by $8 million (Hundertmark et al. 2020). Water stress can have more systemic impacts as well, such as the drought-related 2023 logjam at the Panama Canal, which is a transit point for approximately six percent of global trade (Roy 2023).
- Intense flooding, which has increased in frequency through the 2000s, particularly in the tropics (Najibi and Devineni 2018), in part due to precipitation increases stemming from climate change (Alifu et al. 2022). This sort of flooding can damage buildings, equipment, inventory, and transport networks. For example, in 2011, extreme floods in Thailand that may have been worsened by climate change (Promchote et al. 2016) impacted hundreds of manufacturers, inundating factories and cutting off the supply of components to major foreign automakers (Haraguchi and Lall 2015).
- Sea level rise, which could exceed two meters by 2100 (Bamber et al. 2019), generating $27 trillion in annual costs (Jevrejeva et al. 2018). This owes to increasing temperatures, which cause water to expand and contribute to intense tropical storms (Colgan 2024). Rising seas will affect coastal infrastructure, tourism, fisheries, and agriculture, while threatening to displace coastal populations.[11] Countries such as China, Indonesia, and Vietnam are vulnerable to sea level rise, while the Intergovernmental Panel on Climate Change (IPCC)[12]

[11] Displacement could be massive, as approximately 15 percent of the global population lives near a coast (Cosby et al. 2024).

[12] Details can be found here: https://archive.ipcc.ch/ipccreports/tar/wg2/index.php?idp=671.

warns that islands such as Kiribati, Maldives, Nauru, and Tuvalu may become submerged to the point of being uninhabitable.[13]

Physical climate risks across countries can be assessed quantitatively using the Vulnerability Index from the Notre Dame Global Adaptation Initiative (ND-GAIN), which is composed of thirty-six indicators, covering food, water, ecosystem service, human habitat, and infrastructure (see Figure 3.1). These indicators collectively capture countries' sensitivities and exposure levels to climate change, as well as their adaptive capacities to manage its impacts.[14] According to this measure, the world's five most climate-vulnerable countries are the Democratic Republic of Congo, Eritrea, Guinea-Bissau, the Central African Republic, and Chad.

Physical climate risks can have nonlinear and knock-on effects on global companies. For example, disruptions in one location can propagate through supply chains and affect production and demand in other regions. Extreme weather can also interact with social and economic factors to create systemic shocks that destabilize markets and societies. Therefore, MNCs need to assess their exposure and vulnerability to physical climate risks across their value chains.

3.2.2 *Transition Risk*

Transition risk reflects new rules, regulations, and operations that governments, investors, consumers, and other stakeholders put into force as part of their strategies to mitigate and adapt to climate change. These reforms could lead to financial losses or disruptions for companies, potentially forcing some firms to completely reimagine their business models. Evidence suggests that experts and business managers alike view transition risks as the most impactful sorts of climate risks to companies in the near term, even as physical risks loom large in the more distant future (Sakhel 2017; Stroebel and Wurgler 2021).

Transition risk has several interconnected dimensions, with the first revolving around changing laws and policies. Governments have been instituting new rules and regulations that challenge companies'

[13] It should be noted that rising sea levels are being met with sinking land in many places, due to ground water extraction, glacial rebound, and the weight of infrastructure (see Wu et al. 2024).

[14] Details can be found here: https://gain.nd.edu/our-work/country-index.

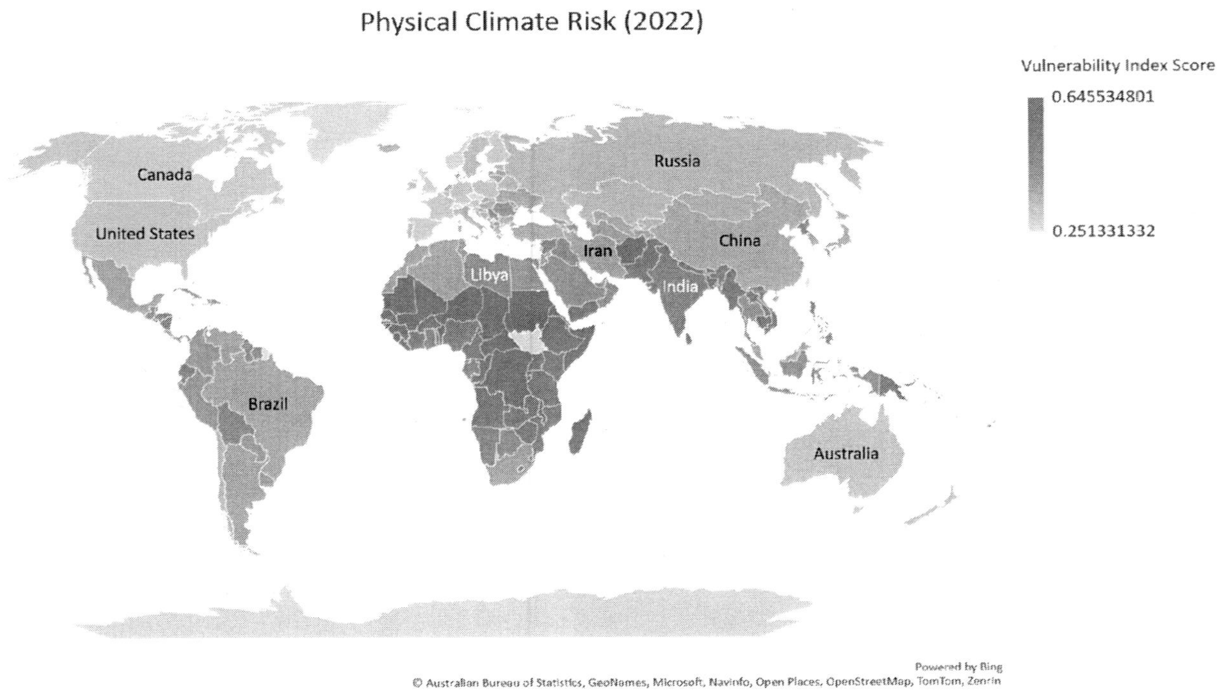

Figure 3.1 Physical climate risk heat map.
Countries coded based on their vulnerability to physical climate risk, using the Vulnerability Index from ND-GAIN. Higher scores correspond to greater climate vulnerability. 2022 is the most recent year for which data is available.

established business practices, such as carbon taxes and fuel efficiency standards, as well as requirements that banks disclose their climate-related exposures and align their lending portfolios with climate goals.[15] For instance, the EU's 2021 Climate Law requires member nations to cut their GHG emissions by 55 percent by 2030, relative to 1990 levels.[16] Likewise, the US has established rules to phase down production and consumption of hydrofluorocarbons by 15 percent by 2035, and to increase GHG emissions standards for new cars and trucks.[17] Additionally, policies promoting sustainable finance have increased tremendously in recent years, growing 40 percent worldwide from 2016 to 2021 (United Nations Conference on Trade and Development 2022).[18]

Policies may be enacted at various levels of government, with some local and state laws going farther than national ones. For example, California recently enacted a law that will force companies doing business in the state to track and report their GHG emissions, including scope 3 emissions that occur in the company's value chain (Hsueh 2023). More generally, governors of states and provinces often step up local climate transition efforts when national leaders are pulling back (see Nichols 2025).[19]

[15] Government policies often reflect the preferences of citizens, particularly in democracies, and evidence suggests that voters are increasingly motivated by climate change (Burgess et al. 2024) and that even citizens of states that rely on fossil fuels are eager for a transition away from carbon-intensive activities (Carrington 2024a).

[16] Details can be found here: https://climate.ec.europa.eu/eu-action/european-climate-law_en.

[17] Details can be found here: https://epa.gov/climate-change/climate-change-regulatory-actions-and-initiatives.

[18] Two interview participants – one who had worked in climate risk management for a major MNC and another who worked in sustainability consulting, with an emphasis on supply chain management – emphasized that the turning point in companies' acknowledgments of transition risk came in 2021, when the UK announced that it would mandate its private companies to disclose their climate risk-related data in accordance with the Task Force on Climate-related Financial Disclosure (TCFD) recommendations, which had been established in 2015 by the Group of 20 countries. Variations on this policy were quickly adopted elsewhere, including the EU. Crucially, one interview participant explained that TCFD recommendations were heavily influenced by capital markets, so that they could more accurately price in the climate risks facing firms.

[19] As this point about national leaders illustrates, the transition trend is not necessarily linear. Political leaders may strengthen or weaken decarbonization policies depending on the interests of their constituents or for other strategic

Another type of transition risk comes from the market itself. Consumers could seek more environmentally friendly goods and services, or investors and lenders could prioritize companies that develop or rely on alternative energy sources. For example, oil and gas companies will likely face lower profits as consumers shift their buying habits away from gas-powered cars and toward EVs, and as investors prioritize ESG. These trends may be encouraged by technological advancements that enable low-carbon solutions or disrupt high-carbon ones, such as innovations in renewable energy generation and energy storage.

Other stakeholders may also demand eco-friendly practices by firms. These could include employees that gravitate toward socially responsible employers or civil society groups that demand environmental sustainability from firms. Sixty-seven percent of respondents to a multicountry survey carried out by IBM said that they were more willing to apply for jobs from environmentally sustainable companies, and 68 percent said that they were more willing to accept such jobs.[20] Evidence also suggests that environmental protests can contribute to pro-environmental attitudes (Kountouris and Williams 2023) and to more robust environmental policies (Muñoz et al. 2018), indicating that growing climate activism could initiate or contribute to transitions.

These facets of transition risk are interconnected to one another. For example, a new policy requiring financial institutions to disclose their loans to fossil fuel companies could lead banks to remove such companies from their portfolios in favor of alternative energy companies, thereby contributing to a market-based transition. Physical and transition risks also intersect, as physically at-risk countries may implement policies to transition their economies and societies to a low-carbon future (Mertz et al. 2009), and climate-exacerbated extreme weather may impact societal attitudes in ways that prompt a different array of consumer decisions (Sloggy et al. 2021).[21]

reasons (Aklin and Mildenberger 2020; Colgan et al. 2021; Kupzok and Nahm 2024).

[20] Details can be found here: https://newsroom.ibm.com/2022-04-13-IBM-Global-Consumer-Study-Sustainability-Actions-Can-Speak-Louder-Than-Intent.

[21] Conversely, climate shocks can lead to consumer behaviors that contribute to further climate change. For example, people often react to extreme heat by

3.2.3 Liability Risk

Liability risk is the danger of being held legally responsible for causing harm or loss to another party. It can arise from contracts, torts, statutes, or regulations. For companies, liability risk can result from business operations or transactions that cause harm or loss to customers, suppliers, employees, shareholders, regulators, or the public. For example, producing or selling defective products, breaching contracts, infringing on intellectual property (IP) rights, or failing to disclose material information can expose a business to liability risk (see Black et al. 2005; Halliday et al. 2011).

Companies increasingly risk being sued for contributing to climate change, or for making false or misleading claims about environmental performance or impact. MNCs face growing exposure to this type of risk (Ganguly et al. 2018), as they operate across jurisdictions and sectors that may have different legal and regulatory frameworks and expectations regarding climate action (Pinkse and Kolk 2012). Climate litigation can result in compensation or damages payments, legal fees and costs, loss of market share and goodwill, regulatory sanctions or restrictions, or divestment pressures. It can also affect access to capital and insurance markets, as well as the ability to attract and retain talent.

Climate change-related litigation cases have increased rapidly since 2015, such that around 800 cases were filed from 1986 to 2014, while over 1,200 have been filed in the subsequent years. These cases have mostly been filed against governments, but corporations have also been targeted (Setzer and Higham 2022); see Figure 3.2. This is particularly common outside of the US, where over 125 climate-related suits have been brought against corporations, according to the Climate Change Litigation Database.[22] A few recent examples include:

- Greenpeace Canada v. Pathways Alliance, which alleged that the Pathways Alliance made false and/or misleading statements to the public through its "Let's clean the air" campaign.
- ClientEarth, Surfrider Foundation Europe, and Zero Waste France v. Danone, which alleged that Danone failed to address risk generated by its plastic production.

increasing their use of air conditioning, which in turn contributes to still greater global warming (Bradsher 2023; Irfan 2022).

[22] The full database is available here: http://climatecasechart.com.

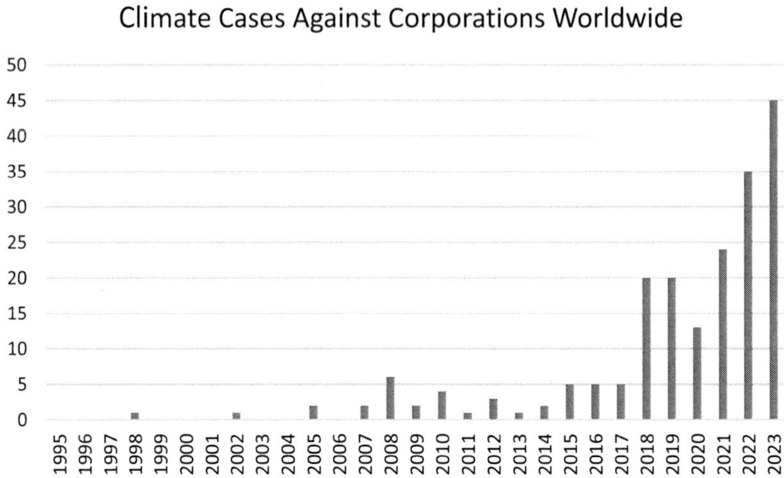

Figure 3.2 Climate litigation.
Climate cases filed against corporations, through 2023. Data is drawn from the Climate Change Litigation Database.

- KlimaAllianz v. FIFA, which was filed in conjunction with several similar suits against FIFA on the basis that the organization made misleading statements regarding the carbon neutrality of the 2022 Football World Cup in Qatar.
- Comissão Pastoral da Terra and Notre Affaire à Tous v. BNP Paribas, which claimed that BNP Paribas was responsible for deforestation in the Amazon.

The proliferation of climate change litigation can be attributed to various factors, including the growing awareness and urgency of the climate crisis and its impacts, the increasing availability and accessibility of scientific evidence and data on climate change attribution and causation, rising expectations and demands from stakeholders for more transparency and accountability on corporate climate actions and disclosures, the emergence of new legal theories and strategies to hold corporations liable for their contributions to climate change, and the development of new laws and regulations on climate change mitigation and adaptation at the local, national, and international levels (see Setzer 2024).[23]

[23] Firms may also face litigation as they attempt to transition away from fossil fuels or integrate climate-conscious investment strategies. In 2024, for example, large asset management firms that had begun shifting investments out of fossil fuels

Individual lawsuits generally have negative effects on the companies they target, with a 2023 study finding that firms saw a 0.41 percent average decrease in their value following a court decision against them in a climate-related case (Sato et al. 2023). Additionally, a ruling may set a precedent that goes beyond the litigants in the case, affecting other companies that carry out similar activities to the defendant. This potential for legal proceedings to cause wider shifts in the business and policy landscapes speaks to the overlap between litigation and transition risks. In fact, litigation risk should arguably be thought of as a component of transition risk.

3.2.4 Reputation Risk

Reputation risk refers to a threat to the good name or standing of a business. It can stem from actions (real or perceived) by the company, associations that it has with other parties, or other negative publicity. Reputational damage can hurt a company's profits, alienate its customer base, drive away investors, or make it difficult to find skilled employees. For example, Nike, Guess, and Liz Claiborne all saw their sales affected by the publicization of their use of sweatshop labor (Bartley and Child 2011). Likewise, Wells Fargo was hit with a flood of complaints from customers, employees, and regulators when it was revealed that its subsidiary, Wells Fargo Bank, had been opening accounts for customers without their consent or knowledge (Shichor and Heeren 2021).

By the same token, MNCs may suffer reputational harm and loss of trust for being seen as irresponsible or unethical in their approach to climate change. Such reputational damage could occur if a firm is perceived by the public to have damaged the environment through negligence, such as in the case of the BP Deepwater Horizon accident (McGuire et al. 2022), or if it is affiliated with other pollution-intensive industries, as when JP Morgan and other major banks faced scrutiny for their financing of fossil fuel projects even as they simultaneously made numerous climate statements and pledges (Rainforest Action Network et al. 2020), or when McKinsey came under scrutiny from

were sued in eleven US states for allegedly conspiring to restrict coal production in a way that would raise electricity prices (Nelson 2025). Similar lawsuits have targeted firms engaged in ESG investing, arguing that these strategies unfairly disadvantage traditional energy sectors (Eaton and Kiernan 2024).

its own employees for providing consulting services to fossil fuel companies (Forsythe and Bogdanich 2021). Companies may also face negative reputational impacts if they are sued by governments, communities, NGOs, or individuals for causing or contributing to climate change, failing to disclose or mitigate climate-related risks, or engaging in greenwashing or other misleading practices (this speaks to the potential for litigation and reputation risks to intersect).

Climate-based reputational damage can have significant negative impacts on companies. For example, firms may lose customers or market share to competitors that are more environmentally friendly or transparent about their climate impacts, have difficulty attracting or retaining employees who value sustainability and social responsibility, and experience lower investor confidence or valuations due to perceived risk exposure or limited growth potential.[24] Like litigation risk, reputation risk may be thought of as a dimension of transition risk, insomuch as it reflects a transition in the attitudes of consumers, investors, and other stakeholders to prioritize climate change and its impacts.

It should be noted that just as some firms experience reputational damage due to their climate impacts, others may find their reputations bolstered by their prioritization of environmental sustainability. A survey carried out by the Economist Intelligence Unit and the World Wide Fund for Nature (2021) found that searches for sustainable products have increased 71 percent since 2016. Likewise, a survey from The Business of Fashion and McKinsey & Co. (2020) found that 66 percent of respondents consider sustainability when shopping. This percentage was even higher for millennials: 75 percent. These data points suggest that firms can appeal to a large segment of customers by signaling their prioritization of environmental sustainability.

3.3 Second- and Third-Order Risks

There are also second- and third-order risks that can stem from changing temperatures. These refer to nonbusiness impacts of climate change that nevertheless threaten to damage MNCs. These impacts fall into three broad categories: health, economy, and social and political

[24] In one interview, a sustainability consultant, emphasized that reputation risk is the most poorly understood climate risk, largely because it is relatively difficult to quantify.

stability. Crucially, these types of risks are interrelated and can have cascading effects on each other. For instance, a public health crisis can lead to economic losses, which in turn generates social unrest. Therefore, as with all climate risks, it is important not to take a siloed view. Each of these three types of risk are discussed in greater detail in the paragraphs that follow.

First, there is the issue of health. While climate change may have varied impacts on human health, reducing the prevalence of diseases and deaths in some cases and increasing them in others, the overall impact is likely to be negative (Haines et al. 2006). As discussed earlier, climate change has been exacerbating the frequency and intensity of extreme weather events, which can, in turn, cause deaths and injuries. Some events, such as violent storms and floods, have immediate impacts, while others have more delayed effects, such as droughts causing crop failures that worsen malnutrition (Patz et al. 2005).[25] These sorts of impacts, which are likely to be most severe in developing countries that lack the resources to carry out successful mitigation and adaptation programs, threaten companies' workforces and their customer bases.

Climate change may also affect human health in other ways, such as via its effect on the spread of infectious diseases. For example, higher temperatures lead salmonella and cholera to proliferate at higher rates (McMichael et al. 2006). Likewise, climate change-induced migration could lead people to move to locations that are more prone to disease outbreaks (Tsui et al. 2024). One only needs to look at the economic disruptiveness of COVID-19 to see how infectious diseases can affect the business community, including via forced closures, intensified sanitation requirements, and heightened border controls (Brakman et al. 2021; Liu et al. 2020; Tang et al. 2021).

Second, there are the macroeconomic impacts of climate change. According to a widely publicized report from the Swiss Re Institute (2021), global warming will lead to an 11 to 14 percent reduction in global output by 2050, which corresponds to approximately a $23 trillion loss. The report finds that some countries and regions will be more severely exposed to climate change than others, with the lower-

[25] In some cases, extreme weather events have both immediate and longer-term impacts. For example, wildfires pose immediate threats to those exposed to the flames and smoke, but they have also been associated with longer-term cancer risks (Grant and Runkle 2022).

income Asian countries and the countries of the Middle East and North Africa (MENA) facing especially severe impacts.[26] Nevertheless, in an interconnected global economy in which supply chains and transportation networks span countries and regions, all nations will be affected. This will obviously have significant impacts on MNCs, even beyond the direct effects discussed earlier.

Finally, climate change can impact social and political stability, both within countries and internationally. These impacts are complex and context-specific, but three general patterns can be identified. First, climate change can exacerbate existing inequalities and vulnerabilities, creating or deepening grievances among disadvantaged groups. Second, climate change can disrupt the functioning and legitimacy of political systems and institutions, creating or worsening instability and violence. Third, climate change can affect relations between countries, generating cooperation and the harmonization of regulations in some cases and conflict and decoupling in others.

Poor countries are more vulnerable to the impacts of climate change than their richer counterparts (Fankhauser and McDermott 2014), but so too are the impacts of climate change likely to be felt most acutely by poorer residents within countries (Paglialunga et al. 2022). Deepening inequality, in terms of income, the availability of food, health services, and education, as well as access to the natural resources that many people depend on for their survival and identity, such as water, land, and forests, is likely to engender frustrations among disadvantaged groups, especially where governance is weak. These threats to human dignity and social cohesion may fuel resentment and protest against authorities or other groups.

Climate change can also disrupt the functioning and legitimacy of political systems. For example, it can weaken the capacity and accountability of governments to provide public goods and services, such as disaster relief, health care, infrastructure, and social protection. This

[26] The MENA region is projected to experience a 4.7 percent decline in gross domestic product (GDP) in a scenario where global warming falls well below 2 degrees Celsius. However, MENA's GDP is projected to fall between 14 and 21.5 percent in a more likely scenario in which global temperatures increase by 2 to 2.6 degrees, and to decline 27.6 percent in the case of severe warming exceeding 3.2 degrees. GDP declines for members of the Association of Southeast Asian Nations (ASEAN) are likely to range from 4.2 percent, if warming stays relatively low, to 37.4 percent in the most extreme scenario.

can erode public trust and confidence in authorities, creating opportunities for opposition groups or extremists to challenge or exploit the situation. Indeed, there is evidence connecting climate change to the outbreak of civil war (Burke et al. 2009; Devitt and Tol 2012), although there is considerable disagreement on this point among researchers (Wischnath and Buhaug 2014). Changing temperatures can also trigger or aggravate migration and displacement within and across borders (Marchiori and Schumacher 2011), which can strain the resources of host communities and countries. This can increase social friction and hostility between newcomers and locals, generating disruptive political backlash (Claassen and McLaren 2022; Lesińska 2014).

Relations between countries can also be affected (see Colgan et al. 2021). Global warming can create new areas of cooperation among countries that share common interests or challenges related to climate action, as a mutual understanding of the threats posed opens up opportunities for collaboration. On the other hand, tensions between countries may emerge or intensify over shared resources, such as rivers, lakes, or fisheries, that are affected by changing temperatures. This could escalate into economic decoupling or diplomatic or military confrontation if not managed properly. Moreover, climate change can affect the balance of power and influence among countries in terms of their economic performance, geopolitical interests, and moral authority. This can alter the dynamics of competition and cooperation in regional or global arenas (Hommel and Murphy 2013).

Social and political unrest generated by climate change, whether within or between countries, will have severe implications for MNCs. For instance, outbreaks of protest or civil unrest in response to heightened inequality could block roads, lead governments to impose societal lockdowns, or threaten public safety, thereby making it difficult for companies to carry out their day-to-day operations and endangering their employees. Likewise, delegitimization of governments leading to political change could affect companies' operations if incoming political leaders opt for a different set of laws or regulations, while the outbreak of civil war would affect firms in many of the same ways as civil unrest or protest, only to a more severe extent. Internationally, regulatory harmonization between like-minded governments would reduce transaction costs for global firms, even as stricter regulations increase their operating costs. Conflicts between countries, on the other hand, would create significant new challenges for companies operating across borders, perhaps necessitating a restructuring of supply chains.

3.4 Climate Risk Management

While climate risks are a relatively new threat to MNCs, they are just the latest in a long line of noncommercial risks that multinationals have faced, including risks stemming from political unrest and social discontent. However, many of the risk management strategies that companies have used to deal with these traditional noncommercial risks are not applicable to climate risk. Therefore, as we will see in Chapter 4, firms will need to draw on a new menu of strategies as they navigate the tumultuous climate challenges on the horizon.

4 *Business Strategies for Climate Risk Management*

While climate risks were almost certainly not on the radars of many companies until recently, recognition of climate change and its likely impacts has become much more prevalent over the course of the twenty-first century (Hornsey et al. 2022), driven by a clear scientific consensus (Maibach et al. 2014), activism from civil society (Fisher and Nasrin 2021; Sabherwal et al. 2021), and the prioritization of the issue by some public and private sector actors (Williams 2004). Yet there remains considerable climate skepticism (Lejano and Nero 2020), as well as inaction among those who accept that climate change is happening (Lamb et al. 2020). Therefore, it is important to begin any analysis of MNCs' climate risk management strategies by exploring the extent to which corporate managers see changing temperatures as a risk to their organizations.

The degree of concern that a given company has about climate risks will depend on how it balances short-term economic pressures against longer-term sustainability, how it responds to the expectations and pressures of its stakeholders, and its level of risk exposure, which varies depending on industry and location (Surminski et al. 2018). Therefore, even as some MNCs may see climate change as an existential threat, others may not be very concerned, either because they do not perceive climate risks as relevant to their business or because they have short-term time horizons.

Survey data from a variety of sources provides insights as to how seriously members of the business community take climate risk:

- Fifty-three percent of the 6,500 companies surveyed by CDP (formerly named the Carbon Disclosure Project) in 2018 reported facing climate-related risks, including 82 percent of the 500 largest companies in the sample. Transition risks were highlighted to a greater extent than physical risks by both the full sample and the subsample of large firms.[1]

[1] The original report is no longer available on CDP's website, but a summary of its findings can be found here: https://preventionweb.net/news/cdp-reporting-data-suggests-worlds-biggest-firms-are-underestimating-climate-risks.

- In a 2021 survey of 750 executives carried out by Deloitte, 82 percent reported that they were "concerned or very concerned" about climate change and 27 percent said that their organizations were being affected by climate-related disasters. Executives expressed concerns about physical, transition, and reputation risks.[2]
- A 2022 Bloomberg poll of over 100 senior executives representing financial services firms from various countries found that 85 percent have started to assess climate risk. Yet most are in the early stages, such that only five percent have collected data and carried out scenario analysis. The survey suggests a host of factors driving companies to prioritize climate risk, including concerns about regulation and disclosure requirements (transition and liability risks), risk management (physical risk), and client and investor pressures (reputation risk).[3]
- A 2022 survey of around 100 US-based firms carried out by the Federal Reserve Bank of San Francisco found 60 percent reporting that climate change is affecting, or is expected to affect, their business operations, whether through its impacts on raw material prices, regulations, or general operating costs. Of that 60 percent, 37 percent reported that they were in the process of designing formal climate risk management plans or that they intended to do so. Many of the firms not pursuing formal risk management plans still reported that they intend to consider climate risks and to implement sustainability initiatives in the future.[4]
- A 2022 survey of sixty-two large financial firms from the Global Association of Risk Professionals found that the majority were attending to climate change and its impacts, with 67 percent having hired staff to work on climate risk. This largely reflects concerns about transition risk, as 90 percent reported that their regulators had published formal expectations for climate risk management and

[2] The full report is available for download here: https://deloitte.com/global/en/services/risk-advisory/research/2021-climate-check-business-views-on-environmental-sustainability.html.

[3] The full report is available for download here: https://bloomberg.com/company/press/financial-firms-see-climate-risks-as-a-top-priority-but-lack-consensus-on-how-to-effectively-analyze-climate-concerns-according-to-bloomberg-survey.

[4] The full report can be found here: https://frbsf.org/economic-research/publications/economic-letter/2022/march/how-are-businesses-responding-to-climate-risk.

80 percent reported being required to report their climate-related risks to regulators.[5]

Other surveys show less immediate concern about climate risk. For example, economic issues dominated the 2022 Executive Opinion Survey from the WEF Centre for the New Economy and Society, in which approximately 12,000 business leaders offered the risks that they expect to be most significant to their home countries in the following two years. Inflation and the cost of living took the lead in both advanced and emerging economies, followed by geoeconomic confrontation and severe commodity price shocks in advanced economies and debt crises and employment and livelihood crises in emerging markets. In advanced economies, the failure of climate change adaptation was the seventh most commonly cited risk, while it was tenth in emerging markets.[6]

Firms clearly vary in their recognition of climate risk, but which risks are most pressing to those that do recognize them? Some research suggests that firms are prioritizing transition risk as the more immediate concern, while physical risk is a more distant threat (Kouloukoui et al. 2019; Sakhel 2017).[7] On the other hand, several studies find that physical risk deters MNCs from investing in climate-vulnerable countries, whereas evidence is mixed on transition risk (see Chen et al. 2022; Gu and Hale 2023; Shear et al. 2023). The potential for reputational damage is also a concern for many firms. For example, 14 percent of executives highlighted reputation risk as a key concern in the previously mentioned Bloomberg survey. Likewise, companies that join voluntary environmental programs do so in large part for the sake of public relations (Potoski and Prakash 2005), and the same is true of those that seek trade and investment partners with strong environmental records (Prakash and Potoski 2006, 2007).

There is also some reason to think that liability risk can deter MNCs from entering new markets (Onoz and Giachetti 2023). However,

[5] The full report is available for download here: https://garp.org/sustainability-climate/fourth-global-climate-risk-survey.

[6] A more detailed breakdown of the results can be found here: https://marshmclennan.com/insights/publications/2022/november/global-risks-for-businesses-country-level-perceptions.html.

[7] One interview participant, the sustainability manager of a consumer packaged goods company, shared the observation that physical risk only becomes salient to companies when it affects them directly.

there is a dearth of empirical research that focuses specifically on climate-related litigation. The only study, to my knowledge, finds that Chinese cities with environmental courts attract significantly less FDI than cities without them (Huang et al. 2022). This is an insightful data point, but more research in this area is necessary to draw meaningful conclusions.

4.1 Corporate Climate Risk Management

The next issue centers on how MNCs manage climate risk. To inform this discussion, I use the *accept*, *transfer*, *adapt*, *diversify*, *avoid* risk management model, which was introduced as a tool for managing geopolitical risks (Grosse et al. 2021). According to this model, MNCs facing country-level risks may use strategies aligning with any of these categories: (1) *accept* the risk and carry on with business as usual, (2) *transfer* the risk to another party, (3) *adapt* to the risk by, for example, shoring up infrastructure to withstand extreme storms, (4) *diversify* risk by establishing operations in various locations, and (5) *avoid* risky locations altogether.

Each of these approaches, which are summarized in Table 4.1 and elaborated on in the pages that follow, carries benefits as well as potential drawbacks. Crucially, these strategies are not mutually exclusive, such that MNCs may consider a combination of strategies to address different aspects of climate risk.

4.1.1 Accept the Risk

Some companies may decide to accept the risk of climate change and continue their normal operations without any adjustments. Indeed, this is the approach that many, if not most, companies have taken so far (see Surminski 2021). For example, almost one in four large fashion brands had no decarbonization plan at all as of 2024, according to a report from Fashion Revolution (Simpliciano et al. 2024). This may be a rational approach for a firm if the risk of climate-related impacts is low in its area of operation or if it has the capacity and resources to cope with potential damages and losses. Moreover, there is always a possibility that climate-related disruptions will not occur at all, even in a place where the probability is high. In that case, a company that did not change its business practices will have avoided the

Table 4.1 *Climate risk management framework.*

Approach	Description	Example
Accept the risk and carry on with business as usual	The company does not take any action to reduce or manage climate risk and accepts the potential consequences.	A company continues to operate in a coastal area that is prone to flooding and storm surges, without investing in flood protection or insurance.
Transfer the risk to another party	The company transfers some or all of the financial responsibility for climate risk to another party, such as an insurer, supplier, or customer.	A company purchases insurance coverage for its assets and operations against climate-related damage.
Adapt to the risk	The company implements measures to increase the resilience of its assets, operations, and supply chains to climate-related disruptions.	A company invests in shoring up its buildings to protect them against extreme winds and rain.
Diversify risk by establishing operations in various locations	The company spreads its assets, operations, and supply chains across different geographic locations that have exposure to different levels and types of climate risk.	A company establishes multiple production facilities in different regions or countries that have different climatic conditions and regulatory regimes.
Avoid the risk by choosing to do business elsewhere	The company decides to exit or not to enter a market that is exposed to high levels of climate risk and focuses on other markets that are less risky.	A company decides to close its facilities in a drought-stricken region, in favor of a different location with a more reliable water supply.

costs of adapting to climate change without suffering any negative consequences.[8]

However, this approach also carries a high level of uncertainty and vulnerability. Climate change is a dynamic and complex phenomenon, and its effects are often unpredictable. A location that is currently low risk may become high risk in the future due to changes in temperature, precipitation, sea level, or other factors. A company that does not anticipate and prepare for these changes may face costly disruptions to its operations, supply chains, markets, or assets. Furthermore, ignoring or downplaying the risk of climate change may damage the reputation and credibility of a company among its investors, customers, employees, regulators, and insurers. Therefore, while accepting climate risk and carrying on with business as usual may seem appealing in the short term, it is probably not a sustainable or prudent long-term strategy for most companies.

4.1.2 Transfer the Risk

A second way that companies can deal with climate risk is to transfer it, typically to an insurer or to customers or suppliers. For example, a company could pay a premium to an insurance company, which would then compensate it for any losses or damage caused by climate-related events, such as floods, droughts, storms, or wildfires. This mirrors political risk insurance, which covers incidents such as war, civil unrest, expropriation, or terrorism (Arel-Bundock et al. 2020; Baroudi 2017). There has been a growing interest in developing similar insurance mechanisms to cover climate risks, especially to promote investment in developing countries and vulnerable communities (see Gamso 2023). Notably, the Paris Agreement has recognized insurance as a key tool for enhancing adaptation and resilience, and the G7 countries have launched a climate risk insurance initiative (Surminski et al. 2016).

[8] Another factor is ownership structure. One interview participant from an MNC that had been purchased by a private equity firm explained that the new owners intended to resell the company in the next few years. This short time horizon means that accepting climate risk is a more rational approach than investing heavily to ensure long-term sustainability, even against the backdrop of growing risk exposure.

However, the market for climate risk insurance is underdeveloped and limited, and there are significant challenges to creating and expanding insurance offerings (Schäfer et al. 2018). These include a lack of reliable analytical tools to assess and price climate risk exposure, low awareness and demand for insurance among potential clients, regulatory and institutional constraints in different countries and regions, and a lack of capacity or willingness among insurance companies to provide coverage. Furthermore, there are ethical and practical concerns about the effectiveness and sustainability of climate risk insurance, such as moral hazard, adverse selection, crowding out of other adaptation measures, or unaffordable premiums in a world where climate-related disasters are becoming more frequent and severe (see Yohe 2025).

Companies can also try to transfer the costs associated with climate change to their customers and suppliers. For example, they may charge higher prices for products or services that are affected by climate-related disruptions or regulations, or impose stricter terms and conditions on their suppliers to ensure compliance with environmental standards. However, this strategy may not work well in the long term, as firms could face resistance from both ends of the value chain: suppliers may not be able to bear the additional costs of climate adaptation and mitigation, while customers may not be willing to pay more for products or services.

Another approach to transferring risk is carbon offsets. Instead of directly reducing their own emissions, firms pay for projects that remove or reduce GHG emissions elsewhere, such as reforestation or carbon capture initiatives. In doing so, they effectively outsource some of the responsibility for emissions reductions to third parties, rather than bearing the full burden of decarbonization internally. This strategy allows businesses to comply with regulatory requirements and meet investor expectations for climate commitments while maintaining their existing high-carbon operations (see Gabbatiss and Pearson 2023).[9]

[9] It should be noted that offsets have faced criticism regarding their effectiveness and transparency (see Delacote et al. 2024). Another concern is moral hazard, as firms continue emitting rather than investing in deeper decarbonization (see Monbiot 2022).

4.1.3 Adapt to the Risk

The next approach is to adapt to climate change. Companies can adapt to physical risk by, for example, forecasting scenarios to determine where and when extreme weather events are most likely to occur and adjusting their operations in response. E-distribuzione, an Italian electricity distribution system operator, used this approach, responding to projected extreme weather events that threatened the electricity grid by investing approximately €345 million to shore up its power distribution system for the 2021–2023 period (D'Aprile et al. 2021). Other companies are adapting by developing new products, such as Starbucks with its engineering of climate-resilient coffee seeds (Uteuova 2023). Still others are shoring up their physical infrastructure to better withstand extreme weather, such as Venture Global LNG, Inc., a gas producer that made headlines after building a 26-foot high seawall around its liquefied natural gas plant in Louisiana (Carioti 2024).

Adapting to transition, liability, or reputation risks typically takes the form of aligning with standards set by governments and other stakeholders. For example, several companies, including PepsiCo, T Mobile, and SAP, have announced plans to reach net zero emissions by 2040, a full decade ahead of the Paris Agreement goal.[10] More generally, over 6,500 companies have set emissions targets through the Science Based Targets initiative (SBTi),[11] which provides frameworks for companies to align their emission reduction efforts with the goals of the Paris Agreement, with the vast majority having done so since 2018 (Toktay et al. 2024). Other firms have undertaken initiatives to demonstrate their dedication to sustainability and climate justice. For instance, Coca-Cola has prioritized the conservation of water, an important ingredient in its products, through its water stewardship program,[12] investing in over 300 community water partnership projects since 2005 and partnering with organizations such as the Water Footprint Network, the Nature Conservancy, the World Wide Fund for Nature, and the Global Environment and Technology Foundation (Thorpe 2011).

[10] See the full list of signatories to this pledge here: https://theclimatepledge.com/us/en/Signatories.

[11] See details on SBTi here: https://sciencebasedtargets.org.

[12] Details on Coca-Cola's water program can be found here: https://coca-colacompany.com/sustainability/water-stewardship.

It should be noted that adaptation does not necessarily mean that companies cease their pollution-intensive operations. On the contrary, some companies have found that changing policies and expectations allow them to overshadow their more problematic activities by emphasizing their climate adaptation efforts. For example, BP sought to offset criticisms of its environmental record during the Gulf of Mexico oil spill by stressing its pro-environmental initiatives through disclosures (Arora and Lodhia 2017). In a similar fashion, some mining firms have branded themselves environmental companies on the basis that the minerals they mine will facilitate the expansion of EVs.[13] However, there are risks, as evidence suggests that public backlash may occur in response to greenwashing – or the appearance of greenwashing (Ioannou et al. 2023).[14]

Adapting is a good strategy for firms hoping to get out ahead of impending transitions or to establish a competitive advantage with a segment of customers. However, doing so can be costly, exceeding the available resources of many enterprises. Companies going all in on adaptation must be prepared to allocate funds to update infrastructure, adopt new technologies, and comply with evolving regulations. Businesses must also invest in their workforce by hiring or training staff with the technical expertise to implement and maintain these adaptations. This need for specialized knowledge can require continuous education and skills development, further burdening companies' financial resources. These costs are compounded in relative terms if a company's competitors decline to adapt and continue to profit from carbon-intensive activities.[15]

The unpredictable nature of the marketplace adds another layer of complexity to climate adaptation strategies. Technological advancements and policy changes occur at a rapid pace, creating an environment where today's solutions may become obsolete tomorrow. Within this context, companies may invest heavily in current adaptation

[13] For example: https://fcx.com/about/copper-at-a-glance.

[14] There could also be legal repercussions for companies, as exemplified by a recent lawsuit against Tyson Foods for its "Climate-Smart" labeling (Zraick 2024).

[15] While this makes adaptation easier for large and well-resourced companies, smaller firms may still adopt small-scale adaptation efforts. In an interview, the sustainability director of a nonprofit that works with local companies in Arizona highlighted that small sustainability efforts, such as installing faucets that reduce water usage or motion sensors that turn off lights to decrease electricity use, can produce meaningful cost savings for small firms.

measures only to find that new technologies or regulatory shifts render their efforts redundant or inadequate. This uncertainty makes it challenging for businesses to develop long-term strategies and can lead to wasted resources if adaptations do not align with future market or policy directions. Additionally, if market dynamics shift and climate adaptation becomes a lower priority, businesses may find that their investments yield little return, affecting their competitiveness and financial stability.[16]

Given these dynamics, it should come as no surprise that companies are often hesitant to adapt their operations (DePillis 2023) and that adaptation can affect firms' productivity for the worse (Greenstone 2002). It is also not unheard of for companies to backtrack because of concerns about cost or changing market dynamics. For example, Ford Motor Company and General Motors scaled down their production of EVs in 2024, citing slower EV sales than had previously been projected (Boudette 2024). Likewise, Shell ended its carbon offset program, reduced plans to invest in renewable power, and abandoned targets for EV charging stations and clean hydrogen sales in 2023 (Marsh and Mathis 2023). These companies, and others like them, are reacting to market dynamics as well as to the ebbs and flows of social and political pressures. This speaks to the wider social ecosystem that companies find themselves operating within when they make strategic business decisions – including decisions related to climate risk and sustainability.

4.1.4 Diversify Risk

The fourth strategy that companies can adopt to cope with the increasing threats of climate change is to diversify their activities across different geographic regions. By doing so, they can reduce the potential losses that a climate-related event or trend may cause in one place. For example, Spirit Airlines, a low-cost carrier based in Miramar, Florida, decided to open a second operations center in Orlando, Florida, in

[16] One interview participant, whose company works in business-to-business distribution, noted that some of their manufacturing partners had invested heavily in green production at a time when decarbonization was a higher priority in North America. Today, these manufacturers continue to use expensive sustainable production processes, even as political priorities have shifted and some of their competitors that have continued to rely on traditional manufacturing approaches enjoy a cost advantage.

2019 as a way of protecting itself from extreme storms and winds that could affect its headquarters (Freedman 2021). The Orlando center serves as a backup facility that can take over Miramar's functions in response to an emergency. This allows Spirit to maintain its flights and services without interruption, thereby avoiding customer and revenue losses.[17]

Diversification can be a useful approach for companies that have the resources and flexibility to operate in multiple locations and that are not tied to a specific geographic area or natural resource. However, diversification can entail significant costs and challenges, such as finding suitable locations, complying with different regulations, managing cultural differences, and coordinating across multiple sites. Moreover, diversification may not be effective if climate risks become too widespread or severe. For instance, a global pandemic stemming from warmer temperatures[18] or a large-scale drought may limit the benefits of diversification, as companies face similar problems and constraints everywhere.

4.1.5 Avoid the Risk

The fifth way that companies can deal with climate risk is to avoid risky settings altogether, declining to conduct business in places where the risks associated with climate change are high.[19] As noted earlier, research suggests that some MNCs are adopting this strategy by curtailing FDI to countries characterized by high risk levels. This investor avoidance is visualized in Figure 4.1, which shows a negative correlation between FDI inflows, measured with data from the World Bank's World Development Indicators (WDIs), and climate vulnerability, measured using the Vulnerability Index from ND-GAIN. This suggests

[17] One interview participant explained that his company had diversified its supply chain in response to COVID-19, which shielded the company from some degree of climate risk as well. In this way, companies that engage in diversification to protect themselves from non-climate disruptions may inadvertently establish resilience to climate risk in the process.

[18] See Baker et al. (2022) on the intersection between climate change and pandemic outbreaks.

[19] For example, one interview participant, who had been a country-level director for an IGO, highlighted a major beverage company that had factored water stress into its supply chain strategy, avoiding locations where the long-term availability of water was a concern.

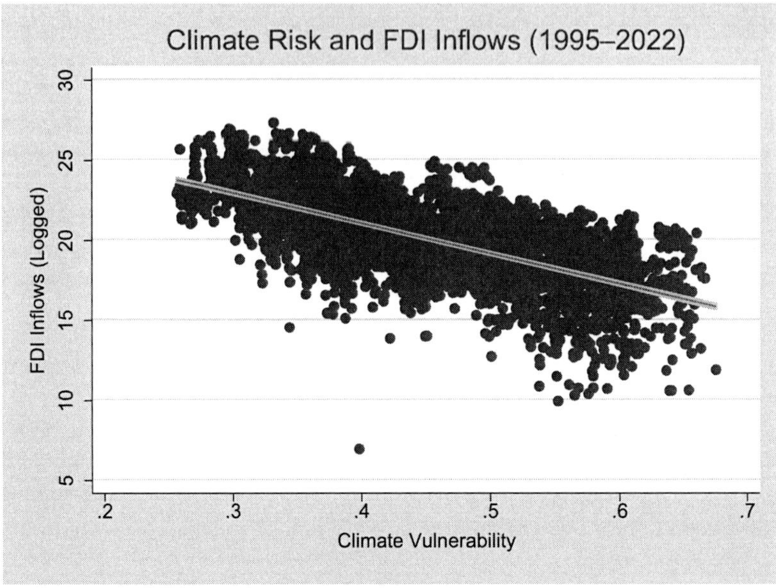

Figure 4.1 Climate risk and investor avoidance.
This figure shows a negative relationship between FDI inflows and climate risk for 184 countries from 1995 to 2022. Climate risk is measured using the Vulnerability Index from ND-GAIN. FDI data is from the World Bank's WDIs. FDI has been logged to account for a heavy skew. The dots are individual observations; the trendline is displayed with 95 percent confidence intervals.

that foreign investors are systematically avoiding countries characterized by high levels of climate risk, presumably because they worry that these risks will threaten their returns.

While avoiding risky countries is a seemingly rational approach for a risk-averse company, the benefits of steering clear of climate risk may be offset by missing out on potential opportunities – including those that arise from climate change. For example, some regions may experience increased agricultural productivity, tourism demand, or renewable energy potential due to changes in climate. Similarly, some sectors may benefit from increased demand for low-carbon products, services, or technologies as a result of changes in policies or consumer preferences. Therefore, avoiding climate risks may not be the best option for companies that want to grow and thrive in a changing world.

Investor avoidance is also concerning from an economic development perspective. FDI is an important contributor to economic growth in less developed countries (see Soumaré 2015), which are often the most vulnerable to climate change (Fankhauser and McDermott 2014). Thus, companies contribute to the persistence of poverty and uneven development when they systematically avoid low- and middle-income countries. This suggests that efforts should be taken to discourage investor avoidance – a topic that will be discussed further in the chapters ahead.

That said, we should exercise caution before drawing strong conclusions from the correlation presented earlier, as it could be spurious. It might be that investors are avoiding developing countries for reasons totally unrelated to climate, even as these countries tend to be quite vulnerable to the impacts of changing temperatures. With that concern in mind, I conduct multiple regression analysis to account for potentially confounding factors. FDI inflows and climate vulnerability serve as the dependent and independent variables, while the following controls are included to isolate the relationship between them:

- GDP (logged), GDP per capita (logged), and annual GDP growth are controlled for on the basis that market size and growth potential are direct and indirect determinants of FDI (Botrić and Ŝkuflić 2006; Iwai and Thompson 2012; Okafor et al. 2022; Sabir et al. 2019). Data for these variables is drawn from the World Bank's WDIs.
- Regime type is included based on evidence that democracies attract more FDI than nondemocracies (Jensen 2008). This variable is measured using the Polity score (Marshall and Gurr 2020), which ranges from −10 (total autocracy) to +10 (total democracy).
- Wars create risks to foreign investors because they threaten safety, damage infrastructure, and introduce uncertainty about the future (see Bussmann 2010). I measure high intensity conflict using data from the UCDP/PRIO Armed Conflict Dataset (Davies et al. 2022; Gleditsch et al. 2002). The variable is coded "1" when over 1,000 people have been killed in conflict and "0" otherwise.
- Oil rich countries are risky environments for investors for various reasons (see Jensen and Johnston 2011). Oil wealth is measured as oil rents as a percentage of GDP, using data from the World Bank's WDIs.

- Bilateral investment treaties (BITs) typically include protections for foreign investors, and they are positively associated with FDI flows (Neumayer and Spess 2005; Tobin and Rose-Ackerman 2011). BIT data is drawn from the World Economics and Politics Dataverse (Graham and Tucker 2019; Graham et al. 2018).

In keeping with statistical best practices, robust standard errors are clustered by country to account for heteroscedasticity and serial correlation, and variables on the right side of the equation are lagged one year to leave them time to affect the dependent variable. The model includes country and year fixed effects to account for unobserved variation across time and space.

Results are presented in Table 4.2, which shows a significant negative relationship between climate vulnerability and FDI inflows, meaning that foreign investment declines as climate risk rises. This suggests that investors are deterred from investing in countries characterized by high levels of climate risk – a finding consistent with various other studies (Chen et al. 2022; Gu and Hale 2023; Shear et al. 2023) and with Figure 4.1.

We can go a step further by analyzing disaggregated FDI[20] to determine whether investor avoidance varies among investors targeting primary, secondary, and tertiary sectors.[21] To do so, I conduct a series of multiple regressions in which each type of FDI serves as a dependent variable. The results are presented in Table 4.3. Here we see significant variation, as primary and tertiary sector investments have positive but nonsignificant relationships to climate risk, whereas the coefficient for secondary sector FDI is negative and statistically significant.

What explains these findings? Primary sector investors are bound to specific locations that offer key natural resources. For example, oil companies must drill where there is oil, regardless of risks. Tertiary sector investors, for their part, may be less affected by climate risks and more mobile if a risk incident does occur. For example, a software company

[20] Disaggregated FDI data is available through the International Trade Centre, which offers data for approximately 70 countries, ranging from 2000 to 2022 – although most countries report data for a subset of years. The data is available here: https://investmentmap.org/investment/time-series-by-country.

[21] Primary sector FDI includes investments targeted toward agriculture, forestry, and fishing, and mining and quarrying. Secondary sector FDI includes investments targeted toward manufacturing as well as repair and installation of machinery and equipment. Tertiary sector FDI includes investments in areas ranging from information and communication to financial and insurance activities to arts, entertainment, and recreation.

Table 4.2 ***Climate risk and investor avoidance.***

Dependent Variable: FDI Inflows	Model 4.1
Climate Vulnerability	-12.97***
	(4.170)
GDP	1.728***
	(0.466)
Per Capita GDP	-1.116**
	(0.432)
Annual GDP Growth	0.0171***
	(0.00500)
Regime Type	0.0256*
	(0.0141)
High Intensity Conflict	-0.109
	(0.130)
Oil Rents	0.0188**
	(0.00868)
BITs	-0.00407
	(0.00263)
Observations	3,329
R-squared	0.439
Number of Countries	159
Country Fixed Effects	Yes
Year Fixed Effects	Yes

Linear panel data model. Robust standard errors in parentheses, clustered by country; independent and control variables lagged one year; ***$p < 0.01$, **$p < 0.05$, *$p < 0.1$.

may be able to relocate its offices or servers to a different country without too much difficulty or cost. In contrast, manufacturing requires considerable physical and human infrastructure that is vulnerable to the impacts of climate change. Moreover, manufacturing is typically neither location specific nor readily mobile once the infrastructure has been set up. For this reason, investors in this sector should be risk-averse, making their avoidance of vulnerable locations quite rational.[22]

[22] One interview participant – a sustainability analyst from an ESG rating agency – noted that manufacturing firms tend to have a relatively strong understanding of climate risks, given their high exposure levels. In contrast, companies in tertiary sectors are often less knowledgeable and, therefore, less inclined to alter their business plans.

Table 4.3 *Climate risk and investor avoidance by sector.*

	Model 4.2	Model 4.3	Model 4.4
Dependent Variables in Parentheses	(Primary Sector FDI Inflows)	(Secondary FDI Inflows)	(Tertiary FDI Inflows)
Climate Vulnerability	30.77	-36.10***	11.76
	(20.19)	(9.609)	(10.95)
GDP	4.521	-1.834	4.679***
	(2.913)	(1.415)	(1.723)
Per Capita GDP	-4.246	1.464	-3.691
	(4.070)	(1.885)	(2.891)
Annual GDP Growth	0.0525**	0.0217*	0.0214*
	(0.0206)	(0.0127)	(0.0114)
Regime Type	-0.0641**	0.00633	-0.0266
	(0.0250)	(0.0232)	(0.0225)
High Intensity Conflict	0.0185	-0.0136	-0.315
	(0.194)	(0.203)	(0.200)
Oil Rents	-0.0546	0.0384	0.0311
	(0.0396)	(0.0262)	(0.0266)
BITs	0.00406	0.00479	-0.00480
	(0.00493)	(0.00439)	(0.00492)
Observations	474	554	593
R-squared	0.171	0.261	0.211
Number of Countries	69	73	73
Country Fixed Effects	Yes	Yes	Yes
Year Fixed Effects	Yes	Yes	Yes

Linear panel data models. Robust standard errors in parentheses, clustered by country; independent and control variables lagged one year; ***$p < 0.01$, **$p < 0.05$, *$p < 0.1$.

The Vulnerability Index, which has six contributing variables, can also be disaggregated to determine which facets of climate risk are driving investor avoidance. Therefore, I analyze a model that includes each of the index components as x-variables: ecosystem vulnerability, food vulnerability, habitat vulnerability, health vulnerability, infrastructure vulnerability, and water vulnerability. The results are visualized in Figure 4.2.

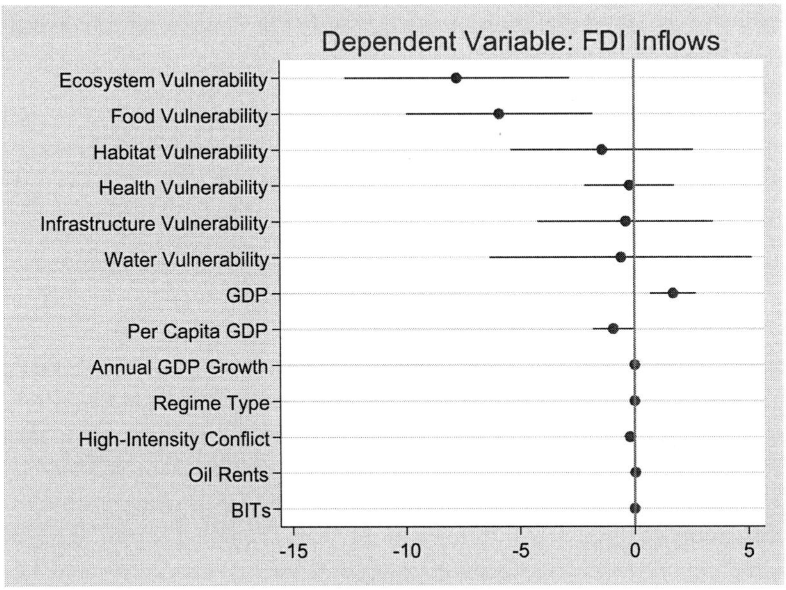

Figure 4.2 Disaggregated climate risk and investor avoidance.
The plot is based on a linear panel data regression model. Country and year fixed effects; robust standard errors, clustered by country; independent and control variables lagged one year.

While all six dimensions of climate vulnerability show a negative association with FDI inflows, only ecosystem and food vulnerability are statistically significant, suggesting that these particular risks are especially salient to foreign investors. One reason may be that ecosystem degradation and food insecurity serve as broader signals of systemic instability, rather than localized or sector-specific challenges. Unlike infrastructure or water-related vulnerabilities, which firms may address through private adaptation measures, ecological collapse and food system fragility often require collective solutions that lie beyond the capacity of individual investors to control. These forms of vulnerability also tend to have cross-sectoral consequences, affecting not just agriculture or resource extraction, but also labor productivity, supply chains, and political stability. In this sense, they may raise red flags about a country's overall investment climate, indicating not only environmental strain but also potential governance failures or social unrest. For foreign investors, such conditions represent uninsurable and poorly bounded risks, making investment less attractive even in otherwise promising markets.[23]

4.2 Climate Risk Management and Resource Dependence Theory (RDT)

The five approaches discussed earlier are best understood as strategic efforts to manage and restructure firms' dependencies in response to a rapidly changing external environment. Climate change has intensified the challenges that firms face in managing their resource dependencies, forcing them to reassess their exposure to climate risk. As firms evaluate their vulnerabilities, they must decide whether to reduce external reliance, shift dependencies to more stable environments, or externalize risks onto other parties. Some firms seek to reduce their exposure to external disruptions by adapting – whether through investing in infrastructure or complying with regulations. This strengthens firms' internal capabilities, thereby reducing their dependence on external systems like public infrastructure and uncertain regulations. Others take a different approach, shifting dependencies by spreading operations across multiple locations or suppliers to avoid excessive reliance on any single climate-vulnerable market. Still others seek to externalize risks onto third parties through risk transfer mechanisms, such as purchasing climate risk insurance or passing costs onto buyers or suppliers.

However, firms do not all have the same ability to restructure their dependencies. MNCs with greater capital reserves, diversified market reach, and regulatory flexibility can adopt proactive strategies, while smaller firms or those in highly location-dependent industries may find themselves with fewer options. For example, while technology firms can relocate some of their data centers or diversify their supply chains, firms in extractive industries or agribusiness must operate where their resources are located, leaving them with more exposure to physical risks. Likewise, risk transfer strategies like purchasing insurance or passing costs onto suppliers may be available only to firms with strong

[23] See Table A.4 in the Appendix for models in which primary, secondary, and tertiary FDI serve as the dependent variables and climate vulnerability components serve as x-variables. These models show that health, infrastructure, and water vulnerability have negative and significant relationships to secondary sector FDI inflows, supporting and adding further nuance to the results presented in Table 4.2.

financial leverage or market power. Even avoidance is not equally accessible to all firms: as suggested by the statistical analysis, investors in manufacturing are relatively able to bypass climate-vulnerable markets, whereas primary sector firms with location-specific needs have little choice but to target high-risk areas.

Meanwhile, firms that appear to accept climate risks without taking proactive steps may actually be engaging in dependency management by negotiating their external environments – using institutional influence, regulatory bargaining power, or consumer market dominance to delay or deflect the worst impacts of climate-related disruptions. By lobbying for regulatory stability, influencing public discourse on sustainability, or securing financial and institutional support, they attempt to maintain the conditions necessary for continued business operations without costly adaptation. This approach reflects a strategic effort to manage key external dependencies, not by reducing their exposure to climate risk, but by shaping the rules and narratives that determine how this risk affects them.

4.3 The Limits of Company-Led Climate Risk Management

While some companies are taking steps to protect themselves from climate risk, the reality is that the threats to companies stemming from global warming cannot be managed entirely through firm-level efforts. This reflects the scale and the nature of climate-related impacts. Two key challenges stand out.

First, as the intensity of extreme weather and natural disasters increases, the infrastructure that companies depend on will face considerable strain. This will be especially significant for MNCs that operate in multiple markets. These companies cannot simply ignore or avoid the problem, as they will inevitably face some degree of physical risk to their operations and supply chains. Nor can they count on insurance, given rising premiums and the likelihood of denial (see Flavelle et al. 2023). Making adaptations to protect infrastructure may be feasible for some assets that are owned or controlled by companies, but not for public infrastructure, such as roads, bridges, power grids, water systems, and communication networks.

This presents a massive problem for MNCs. Public infrastructure enables them to produce and deliver goods and services, to access markets and customers, and to manage their finances and operations.

However, the very same infrastructure is also vulnerable to the physical impacts of climate change, which may cause disruptions, damages, or losses for the companies that depend on it. For example, a manufacturing company may face disruptions in its production and supply chain if public roads are flooded or if the electricity grid is overloaded due to extreme heat. A retail company may lose customers and revenue if local communities are damaged by hurricanes or if the local population is affected by heat stress. A financial company may face increased loan defaults and credit losses if its borrowers are affected by wildfires or coastal erosion. It is simply not realistic for companies to protect all of this infrastructure on their own.

The second challenge revolves around the interdisciplinary nature of climate risk. Climate change is not only a technical or financial problem, but also a social, political, ethical, and legal one. It involves multiple dimensions and domains of knowledge and action that need to be integrated and coordinated to address causes, consequences, and solutions:

- One dimension of climate risk is scientific, requiring an understanding of the physical processes and mechanisms that drive climate change, such as GHG emissions, radiative forcing, feedback loops, and tipping points. It also requires an understanding of the impacts and uncertainties of climate change on the natural environment and human systems, such as temperature changes, sea level rise, extreme weather events, biodiversity loss, food security, health, and migration.
- A second dimension of climate risk is engineering. It requires an understanding of the technologies and innovations that can help mitigate or adapt to climate change, such as renewable energy sources, carbon capture and storage (CCS), energy efficiency, smart grids, green buildings, and climate-resilient infrastructure, as well as the costs, benefits, trade-offs, and barriers of implementing these technologies and innovations in different contexts and sectors.
- Policy is a third dimension of climate risk. One must understand the laws and regulations that govern the actions and responsibilities of different actors and stakeholders in relation to climate change, such as national governments, IGOs, subnational entities, businesses, civil society groups, and individuals. The incentives and disincentives that shape the behaviors and choices of these actors in terms of reducing

emissions, enhancing adaptation, or supporting finance and cooperation are also key.

- A fourth dimension of climate risk is economic, which necessitates an appreciation for the markets and mechanisms that influence the supply and demand of goods and services related to climate change, such as carbon pricing, emissions trading schemes, subsidies, taxes, green bonds, and green funds, in addition to the risks and opportunities that climate change creates for different industries and sectors in terms of competitiveness, profitability, growth potential, and value creation.
- A fifth dimension of climate risk is psychological. This corresponds to the attitudes and beliefs that affect the perceptions of climate change among different groups and individuals, such as cognitive biases, heuristics, framing effects, social norms, and values. A psychological lens is also necessary to understand the motivations and emotions that influence the willingness to act on climate change among different groups and individuals, such as self-interest, altruism, fear, anger, guilt, hope, and trust.
- Sixth, unpacking the moral principles and values that guide judgments and decisions about what is right or wrong in relation to climate change, such as justice, equity, responsibility, accountability, and solidarity, is essential to fully capturing climate risk. Ethics are also necessary to comprehend the dilemmas and conflicts that arise from competing or conflicting interests and values among different actors and stakeholders in relation to climate change, such as inter- and intra-generational equity, human rights, and ecological rights.

Its interdisciplinary nature makes climate risk quite different from other kinds of noncommercial risks that companies face, such as those related to politics or culture. While managing these risks requires an understanding of countries' political systems, social norms, and cultural characteristics, there is not generally a need to understand complex scientific phenomena or transportation and facilities engineering. Climate change presents a different sort of challenge than companies are used to dealing with, and most are not equipped to handle it on their own.

Within this context, companies will need to collaborate with local, national, and international governing bodies to protect and adapt the public infrastructure that they share and use. More generally, companies will need governments to take on the brunt of the burden of climate change adaptation. Governments have the authority and responsibility to set the rules and standards that shape the behaviors of businesses and other actors in relation to climate change. They also often have the resources and capabilities to provide the public goods and services that are essential for building climate resilience and sustainability.

Chapter 5 and 6 will turn attention away from climate risk and toward climate opportunities. However, in Chapter 7 we will return to climate risk and the role of governments in risk management.

5 International Business Opportunities Amid Climate Disruption

As we have established, climate change is creating challenges for many firms, threatening the infrastructure that they rely on, leading to new regulations and laws, exposing them to costly litigation, and affecting their reputations among investors and consumers. Yet even as many companies are facing heightened risk as a result of warming temperatures, others are finding opportunities in the evolving marketplace. In particular, those MNCs that are willing and able to develop and adopt green technologies and solutions can simultaneously enhance their reputations, attract investors and customers, create new markets and jobs, and generate positive environmental impacts.

5.1 Business Opportunities Amid Non-Climate Disruptions

Before focusing on climate change specifically, it is useful to reflect on the ways in which companies have found opportunities amid other sorts of large-scale crises, be those wars, economic recessions, or major public health disruptions. These sorts of crises had devastating impacts on the operations of many companies around the world. Yet, at the same time, innovative, adaptable, and forward-thinking firms found opportunities to prosper even as many of their counterparts failed.

We can begin with the example of World War II, a period of widespread devastation and economic upheaval that had profound impacts on many businesses. Industries not essential to the war effort experienced severe shortages as access to raw materials became limited and scarce resources were diverted to support military needs (Wendt 1947). Workforces were also affected as millions of men enlisted in the military and many other workers were recruited into strategic war industries, leaving labor shortages in many sectors (Dechter and Elder, Jr. 2004). The impacts were still more acute for companies that relied on global markets, as international trade disruptions were caused by naval blockades and the destruction of trade routes (Krpec and Hodulak 2019; Martin 2021).

At the same time, the war created opportunities in industries like manufacturing, technology, and logistics, which boomed because of unprecedented demand for military equipment and supplies (Klein 2013). Companies that could pivot to support the war effort flourished, such as automakers retooling factories to produce tanks, airplanes, and military vehicles (Hyde 2013). The war also accelerated technological and industrial advancements. For instance, the development of radar, jet engines, and nuclear technology during this period opened new avenues for future business and innovation (Giffard 2016; Hewlett 1976; Zaloga 1989). Furthermore, the war effort led to significant government investment in infrastructure and industry (Jaworski 2017), laying the foundation for postwar economic growth in several countries (Marglin and Schor 1992). Thus, while World War II brought immense challenges for some businesses, it simultaneously laid the groundwork for others to prosper and innovate.

Likewise, the 2007–2008 global financial crisis, marked by the collapse of major financial institutions and a severe credit crunch, affected businesses across countries and sectors.[1] Numerous companies, including many in the finance, real estate, and automotive sectors, faced extreme difficulties. The tightening of credit markets meant that many businesses struggled to secure loans for operations and expansion.[2] At the same time, consumer spending plummeted, deeply impacting industries that relied on discretionary spending, such as retail and leisure.[3]

Conversely, the recession created substantial opportunities in some sectors. Financial turmoil led to a surge in demand for discount and value-based retailers as consumers became more budget-conscious (Rosenbloom 2009), enabling companies in these spaces to expand their market shares (Dizik 2015). Furthermore, the crisis prompted a renewed focus on financial regulation and risk management, providing a boost to firms specializing in compliance, auditing, and consulting (Singh 2008). Companies in the technology sector also saw growth

[1] See Brunnermeier (2009) and Tooze (2019) for detailed overviews of the crisis.

[2] New loans for large borrowers fell 79 percent from the second quarter of 2007 to the fourth quarter of 2008 (Ivashina and Scharfstein 2010).

[3] For example, US department store sales declined 13.3 percent and specialty apparel retailer sales declined 10.4 percent in 2008 (Rosenbloom 2008).

opportunities as businesses sought more efficient solutions in a challenging economic environment (e.g., Barroso and Laborda 2022). Additionally, the recession paved the way for the rise of the sharing economy, with companies like Airbnb and Uber capitalizing on changing consumer behaviors and preferences (Habibi and Kohli 2022).

The COVID-19 pandemic, a global health crisis that began in early 2020, serves as a final example. Many companies faced severe hardships because of the pandemic. Travel restrictions and lockdowns led to rapid declines in airline and tourism activities (Liu et al. 2023), while social distancing and consumer caution impacted restaurants, hotels, and brick-and-mortar stores (Gunay and Kurtulmuş 2021). The pandemic also disrupted global supply chains, causing significant operational challenges for manufacturing and export-dependent industries (McGillvray 2021). Small businesses were hit particularly hard because of their limited financial buffers and reliance on foot traffic (Kang and Wang 2023).

On the flip side, the pandemic presented opportunities for growth in several areas. E-commerce and online retail experienced a massive surge as consumers shifted to online shopping amid lockdowns and physical store closures (United Nations 2021). Companies offering remote work technologies, such as video conferencing, cloud services, and cybersecurity, saw increased demand as the workforce transitioned to working from home (Ellsworth-Krebs et al. 2021). The healthcare sector, particularly pharmaceuticals and biotech companies involved in developing COVID-19 vaccines and treatments, experienced significant growth (Cancherini et al. 2021; Kimball 2023). Additionally, the pandemic spurred innovation in areas like telemedicine, online education, and digital entertainment, with companies in these fields finding new customers and markets (Adgate 2021; Diaz-Infante et al. 2022; Shaver 2022).

5.2 The Value of Sustainable Business

In each of the cases noted earlier, innovative and forward-thinking companies identified and filled voids in a challenging marketplace. Climate change will similarly offer opportunities for certain firms – particularly those that are willing and able to lean into environmental sustainability. The scholarly literature offers two broad frameworks to

Table 5.1 *Frameworks for conceptualizing the value of sustainability.*

	Triple Bottom Line	Sustainable Value Framework
Definition	A sustainability framework that examines a company's social, environmental, and economic impacts.	A strategy that integrates sustainability into business operations and decision-making, aiming to create long-term value.
Key Focus	Balancing social, environmental, and economic considerations.	Creating value through sustainability for different stakeholders and timeframes.
Components	People (social); planet (environmental); profit (economic).	Present/internal; present/external; future/internal; future/external.
Example	A company implements fair labor practices, reduces carbon emissions, and maintains profitability.	A company improves operational efficiency (present/internal); a company enhances community relations (present/external); a company invests in renewable energy (future/internal); a company invests in the development of sustainable products (future/external).

explain how companies can incorporate sustainability into their planning strategies: the triple bottom line and the sustainable value framework (see Table 5.1).

The triple bottom line posits that companies should undertake a shift in mindset to move from focusing solely on generating profits to taking a more holistic approach that simultaneously advances people, the planet, and profits (Elkington 1998). To achieve this shift, companies should cater not only to their shareholders but also to their stakeholders, including employees, advocacy groups, and subject matter experts. Advocates of the triple bottom line emphasize that companies can derive a competitive advantage by adopting a strategy of advancing social and environmental progress, as consumers increasingly shift toward responsible firms (Schulz and Flanigan 2016). More generally, companies such as these will be well positioned to thrive in the emerging market landscape in which regulators, customers, and investors expect firms to incorporate sustainable planning into their wider business activities.

This framework, while appealingly simple, faces several critiques. One of the primary concerns is that it lends itself to vague promises and greenwashing. Companies may use the language of the triple bottom line to present themselves as socially and environmentally responsible without committing to substantial or measurable changes, which allows them to reap the reputational benefits of sustainability without implementing impactful practices (Norman and MacDonald 2004). Additionally, the triple bottom line can be challenging to operationalize because it requires balancing sometimes competing priorities of economic performance, social equity, and environmental stewardship. This balancing act can result in conflicts and trade-offs that are difficult to manage and may not always align with the core profit-driven motives of traditional business models (Ozanne et al. 2016). Furthermore, this framework lacks a standardized method for measuring social and environmental outcomes, making it difficult to assess and compare the performance of different companies objectively (Hubbard 2009).

The sustainable value framework addresses some of these concerns by more explicitly and systematically explaining how sustainability planning enhances shareholder value (Hart and Milstein 2003). The starting point is that shareholder value has four key dimensions that stem, first, from the need for firms to be successful both in the present and in the future and, second, from the importance of building capabilities within the firm while also engaging productively with external sources. These dimensions are: (1) cost and risk reduction, which generates immediate impacts and internal development, (2) reputation and legitimacy, which leads to present success and external validation, (3) innovation and repositioning, which supports future planning and internal development, and (4) growth path and trajectory, which corresponds to future planning and external engagement. Each dimension of shareholder value can be enhanced by means of a sustainability-oriented strategy. For example, the development of clean technology advances innovation and repositioning, a sustainability vision supports growth trajectory, pollution prevention contributes to cost and risk reduction, and product stewardship acts as a catalyst for reputation and legitimacy.

5.3 Three Pillars of Sustainable Business Opportunity

The triple bottom line and sustainable value framework provide insights into how business analysts can conceptualize the value of sustainability in the emerging green economy, which the UNEP defines as an economy that results in "improved human well-being and social equity, while significantly reducing environmental risks and ecological scarcities."[4] While understanding the value of sustainability is an important step, carving out a competitive advantage in the green economy will require companies to innovate by developing or advancing into new areas – that is, into the blue ocean.

The blue ocean refers to the array of industries and markets that do not yet exist in today's world. This new market space is uncontested, such that innovative firms that create opportunities for themselves in the blue ocean can build and corner the market in the initial absence of competition. Firms can do so either by creating entirely new industries or by stretching the boundaries of existing industries (within the red ocean) into new spaces (Kim and Mauborgne 2005).

To reflect on market space within and around the blue ocean, I draw on a framework from ARUP and Oxford Economics (Richard and Lambert 2023) that identifies three interconnected and, at times, overlapping pillars of sustainable business opportunity that are emerging in the climate transition: (1) early adopters can establish an advantage relative to slow-to-adapt competitors, (2) new green markets for low-carbon goods and services are emerging and prospering, and (3) there are opportunities for developing and advancing climate solutions. These are summarized in Table 5.2 and discussed in the pages that follow.

Before diving into these pillars, it must be noted that the strategy of pursuing blue ocean innovation is inherently risky and unpredictable. The process of discovering or inventing in the blue ocean requires

[4] The UNEP's full statement is available here: https://sustainabledevelopment.un.org/index.php?menu=1446.

Table 5.2 ***Pillars of sustainable business opportunity stemming from climate change.***

Pillar	Description	Benefits	Risks
Early Adopters	Firms that quickly adopt and integrate new technologies, practices, or innovations ahead of competitors.	Enhanced brand recognition and corporate image; customer loyalty; employee retention; operational efficiencies and cost savings; compliance with evolving regulations; access to government incentives.	Risk of investing in unproven technologies; potential operational inefficiencies; regulatory uncertainties.
Green Markets	Emergence of new markets for carbon-neutral goods and services.	First mover advantage; influence on regulatory frameworks; alignment with global sustainability trends.	Significant upfront investments; potential for lower-than-expected investment returns; increased competition from later entrants.
Climate Solutions	Developing technologies to mitigate global warming directly.	Capitalize on emerging demand for climate solutions.	High costs; unproven scalability; environmental uncertainties; ethical concerns; potential for geopolitical conflicts.

significant investment in R&D, as well as a deep understanding of emerging trends and consumer needs. However, these investments do not guarantee success, and many firms may struggle to generate innovative ideas or to accurately judge market demand. Additionally, the initial absence of competition in a blue ocean can be short-lived. Once a new market is proven profitable, it will quickly attract competitors, turning the once uncontested space into a competitive red ocean. Lastly, the focus on creating new markets may lead companies to overlook opportunities for improvement and innovation within their existing markets, where they already possess expertise and customers. Thus, while blue ocean innovation offers the potential for growth and market leadership, it also entails considerable risks and challenges.

5.3.1 Pillar #1: Early Adopters

The first pillar is early adopters – which can be thought of as operating in the coastal areas around the blue ocean. These are firms that quickly adopt and integrate new technologies, practices, or innovations into their operations ahead of competitors. By positioning themselves at the forefront of change, these companies are well placed to seize emerging opportunities, set industry standards, and establish a competitive edge (Rogers 1962). Companies that adapt early to global warming adopt sustainable practices, invest in green technologies, and align their business models with environmental stewardship, often setting the pace for others in their industries. Being an early adopter can boost a company's competitive advantage by enhancing its brand recognition, corporate image, and performance (Su et al. 2015).

These benefits can be seen across various sectors. For example, Vestas and Siemens invested in wind turbine technology before it became mainstream, which allowed them to develop advanced technologies, secure patents, and build extensive networks – all of which now serve as barriers to entry for new competitors (Sovacool and Enevoldsen 2015). In the retail sector, Patagonia's commitment to environmental responsibility, including using recycled materials and promoting product longevity, has enhanced its brand reputation and attracted a loyal customer base that values sustainability (Rattalino 2018). Similarly, IKEA's early investments in sustainable supply chains and eco-friendly products have set industry standards and drawn environmentally conscious consumers (Alänge et al. 2016; Gao and Souza 2022). In the technology sector, Google and Microsoft invested early in renewable energy-powered data centers. This adaptation stands to reduce their carbon footprints and to result in long-term operational cost savings (Oberhaus 2019).

Research shows that leaning into sustainability in this manner can lead to increased customer loyalty (Yuan et al. 2024) and better employee retention (Lee and Chen 2018), among other things (Alhouti and D'Souza 2018). Furthermore, early adaptation may translate into tangible benefits like operational efficiencies and cost savings (Link and Naveh 2006). Early adopters are also better positioned to comply with evolving environmental regulations, as proactively incorporating sustainable practices helps them avoid the costs and disruptions associated with retrofitting operations to meet new standards (Potoski and Prakash 2005). They are also often first in line to benefit from government incentives, such as tax breaks, grants, or subsidies for sustainable practices (Giuli and Kostovetsky 2014).

In the context of RDT, early adoption helps companies manage their dependencies in three ways. First, they reduce reliance on natural and institutional resources that are likely to lose viability, such as fossil fuels and weak regulations, instead aligning themselves with renewable energy sources and stricter environmental standards. In doing so, they preemptively adjust to future policy and market shifts rather than being forced to react under pressure. Second, early adopters secure key resources before competitors. These include customers who prioritize sustainability, policy support, and product inputs that may become scarce as demand for green technologies grows. By locking in these resources early, firms create barriers to entry for laggards that wait too long to transition. Third, they negotiate their environment by influencing industry standards and regulatory frameworks in ways that reinforce their strategic advantages, again making it more difficult for later entrants to compete.

While being an early adopter offers numerous advantages, it is not without risk. Adopting sustainable technologies and practices often requires significant upfront investment, which can strain financial resources, particularly for smaller or less established companies (Jaramillo et al. 2019). Additionally, the regulatory landscape for environmental practices remains in flux, with the possibility of future regulations rendering current investments less effective or even obsolete. These risks reflect the double-edged nature of dependency management for early adopters: they attempt to restructure dependencies before others, but they may find themselves committed to dependencies that do not materialize as expected if they miscalculate future trends.

5.3.2 Pillar #2: Green Markets

The second pillar is green markets for low-carbon goods and services. The green market is largely in the blue ocean, such that firms innovating in this space have an opportunity to corner their respective markets and build strong relationships with the growing, yet still underserved, segment of environmentally conscious consumers. Moreover, by pioneering sustainable solutions, these companies often influence regulatory frameworks, which are frequently shaped around emerging technologies and practices (Puller 2006). This can, in turn, contribute to relatively high barriers to entry for latecomer companies seeking to enter the space subsequently (Kerin et al. 1992).

EVs, for example, were a blue ocean innovation that stemmed from the stretching of an existing industry. Yet it involved a complete reimagining of vehicle design, production, and infrastructure. Since this sector emerged, it has been experiencing rapid growth because of increasing environmental concerns, stricter emissions regulations, and breakthroughs in battery technology (Brothers et al. 2023), as well as policy support (Baumgarte et al. 2021; Langbroek et al. 2016). Environmentally, EVs offer a significant reduction in CO_2 emissions (Ahmadi 2019; Franzó and Nasca 2021) – which should be further amplified as electricity generation becomes greener – while also contributing to improved air quality (Liang et al. 2019).[5]

Venturing into EV manufacturing secures new markets and aligns with the global trend toward sustainability (Yang et al. 2022). Tesla's early commitment to electric cars and trucks allowed it to develop a robust charging infrastructure (LaMonaca and Ryan 2022) and a strong brand identity associated with environmental responsibility (Long et al. 2019), effectively making it the poster child for EVs in

[5] EVs also carry some negative environmental impacts (see Tabuchi and Plumer 2023).

the US.[6] Traditional automakers like Volkswagen and General Motors have responded by accelerating their own EV programs, yet these companies have struggled to eat into Tesla's market share (Lienert and White 2023), while other firms have struggled to enter the EV market at all (Ewing and Dooley 2023).

Likewise, renewable fuel production is an emerging green market responding to the need for sustainable fuel options, particularly in sectors that are difficult to electrify, such as aviation and heavy industry (Gelles 2023). This market has grown because of advancements in technology (Ebadian et al. 2020), increased environmental concerns (Hao and Shao 2021), and the push for energy diversification (Bird et al. 2005). While solar, wind, and hydro energy are well established at this point, the markets for green hydrogen and geothermal energy are poised to expand rapidly as technology advances and production costs decline (Ordóñez et al. 2023; Center for Sustainable Systems, University of Michigan 2023). Thus, for companies like Greenergy, Rentech, Binatural, and others, engaging in renewable fuel production offers a strategic opportunity to be part of an evolving energy landscape in a market that is likely to see increased demand as global efforts to reduce emissions intensify.

Green market firms share many of the same dependency management advantages as early adopters. They reduce their reliance on unsustainable natural resources, outdated regulatory systems, and carbon-intensive supply chains before market pressures force a transition. By securing key natural resources and government support before competitors, they position themselves ahead of industry shifts. Additionally, they influence policy and regulatory frameworks, ensuring that emerging environmental standards align with their business models. By proactively managing these dependencies, green market firms can insulate themselves from future disruptions and reinforce their competitive advantages as sustainability gains traction.

Yet green market firms also create new dependencies for those who enter later. For example, later entrants in the US marketplace for EVs have little choice but to integrate into Tesla's extensive EV charging network, rather than create their own (Rogers 2023). This reinforces

[6] At the time of this writing, BYD has displaced Tesla in EV manufacturing and sales worldwide, even as trade barriers have locked it out of the US market (Walt 2025).

Tesla's ability to shape the marketplace to its advantage, dictating the terms of engagement for those who follow by controlling a key resource that its rivals depend on.

However, green market firms are not immune to dependency risks of their own. Many rely on government incentives and subsidies to make their products competitive, leaving them vulnerable to policy shifts (Fonseca 2024). Additionally, consumers and businesses may transition to green products more slowly than anticipated, leaving first movers overexposed to high upfront costs with lower-than-expected returns. For example, Beyond Meat and Impossible Foods were pioneers in sustainable food production after developing plant-based meat alternatives to great fanfare (Hart 2023), yet the growth of both companies stalled as the market for plant-based meat hit a ceiling (Torrella 2023). Finally, while first movers enjoy early competitive advantages, late entrants may benefit from observing their mistakes, entering with cheaper, refined solutions once the market is more developed. Thus, if green market firms fail to continuously innovate, they risk losing dominance to second movers who leverage existing infrastructure without bearing the costs of creating it (Tran et al. 2012).

5.3.3 Pillar #3: Climate Solutions

Demand for large-scale solutions to directly mitigate global warming is supporting the third pillar of green business opportunity, which centers on putting the world on a sustainable path (Gelles and Flavelle 2024; Twidale 2024). The companies in this space will be the ones that develop products and services aimed at slowing, stalling, or even reversing the rise in global temperatures. This pillar is best exemplified by the emerging sector of climate engineering, sometimes called climate intervention, which includes technologies focused on CO_2 removal (Carbon Dioxiide Removal or CDR) and solar radiation modification (SRM).[7]

CDR technologies have generated great excitement in recent years, in part because companies in carbon-intensive industries, such as oil and gas, hope that CDR will allow them to continue engaging in business as usual (Temple 2021). These technologies, which have been advocated by the IPCC as a necessary tool for reining in global

[7] See Gordon (2017) and Keith (2013) for overviews and discussions of climate engineering.

temperature increases, aim to extract CO_2 from the atmosphere and store it, either through natural means or engineered processes (see Mannion et al. 2023). The potential market for CDR has drawn interest from hundreds of companies and attracted billions of dollars from venture investors (Temple 2024). Carbon Engineering, for example, has been focused on developing technologies that capture CO_2 from the air and then permanently sequester it underground or convert it to carbon-neutral fuel.[8]

On the more experimental side of climate engineering is SRM, a technique aimed at reflecting a portion of the sun's energy back into space to cool the planet (National Research Council et al. 2015). Though SRM remains largely theoretical, and its commercial application uncertain, its potential to help mitigate global heating is attracting interest from both scientific and business communities (see Buck and Nicholson 2023; Irvine et al. 2019). For example, the Harvard Solar Geoengineering Research Program is investigating the feasibility of methods like stratospheric aerosol injection and marine cloud brightening.[9]

Like green market firms, companies in the climate engineering space have the potential to reshape industries by controlling essential resources that others will depend on in a decarbonizing world. As carbon pricing and emissions targets become more stringent, fossil fuel producers, airlines, and heavy manufacturers may rely on CDR technologies to remain compliant. Similarly, SRM could create dependencies at the national or global level, with governments relying on geoengineering firms to stabilize temperatures and prevent extreme climate impacts.

However, climate engineering firms face great uncertainty in their external dependencies. Unlike EVs or biofuels, where the emergence of consumer demand, infrastructure, and supply chains are already well underway, the viability of climate engineering solutions is uncertain (Temple 2024), particularly given the enormous costs of developing and scaling these technologies (Heid et al. 2023). At present, most CDR methods remain expensive and energy-intensive, and even the most advanced systems capture only a fraction of the CO_2 emitted

[8] More information about Carbon Engineering can be found at their website: https://carbonengineering.com.

[9] Details on this research are available here: https://salatainstitute.harvard.edu/sgrp.

annually (Aeschlimann et al. 2023). This is compounded by concerns about where to store the captured carbon safely and permanently, with the risk of leakage undermining the long-term effectiveness of these efforts (van der Zwaan and Smekens 2009). SRM also comes with significant challenges and uncertainties (Baur et al. 2023), including its potential side effects (Zürn and Schäfer 2013). Techniques like stratospheric aerosol injection, which involves dispersing reflective particles into the atmosphere, could disrupt regional and global climate patterns, potentially affecting monsoons, agricultural systems, and water supplies in certain regions (see Hegerl and Solomon 2009). Crucially, there is no international framework in place to regulate or direct the deployment of SRM. Thus, unilateral deployment by individual countries or groups of countries could have serious negative impacts elsewhere, prompting geopolitical conflicts and threatening human development (Kravitz and Felgenhauer 2024; Pasztor et al. 2023).

In this context, support from governments, investors, and the scientific community – which climate engineering firms will depend on for the foreseeable future – remains highly uncertain. If governments decline to provide subsidies, incentives, or regulatory mandates, or if investor enthusiasm wanes (in the case of CDR) or fails to take off (in the case of SRM), then these industries will struggle to develop or scale up. Perhaps the most fundamental challenge for climate engineering firms is their reliance on infrastructure and scientific advancements that may never fully materialize. Thus, while climate engineering firms may come to shape dependencies for others, they remain more vulnerable than early adopters or green market firms because they lack the same level of control over their external dependencies, making them the most structurally uncertain of the three pillars of climate opportunity.[10]

5.4 Additional Areas of Opportunity

Additional areas of business opportunity that do not fit comfortably into the three-pillar framework are in the realms of consulting,

[10] While not necessarily an obstacle for companies looking to operate in this space, concerns about moral hazard should be noted. The mere promise of climate engineering technologies may encourage carbon-intensive industries and governments to delay necessary emission reductions. This is particularly troubling given the uncertainty of these technologies, as they could ultimately prove unsuccessful (see Andrews et al. 2022; Tsipiras and Grant 2022).

construction, logistics, and insurance. As physical climate risks multiply, demand for consulting services will grow. Firms like the Boston Consulting Group[11] and KPMG[12] are developing advanced, technology-driven early warning systems to predict and mitigate the impacts of natural disasters. Consulting related to transition risk is also likely to grow, driven by the evolving regulatory landscape and changing societal expectations. As governments worldwide implement stricter environmental regulations, businesses will seek expert guidance to navigate new rules and capitalize on any associated incentives. Among other things, consultants can provide advice on carbon trading and adapting to green building standards.[13] Consultants can also help companies appeal to more environmentally conscientious consumers by aligning their business strategies with sustainable practices. Firms will find these services increasingly crucial for maintaining brand reputation, enhancing customer loyalty, and securing investor confidence in an eco-aware market.[14]

There is also sure to be heightened demand for resilient infrastructure, such that companies in and around the construction sector should find opportunities to create structures that can withstand extreme weather events. Another key area is logistics and supply chain management, which will increasingly be called upon to create robust, adaptable networks that can function effectively in the aftermath of an extreme weather event.

Climate risk insurance is another area of opportunity, as demand rises for protection in the face of extreme weather and climate-related

[11] Details on Boston Consulting Group's climate-related services can be found here: https://bcg.com/capabilities/climate-change-sustainability/climate-risk-adaptation-resilience.

[12] Details on KPMG's climate risk services are available here: https://kpmg.com/xx/en/home/services/advisory/risk-consulting/internal-audit-risk/sustainability-services/climate-risk-services.html.

[13] One interview participant highlighted energy service contracts as an emerging area of consulting opportunity, given regulatory variation within and across countries. Service providers audit energy use and regulations across a company's locations, identifying opportunities to integrate renewable energy to remain compliant and reduce costs.

[14] ESG rating agencies, which often have a consulting arm, have also emerged in response to climate change. I spoke to a sustainability analyst at one such agency, who told me that her company emerged in response to companies' concerns about reputation risk and thrived as transition risk came to the forefront in the 2010s and 2020s.

disruptions (see Grimaldi et al. 2020). This demand will come from individuals as well as businesses seeking ways to manage the financial fallout from intensifying storms, floods, and wildfires. Against this backdrop, insurers will see growing demand for products such as supply chain disruption insurance, climate liability insurance, and multi-peril insurance.

5.5 Change Management and Leadership

This chapter speaks to a duality of climate change, which presents unique opportunities for innovative and adaptable businesses, even as it threatens the very existence of others. To successfully navigate the evolving landscape, companies must shift their mindsets to adapt to the new reality. This requires a proactive and visionary approach to climate-related challenges: instead of viewing them solely as threats, firms should see them as opportunities for growth and innovation. This perspective is crucial for ensuring long-term sustainability and profitability against the backdrop of rising temperatures.

The companies that will thrive in this new era are those that embrace change and invest in sustainable practices and technologies. In doing so, these firms can capture emerging green markets, differentiate themselves from competitors, and comply with increasingly stringent environmental regulations. Such companies can also build stronger relationships with customers, employees, investors, and regulators, resulting in increased loyalty, better retention, and access to new markets. Beyond economic benefits, these firms can drive environmental progress, contributing to global efforts to combat climate change and promote a more sustainable future.

6 *Navigating Climate Change in the Energy Industry*

While Chapters 4 and 5 provided conceptual frameworks for understanding how MNCs manage climate risks and opportunities, case studies can offer deeper insights into how they execute climate management in practice. To that end, this chapter investigates three companies in the energy sector: ExxonMobil, Saudi Aramco, and Ørsted. These firms have each adopted a different approach, with Exxon opting to conduct business as usual by continuing to focus exclusively on oil and gas, Aramco beginning to shift into a diversified energy company, and Ørsted transitioning away from fossil fuels altogether. These firms present the full spectrum of climate management strategies, while also spanning geographies and ownership structures.[1]

I concentrate on energy firms that focus (or focused until recently) on fossil fuels for several reasons. First, these companies face existential threats from climate change, as well as potential opportunities. Oil and gas companies operate all over the world, including in the locations that are most vulnerable to physical climate risk.[2] They are also in a location-specific industry, such that avoiding climate-vulnerable settings is not a viable strategy (Gamso et al. 2024). This risk is compounded by their reliance on extensive physical infrastructure, which may be impacted by extreme weather (Cruz and Krausmann 2013). They are also highly vulnerable to transition, litigation, and reputation

[1] It should be noted that companies sometimes shift from one strategic approach to another. For example, BP adopted a diversified energy strategy in 2020, investing heavily in renewable resources and promising to reduce fossil fuel production. Yet it reversed course a few years later as its value fell, redirecting investment back to oil and gas (Elliott 2024). Thus, any or all of these companies may change course as stakeholder demands, market dynamics, or risk exposure levels change.

[2] Over 40 percent of oil and gas reserves are vulnerable to the physical impacts of climate change (Nichols and Clisby 2021). Notably, the Middle Eastern countries that contain around 50 percent of known oil reserves are becoming increasingly uninhabitable because of extreme heat (Cook and Bouri 2024), while rising sea levels threaten oil ports around the world (Carrington 2025).

risks, as their very business models are threatened by the policies, laws, and social forces pushing for decarbonization.[3] At the same time, these companies have the engineering know-how, infrastructure, and capital to be at the forefront of clean energy innovation, production, and distribution, putting them in position to take a leading role in post-carbon energy markets.

Second, fossil fuel firms face complex risk management challenges. This reflects their reliance on physical infrastructure in multiple countries and their sensitivity to changes in policy and law, but it also reflects external factors that impact their operations. For example, geopolitics affects oil and gas companies to a greater extent than firms in industries of less strategic importance (Gamso et al. 2024). For this reason, studying fossil fuel companies gives us insights into how external factors, beyond extreme weather or sociopolitical pressures to decarbonize, can affect a company's approach to managing the risks and opportunities associated with rising temperatures.

Third, the companies in this industry are major contributors to global GHG emissions. Since these are among the most problematic firms in this regard, it is important to evaluate their responses to the growing pressures to reduce emissions. This is especially true given the extensive lobbying that some oil and gas companies have undertaken to slow the transition to renewable energy (Lantushenko and Schellhorn 2023).

Finally, as some of the largest and most profitable corporations in the world, the economic power of fossil fuel firms gives them substantial leverage over national and international policy-making (Skjærseth 2005). A major energy company's commitment to reducing emissions or investing in renewables could potentially encourage governments to impose their own guidelines or mandates (see Saikawa 2013). More typically, however, their resistance to environmental regulations or to policies promoting the adoption of clean energy hinders progress toward climate goals (see Gutstein 2018; McBeath 2016; Stokes 2020).

[3] See Bogmans et al. (2024) on the impacts that climate change policy has on oil and gas. Also see a recent poll from the United Nations Development Programme and Oxford University (Flynn et al. 2024), which found that 72 percent of the global population want their country to quickly shift away from fossil fuels and toward clean energy – including majorities in fossil fuel producing countries such as Iran (79 percent), Nigeria (89 percent), and Saudi Arabia (75 percent).

The focus on energy is not to diminish the importance of companies outside of this sector. As we have seen, climate pressures are facing firms across industries. Yet the extensive challenges and opportunities that energy companies face make them ideal case studies. Moreover, their strategies and actions offer valuable lessons for companies in other sectors that are facing similar pressures to innovate and adapt.

6.1 ExxonMobil: Business as Usual

ExxonMobil, headquartered in Irving, Texas, operates major business hubs across North America, Europe, Asia, and the Middle East. Its activities span the entire oil and gas value chain, from exploration and production to refining and marketing (see Coll 2012). Exxon has faced significant criticism from environmental groups and regulators for its historical reluctance to acknowledge the full extent of climate change (Brady 2023). Yet despite these criticisms and growing global momentum toward decarbonization, Exxon remains committed to exploring and developing new oil and gas fields, expanding its refining capabilities, and optimizing its global supply chain, rather than diversifying into renewable or clean energy.[4]

This business-as-usual approach aligns most closely with the *accept* strategy discussed in Chapter 4, in which companies take little to no action to reduce or manage climate risk and accept the potential consequences. Yet there is also a facet of the *adapt* strategy in Exxon's case, as it has taken some steps to reduce emissions in an effort to cut costs and comply with regulations.

Exxon's decision to move forward this way is influenced by a combination of regulatory, stakeholder, and market factors. The regulatory system that Exxon operates within is relatively lax, as the US federal government has been less aggressive in imposing stringent climate regulations compared to the EU or other global leaders in environmental policy (Löfstedt and Vogel 2001; Smith 2012), while Texas maintains a regulatory environment that is generally favorable to fossil fuel companies (Miller 2020). These dynamics have allowed Exxon to continue its operations with minimal pushback from

[4] Exxon's plans are elaborated on in greater detail here: https://corporate.exxonmobil.com/news/news-releases/2024/1211_exxonmobil-announces-plans-to-2030-that-build-on-its-unique-advantages.

regulators. Nor have internal stakeholders imposed significant roadblocks: while a small share of activist investors have pressured Exxon to adopt a more ambitious strategy for cutting emissions, the critical mass of Exxon's investor base remains supportive of its focus on fossil fuels (Kerber and Kumar 2024). Furthermore, the market has rewarded the business-as-usual strategy so far, with Exxon enjoying record profits and paying out large dividends to investors (Ambrose 2024).[5]

At the same time, Exxon has acknowledged a need to address climate-related concerns, and the company has implemented various measures aimed at reducing its GHG emissions.[6] For example, it has made significant investments in CCS, which captures CO_2 emissions from industrial processes and stores them underground to prevent their release into the atmosphere (Eaton 2023).[7] Exxon has also undertaken projects to modernize refineries and production facilities and replace older, less efficient equipment with newer, more energy-efficient alternatives (Krauss 2017). These investments allow Exxon to signal that it is not ignoring climate change entirely.

There are pros and cons to the business-as-usual approach. One of the key pros is that it allows Exxon (and other companies using this strategy) to achieve quick improvements in efficiency and reductions in emissions without overhauling their operations. For instance, implementing advanced methane detection and reduction technologies or upgrading equipment to minimize energy waste can yield benefits with minimal disruptions to core business activities. These incremental

[5] Kenner and Heede (2021) show evidence that Exxon's executives are incentivized financially to continue down the business-as-usual path. Additionally, one interview participant – a sustainability specialist with a background in the energy industry – pointed out a legacy effect, whereby oil and gas executives, having been socialized within the industry and shaped by its historical successes, often remain confident in their ability to expand market share and maintain profitability using a fossil fuel-based model.

[6] Exxon's statement on reducing GHG emissions can be read here: https://corporate.exxonmobil.com/news/news-releases/2022/0118_exxonmobil-announces-ambition-for-net-zero-greenhouse-gas-emissions-by-2050. It should be noted that Exxon's climate statements have often been stronger than its actions (Li et al. 2022).

[7] CCS is related to CDR, which was discussed in Chapter 5. However, while CDR focuses on removing CO_2 already in the atmosphere, CCS primarily captures CO_2 from industrial processes before it enters the atmosphere. It should be noted that there are considerable questions about the scalability of CCS and about its capacity to significantly reduce CO_2 emissions (Westervelt 2024).

changes can lead to measurable emissions reductions, helping to align the company with immediate regulatory requirements and industry standards.

Another benefit is its cost-effectiveness compared to more radical changes. Diversifying or shifting fully into renewable energy requires substantial investments in new technologies, infrastructure, and talent. In contrast, improving efficiency within the existing operational framework tends to be less costly and can often be funded through internal capital rather than requiring external financing or new business partnerships. This strategy has enabled Exxon to continue generating significant revenue from its oil and gas operations while modestly improving its sustainability profile.

The business-as-usual strategy also has significant limitations, particularly when considering the long-term risks of relying heavily on fossil fuels in a changing global energy market. Companies that lean heavily into efficiency gains without making more substantial changes to their energy mix or business model may become complacent, believing that incremental improvements are enough. In Exxon's case, the company's confidence in the long-term viability of oil and gas could lead to underestimating the urgency of transitioning to renewable energy sources. This mindset can create a false sense of security, leading to heightened vulnerability to market shifts, regulatory changes, and increased competition from more forward-thinking firms.

Relatedly, this strategy is a gamble of sorts that the impacts of climate change will not be as severe as most analysts believe. This gamble can pay off, particularly if markets swing away from renewable energy (see Elliott 2024). Yet, as awareness of global warming intensifies, there is likely to be greater pressure from investors, consumers, and civil society for companies to take bold actions to address their environmental impacts. Companies that stick too closely to the business-as-usual model may face reputation costs, as stakeholders perceive their efforts as insufficient or out of touch with the broader societal push toward sustainability. Indeed, Exxon has faced criticism from environmental groups and some investors who argue that its efforts to reduce emissions do not go far enough (Quinson and Crowley 2024). This could ultimately result in decreased sales, divestment, and challenges in attracting and retaining top talent.

Overall, then, while the business-as-usual strategy offers some immediate and cost-effective benefits, it carries significant risks and limitations in the long term. As we will see in the next section, some companies have sought to hedge by diversifying their investments toward renewable energy, even while continuing to focus much of their business on fossil fuels.

6.2 Saudi Aramco: Diversified Energy Company

Recognizing the growing pressures of climate change and a desire from policymakers to diversify into more sustainable energy sources, Aramco – the world's largest energy company – is beginning to expand its portfolio beyond oil and gas. This involves maintaining its core fossil fuel business while also making large investments in renewable energy, hydrogen production, and alternative fuels. By diversifying its energy mix, Aramco aims to position itself as a key player in the emerging green energy market while continuing to leverage its vast resources and expertise in oil and gas.

This approach aligns with the *diversify* risk management strategy, discussed in Chapter 4, as well as with the *green markets* pillar of opportunity, presented in Chapter 5. Companies that are diversifying their energy portfolios reduce the climate risks associated with fossil fuels, as well as their reliance on a single commodity. They are also attempting to open new revenue streams in the rapidly expanding renewable energy sector.

For its part, Aramco invested approximately $920 million to secure 30 percent of Sudair, a massive solar photovoltaic power plant in Sudair Industrial City that plans to build a 40-gigawatt solar platform (Reed 2024). It also bought a 50 percent stake in Air Products Qudra's Blue Hydrogen Industrial Gases Company, signaling its moves into blue hydrogen production and CCS (Ojea 2024).[8] It also plans to open two plants in 2025 to produce synthetic fuels, which emit less CO_2 than petroleum (Martin and Di Paola 2023). Crucially, Aramco continues to invest heavily in oil and gas, which remains its primary source of revenue (Reed 2024), and has rejected calls to transition away from fossil fuels entirely (Kimball 2024).

[8] Blue hydrogen is produced using natural gas, but unlike grey hydrogen, the emitted CO_2 is captured and stored using CCS technology. Green hydrogen, which is the most environmentally friendly option, is produced using electricity generated from renewable resources like sunlight or wind.

Aramco's strategy is rooted in its position as both the world's largest oil producer and a state-owned enterprise responsible for supporting the broader economic goals of Saudi Arabia.[9] Saudi Arabia sits atop around 27 billion barrels of crude oil, second only to Venezuela in proven reserves, and it is one of the world's leading exporters of petroleum.[10] Oil and gas are central to the economy, accounting for 87 percent of budget revenues, 42 percent of GDP, and 90 percent of export earnings in 2018.[11] Not surprisingly, given this context, Saudi officials have taken steps to discourage a global shift away from oil and gas through pressure and lobbying campaigns (Friedman 2024; Tabuchi 2022). Yet the government is also seeking to diversify its economy, given the finite nature of oil and the global movement to shift away from fossil fuels.[12] Aramco's strategy reflects this multifaceted imperative: it is driven by the need to adapt to the evolving global energy market, where demand for renewable energy is rapidly growing, it has a mandate to support Saudi Arabia's aims to reduce the country's dependence on fossil fuels, and it must continue to generate oil revenue for the foreseeable future.

The diversified energy company strategy has several advantages. By investing in renewable energy sources like wind, solar, and bioenergy, companies like Aramco participate in, and benefit from, the growing clean energy market, ensuring that they remain key players in the energy industry even as traditional fossil fuel demand declines in relative terms. In the meantime, they can continue to sell fossil fuels to satisfy near-term demand, thereby maintaining the core facet of their business operations in case alternative energy markets do not expand as quickly as some anticipate (Garrett et al. 2024).

Additionally, even a modest shift away from fossil fuels is likely to be viewed favorably by investors, customers, and governments that prioritize sustainability. Companies that demonstrate a commitment to reducing their environmental impacts and contributing to the global energy transition can attract investment from environmentally conscious

[9] See Cuervo-Cazurra et al. (2014) on the unique characteristics of state-owned MNCs.

[10] Details on Saudi Arabia's oil reserves and exports are available here: https://trade.gov/country-commercial-guides/saudi-arabia-oil-gas-petrochemicals.

[11] These and other data points can be found here: https://forbes.com/places/saudi-arabia.

[12] Saudi plans and ambitions are detailed here: https://vision2030.gov.sa.

funds and receive support from governments. Additionally, consumers are becoming more discerning about the environmental practices of the companies they support, such that a diversified energy portfolio can enhance a company's brand reputation and customer loyalty. In Aramco's case, there is a direct imperative to align its operations with the objectives of policymakers, who have their own complex stakeholder maps.

This strategy also comes with significant challenges. There are high upfront costs associated with R&D, as well as with creating infrastructure to support clean energy production. Synthetic fuels and clean hydrogen are, perhaps, the clean energies of the future, but they are still at relatively early stages of development and are not yet economically viable or scalable. Solar and wind energy are more well developed, but they too are characterized by costly challenges associated with land use, storage, and environmental and resource management.

Relatedly, companies venturing into renewable or alternative energy production find themselves navigating unfamiliar territories that lie outside their core competencies.[13] For Aramco, which has a long history rooted in oil and gas, the shift will involve significant learning curves and the need to build expertise. At the same time, diversifying companies risk diluting their focus in traditional operations. As Aramco allocates resources and attention to new energy ventures, it may inadvertently weaken its core oil and gas business. If not managed carefully, this shift in focus could lead to poor performance in both traditional and diversified sectors.

Finally, while diversification into renewables mitigates some climate risk, continued investment in fossil fuels and reliance on carbon-intensive energy sources do not align with the rapid decarbonization needed to meet international climate targets. Aramco, while expanding into new energy markets, continues to rely primarily on oil production. This stands to lead to some of the same risks that face firms continuing to engage in business as usual.

In sum, a diversified energy strategy allows companies to wade into new areas while maintaining their core business functions. Yet it also presents financial, operational, and strategic challenges. Aramco's experience illustrates both the potential benefits and risks of pursuing

[13] See Hashai (2015) and Zahavi and Lavie (2013) on the challenges that can face firms as they diversify their business operations.

such a strategy, particularly given the political pressures it faces as a state-owned firm. These dynamics are amplified further for companies that shift entirely away from fossil fuels, such as Ørsted.

6.3 Ørsted: Pioneer of Complete Transition

Ørsted, a company that was generating the large majority of its revenue from fossil fuels just sixteen years ago, has fully embraced green energy – especially wind.[14] By focusing decisively on sustainability and innovation, Ørsted has become an industry leader, capturing significant market share in the process (Rendtorff 2023). Yet it also faces substantial challenges.

Fossil fuel companies adopting a complete transition strategy make significant investments in established renewable energy sources like wind, solar, hydro, and bioenergy. They may also invest in emerging energy technologies that have the potential to transform the industry in the future, such as green hydrogen and geothermal energy. This approach can also involve fostering innovation through partnerships with tech companies, startups, and other industries to develop smart grids, energy storage, and advanced digital technologies. As was true of companies using the diversified energy company approach, those transitioning completely away from fossil fuels are in alignment with the *diversify* risk management strategy and the *green markets* pillar of opportunity. Yet unlike companies such as Aramco, pioneers of complete transition are gearing their entire business model toward emerging green markets, such that diversification from fossil fuels is a means to an end, as opposed to an end unto itself.

Ørsted, formerly Danish Oil and Natural Gas (DONG),[15] was engaged in significant oil and gas exploration and production, primarily in the North Sea. It also held a near-monopoly on gas distribution in Denmark, deriving the bulk of its revenue from coal-generated heat and power. However, a combination of external pressures and internal dynamics led the company to embark on a dramatic reorientation away from fossil fuels. Ørsted went on to become the world's largest

[14] Ørsted is a very rare company in this regard, as becoming a diversified energy company that maintains oil and gas operations (as exemplified by Aramco) is the farthest extent to which firms have generally gone (Green et al. 2022).

[15] DONG was established in the early 1970s by the Danish government, which continues to own a 50.1 percent stake in Ørsted.

producer of wind energy, which now accounts for approximately 90 percent of its energy generation (see McFarlane 2021; Storrow 2020).

A key external factor driving Ørsted's transition was the evolving regulatory landscape in Europe (Voldsgaard and Rüdiger 2022). The EU has been at the forefront of global efforts to reduce carbon emissions and to promote the formation of green markets (Oberthür and Dupont 2021; Veugelers et al. 2024), while also taking steps to liberalize energy markets across the continent (Pepermans 2019). These policies coincided with declining returns from Ørsted's investments in natural gas, which proved uncompetitive relative to coal-generated electricity. Faced with the changing policy landscape and a failing business, Ørsted opted to completely overhaul its approach.

With the support of a major investment from Goldman Sachs Group Inc., Ørsted leaned into offshore wind, which it had been dabbling in since the early 2000s (McFarlane 2021). In the years that followed, it launched wind projects in Germany, Sweden, the Netherlands, Norway, the UK, and the US, in addition to Denmark. As Ørsted focused more on wind, it shed its fossil fuel operations, closing plants and selling off what remained of its oil and gas business in 2017 (Storrow 2020). Like Aramco, Ørsted has made investments in next-generation clean energy technologies, including CCS,[16] e-fuels, and green hydrogen,[17] but its primary focal point remains offshore wind.[18]

Being a pioneer of complete transition carries potential rewards. One of the most significant benefits is the first-mover advantage, which secures early market share (Robinson et al. 1994), while putting the firm in a position to act as an industry leader that can drive future trends to its advantage (Afewerki and Steen 2023). Indeed, by leading the way in offshore wind production, Ørsted has been able to set the pace for technological advancements and regulatory frameworks,

[16] More information on Ørsted's CCS investments can be found here: https://orsted.com/en/what-we-do/renewable-energy-solutions/bioenergy/carbon-capture-and-storage.

[17] More information on Ørsted's e-fuel and green hydrogen investments is available here: https://us.orsted.com/renewable-energy-solutions/power-to-x.

[18] Focusing intensively on wind, as opposed to a panoply of renewable energy sources, has arguably been key to the company's success (McFarlane 2021).

particularly in Europe.[19] Ørsted's role in shaping the offshore wind market, along with its investments in green hydrogen and other emerging technologies, has also attracted significant partnerships and collaborations, further solidifying its leadership position. For example, Ørsted partnered with BP in 2020 to develop green hydrogen at BP's Lingen Refinery in Germany (Frangoul 2020), and it partnered with the World Wildlife Fund in 2022 to limit the impact of offshore wind on biodiversity (Shain 2022).

Additionally, firms like Ørsted can generate great excitement among a segment of stakeholders. Investors increasingly target companies that are leading the charge in sustainability,[20] while a growing number of customers are drawn to brands that align their values to environmental responsibility (Reichheld et al. 2023). Governments may also offer incentives and support to firms that are pushing the boundaries of clean energy development. Additionally, this strategy is attractive to top talent looking to work on cutting-edge projects that promise to change the world for the better (Magbool et al. 2016).

However, this strategy also comes with risks and challenges. First, while it offers companies an early mover advantage, new entrants will not be far behind as the market takes off. Sure enough, while Ørsted was able to develop an impressive market share in wind, particularly in Europe, various other companies have since entered this space (Ambrose 2021). While these firms started at a place of relative disadvantage, they learned from Ørsted's experience and are enjoying the fruits of its technological and managerial innovations (see Tran et al. 2012).

Second, investing in new and sometimes unproven technologies may not generate strong returns, which can strain a firm's financial stability and limit its ability to pursue other opportunities. Indeed, Ørsted experienced challenges with wind technologies early on (McFarlane 2021) and, more recently, high costs led it to scrap once-promising wind projects.[21] Even if investments are ultimately successful, there can

[19] An overview of Ørsted's policy advocacy can be found here: https://lobbymap.org/company/-rsted-A-S-551f3d7a1a6932d29d976a3e9233c875.

[20] A 2024 Morgan Stanley report highlighting investor interest in sustainability can be downloaded here: https://morganstanley.com/ideas/sustainable-investing-on-the-rise.

[21] Details on one scrapped project can be found here: https://orsted.com/en/company-announcement-list/2023/10/oersted-ceases-development-of-its-us-offshore-wind-73751.

be a long timeframe required for new technologies to become commercially viable and contribute to profits. During this time, companies must continue to sustain their investments without immediate financial returns, which can be challenging in a competitive environment. The extended period of waiting for profitability can also lead to pressure from investors and shareholders who are seeking quick results.

Third, while renewable energy use is likely to tick up, ultimately becoming a large share of the total global energy mix, this upward trend will probably feature valleys as well as peaks. During periods in which fossil fuels gain ground, energy companies like Ørsted that have turned completely away from oil and gas will not be able to fall back on their traditional business models. This has been demonstrated by political and market trends in the mid 2020s that put wind-oriented firms at a disadvantage relative to fossil fuel producers, undermining Ørsted's position in key markets (Elliott 2024; Prakash 2025).

6.4 Comparative and Theoretical Analyses

As global momentum toward decarbonization continues to build, the oil and gas industry faces increasing pressure to reduce its carbon footprint and transition to more sustainable energy sources. The cases of ExxonMobil, Saudi Aramco, and Ørsted illustrate the manners in which companies are responding to these pressures. Through the lens of RDT, these companies' strategies can be understood as distinct approaches to managing their external dependencies – whether by reinforcing control over existing resources or fully transitioning away from one set of dependencies in favor of another.

Exxon's business-as-usual strategy can be understood as an attempt to maintain control over the critical resources on which it depends: its vast oil and gas reserves and the infrastructure required to extract and process these resources. By continuing to lean into oil and gas, Exxon ensures a steady supply of the resources that underpin its profitability, but it also avoids the costly and uncertain shift to new dependencies associated with renewable energy markets, including new materials, technologies, and stakeholder relationships. To maintain its approach, Exxon has negotiated its environment by lobbying for favorable policies and managing stakeholders to minimize external pressures that could force a transition. Even Exxon's limited adaptation efforts serve this function, helping to neutralize criticisms without requiring a full-scale shift in operations. However, while business as usual may be profitable in the short term, it carries risk going forward: external conditions could shift quickly, leaving Exxon with diminished leverage over resources, regulators, and investors.

Aramco's effort to balance traditional fossil fuel dominance with strategic diversification into clean fuels has some overlap with Exxon's approach. Like Exxon, Aramco retains control over its most critical resource – Saudi Arabia's vast oil reserves and the infrastructure needed to exploit them. However, unlike Exxon, Aramco is actively developing new resource dependencies through its pursuit of solar energy, hydrogen, and synthetic fuels, including key minerals, new infrastructure, and still-developing technologies. This diversification serves as a hedging strategy, allowing Aramco to remain viable whether fossil fuels maintain dominance, a mixed energy system prevails, or renewables accelerate. A further distinguishing factor is Aramco's state ownership, which ties its corporate strategy to Saudi Arabia's policy objectives. This creates a complex dependency matrix, in which Aramco must balance resource control, new market expansion, and alignment with government interests. While Aramco's approach increases strategic flexibility, it also presents management challenges, as maintaining competitiveness in both traditional and emerging energy sectors requires significant investment, operational coordination, and the ability to navigate shifting regulatory and market landscapes.

Ørsted is the purest example of a company completely reshaping its resource dependencies. This has meant abandoning its traditional reliance on oil, gas, and coal resources in favor of new dependencies on offshore wind infrastructure, critical minerals, and partnerships with utilities and policymakers. Ørsted also negotiated its environment. Yet unlike Exxon, which has resisted regulatory shifts, Ørsted capitalized on evolving policies and investor preferences, securing subsidies and market support to become a leader in offshore wind. This strategy granted Ørsted an early-mover advantage, industry leadership, and access to green capital. However, it also comes with significant risks. Unlike Aramco, which retains fossil fuel revenue as a hedge, Ørsted has no fallback if renewables face setbacks. The company's success is contingent on continued policy support, technological advancements, and stable investor and consumer interest in clean energy, which could make it either a long-term winner or a casualty of market swings away from renewables.

6.5 Looking Beyond the Energy Sector

The global energy transition is a microcosm of the broader shift that is reshaping industries worldwide. As companies across sectors face pressures to reduce their environmental impacts and adapt to changing market conditions, they should consider several key insights from the strategies undertaken by Exxon, Aramco, and Ørsted.

First, nearly all MNCs – even those firmly dedicated to their existing business models – will need to take some actions in light of climate change. Those actions might be incremental, as in the case of Exxon, or comprehensive, in the mold of Ørsted, but they will need to exist in some form or fashion for companies to remain competitive in the context of rising physical risk, as well as shifting regulations and expectations. Thus, adaptability and innovation are crucial, even for companies attempting to stay the course and practice business as usual.

Balancing short- and long-term goals is another critical aspect of strategic planning. Absent policy support that allows firms to operate at a loss while building for future success, companies must find ways to pursue immediate financial returns while also investing in long-term sustainability. For Aramco, this has meant maintaining its core business in oil and gas, even as it invests in renewable energy resources and next-generation technologies. For Ørsted, it has meant cornering a new marketplace quickly and comprehensively, with the support of relatively patient stakeholders.

On that note, the importance of stakeholder engagement cannot be overstated. Companies do not operate in isolation, and stakeholder pressures can drive their strategies in one direction or another. For a state-owned company, like Aramco, business strategy reflects the state's strategic interests in whole or in part, potentially pushing the company in seemingly contradictory directions that result in a diversification strategy. For a private company, like Exxon, shareholder pressures are paramount, although the interests of various other stakeholders hold some weight, including indirectly through their influence on policies and regulations.

Finally, the need for bold leadership is evident in companies like Ørsted, which demonstrates how a clear vision and decisive actions can set a company apart in a rapidly changing market. Opportunities for transformation can come at times of immense challenge, as was the case for Ørsted in the context of its failing natural gas business in the early 2000s. But even in this context, Ørsted's leadership needed to take risks, invest in innovation, and manage uncertainties to become an industry pioneer.

7 *Public Policy and Climate Risk Management*

The chapters so far have focused on the activities of firms – both in terms of managing climate risks and seizing opportunities amid rising global temperatures. However, it would be reductive to examine corporate strategies without considering the broader institutional contexts within which companies are embedded. These contexts can shape firms' behaviors, constraining them in some respects and enabling them in others (see Macdonald 2013). For MNCs, embeddedness is especially complex, since their operations span multiple nations (Kostova et al. 2008; Pinkse and Kolk 2012).

Against this backdrop, this chapter explores strategies that national governments employ to manage the impacts of climate change.[1] I also consider the signals that these policies send to companies by investigating whether MNCs have greater confidence in host governments that appear ready, willing, and able to shore up their nations against the impacts of climate change. The statistical analysis that I carry out suggests that they do, but that not all policies are equally effective in this regard. After laying out these empirical findings, the chapter offers insights as to how governments should allocate scarce policy resources if the goal is to ensure that their nations remain active participants in the global economy.

7.1 Government Policies Through the Lens of RDT

It is instructive to begin the discussion by framing public policy through the lens of RDT. Firms rely on national governments, just as

[1] Three points should be noted. First, while national-level policies and political institutions are clearly important, so too are those at local levels (Broto 2017). Second, while political institutions are important, companies' embeddedness goes beyond politics, to social, economic, and cultural norms and systems (see Heidenreich 2012). Third, these other levels and dimensions often intersect with national-level political institutions (see Harring and Jagers 2018).

they depend on suppliers for raw materials, financial institutions for capital, and technology providers for innovation. Government policies influence the availability of essential resources, such as climate-resilient infrastructure that shields supply chains and assets from extreme weather events, legal and regulatory protections that establish clear, predictable compliance frameworks, and financial incentives that shape investment in green technologies and sustainability. MNCs must therefore strategically manage their dependence on governments, just as they manage relationships with suppliers or investors.

At the same time, government policies actively reshape MNCs' dependencies. As governments craft decarbonization strategies, implement carbon pricing, and incentivize clean energy, they push firms to transition away from carbon-intensive resources and toward low-carbon technologies, renewable energy, and sustainable supply chains. This shift fundamentally alters which industries and supply networks MNCs depend on. For example, as governments phase out fossil fuel subsidies and introduce carbon taxation, MNCs may relocate production to regions with cleaner energy grids or invest in decarbonization technologies to maintain regulatory compliance.

Yet MNCs retain agency in negotiating regulatory environments to create more favorable conditions. They can do so directly by lobbying policymakers to shape climate regulations in ways that align with their interests. Some MNCs also engage in forum shopping, choosing to expand operations in countries with policy environments that align with their business models, while scaling back investments in countries with unfavorable regulations or a weaker capacity to manage climate change.

Thus, government policies do more than just regulate firms. They structure the external environment that determines which resources firms need, how they access them, and where they choose to do business. As the chapter proceeds, we will see how governments' policy strategies encourage MNCs to reevaluate their dependencies and negotiate their positions.

7.2 Policies for Climate Change Management

Before delving into governments' efforts to shield their nations against the impacts of climate change, it is worth reflecting on why they undertake such efforts in the first place. Governments' motives to address climate change – whether through mitigation or adaptation[2] – stem from a combination of economic, social, and political imperatives. Economically, climate disruptions threaten industries, infrastructure, and growth, risking instability and loss of investor confidence (Bosello et al. 2012; Hsiang et al. 2017). Socially, climate change threatens public health and well-being (Adger 2010; Costello et al. 2023). Politically, climate change could potentially lead to political destabilization and conflict (Koubi 2019; Omelicheva 2011). Political leaders facing these challenges may be compelled to act, whether out of an altruistic desire to solve these pressing problems or because they think that doing so will enhance their political standing or ensure their political survival.[3]

By the same token, policymakers may be deterred from implementing climate management policies for various reasons. As was discussed in Chapter 2, fossil fuel companies and others that wish to avoid costly regulations often lobby to delay or prevent the establishment of new green policies or to roll back existing rules. When policymakers face greater pressure from firms representing carbon-intensive industries than they do from pro-environmental forces, they are likely to eschew greening policies (Colgan et al. 2021). This effect may be amplified when governments worry about the negative impacts that can accompany environmental reforms (Fails 2022; Mahdavi et al. 2022; McCulloch et al. 2022).

Governments that do attempt to manage climate change have developed a variety of policy strategies. These range from large and audacious proposals, such as Indonesia's plan to move its capital from Jakarta (Beech 2023) or Kiribati's plan to lift the island several meters to protect it from rising sea levels (Milman 2022), to less grandiose efforts, such as China's implementation of community-led early

[2] Climate mitigation efforts aim to reduce GHG emissions and curb global warming. Adaptation involves adjusting systems and infrastructure to cope with the inevitable impacts of climate change, building resilience in the face of rising sea levels, extreme weather events, and other climate-related disruptions. See Hoppe et al. (2023) on mitigation, Fankhauser (2017) on adaptation, and Watkiss et al. (2015) on the intersections between them.

[3] Leaders may see their political survival threatened when they alienate the supporters that they depend on to retain power (Bueno de Mesquita et al. 2003). Failure to act on climate change or the wrong choice of actions could lead to backlash from key stakeholders. See Dolšak and Prakash (2018) on the political calculations associated with climate policy.

warning systems for flash floods.[4] These sorts of projects can have profound impacts on MNCs, including on the climate risks that they face.

National policies can be bundled into three broad categories: (1) governance and planning, (2) capacity building, and (3) incentives and regulations (see Nachmany et al. 2019). The pages that follow explain each strategy and reflect on their impacts for MNCs. This information is presented briefly in Table 7.1.

7.2.1 Governance and Planning

Governance and planning initiatives encourage or require governments at various levels to carry out climate-related planning, establish dedicated institutions, and implement processes to monitor and report progress. Policies along these lines include national climate action plans, the establishment of climate councils or task forces, and the legal requirement for municipalities to develop local adaptation strategies. For example, the UK's Climate Change Act legally requires the government to set carbon budgets and develop a national adaptation plan.[5] Along the same lines, India's National Action Plan on Climate Change includes missions aimed at building climate resilience across various sectors (Pandve 2009).

We can proxy for governance and planning using the governance readiness indicator from ND-GAIN, which is designed to reflect the institutional elements that improve the effectiveness of investment in adaptation efforts.[6] Figure 7.1 provides a snapshot of governance readiness across countries for 2022, the most recent year for which data is available. Generally speaking, the readiest countries are wealthy Western nations, such as the US, Canada, Australia, and the countries of western Europe, which generally have strong political institutions. Japan, South Korea, Botswana, Costa Rica, and Uruguay also score

[4] See details on China's adaptation strategy here: https://development.asia/summary/climate-change-adaptation-strategy-peoples-republic-china.

[5] Details on the UK's Climate Change Act can be seen here: https://legislation.gov.uk/ukpga/2008/27/contents.

[6] The governance readiness indicator is an index that uses several measures from the World Bank's World Governance Indicators: political stability and non-violence, control of corruption, regulatory quality, and rule of law.

Table 7.1 *Public policy strategies for climate change management.*

Policy Strategy	Description	Hypothetical Example	Implications for MNCs
Governance and Planning	Mandating adaptation planning, establishing institutions for adaptation, and reviewing progress toward adaptation objectives.	A national policy requiring all municipalities to develop and submit climate adaptation plans to a newly established Climate Adaptation Authority.	Physical risk (↓); transition risk (↓/↑); litigation risk (↑); reputation risk (↑).
Capacity Building	Generating knowledge about climate risk, identifying best practices, and harnessing resources for mitigation and adaptation.	A government-funded program that trains local communities on climate risk management and disaster preparedness.	Physical risk (↓); transition risk (↑); litigation risk (↑); reputation risk (↑).
Incentives and Regulations	Incentives encourage private-sector support for national policy goals. Regulations require private-sector actors to follow national policy guidelines.	A tax credit program that incentivizes companies to invest in renewable energy projects or climate-resilient infrastructure. A regulation mandating that all new buildings in coastal areas must adhere to flood-resistant construction standards.	Physical risk (↓); transition risk (↑/↓); litigation risk (↑).

well above average. Conversely, the least ready countries are Somalia, Syria, Yemen, Libya, and Venezuela.

Governments that have planned adequately should be relatively able to manage extreme weather events, thereby protecting those companies operating within their borders from physical climate risk. Likewise, when governments set out detailed adaptation plans and frameworks, they provide businesses with the guidance needed to align their operations with national climate goals, which should help them keep pace with policy changes. In this context, adequate governance and planning should allow companies to plan and invest with confidence, knowing that physical risk is low and understanding the contours of transition risk.

However, while governance and planning offers stability, it can nevertheless disrupt business operations or threaten companies' returns. Those companies that are unwilling or unable to adapt may face fines or legal penalties. Moreover, national adaptation plans can raise awareness of climate change among consumers, investors, and other important stakeholders, in turn generating backlash against companies that are perceived to be poor environmental performers.

7.2.2 Capacity Building

Capacity building involves generating knowledge about climate risk, developing best practices, and harnessing resources for mitigation and adaptation. Policy strategies along these lines could include national education campaigns on the impacts of climate change, training programs for local governments and businesses, and initiatives to improve data collection and climate modeling capabilities. For example, Norway's Svalbard Environmental Protection Fund provides grants to individuals and organizations for projects aimed at understanding and addressing environmental challenges to the Svalbard islands.[7]

Capacity building can also take the form of direct government investments in the physical infrastructure that supports adaptation. The Netherlands, for example, invested heavily in the Delta Works, a series of flood defenses designed to protect against rising sea levels

[7] More information about the Svalbard Environmental Protection Fund is available here: https://regjeringen.no/en/dep/kld/organisation/Subordinate-agencies/the-svalbard-environmental-protection-fund/id2360870.

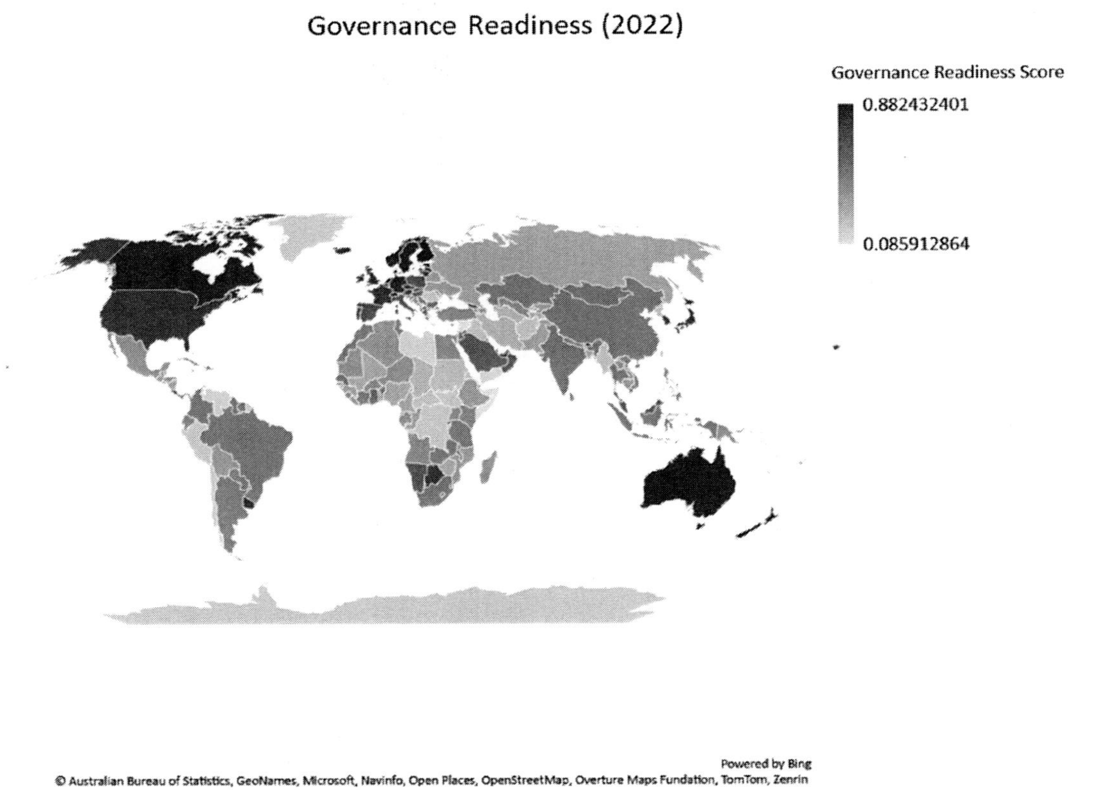

Figure 7.1 Governance readiness heat map.
Countries have been coded using the governance readiness indicator from ND-GAIN. A higher score corresponds to greater readiness.

(Stokkom et al. 2005). Likewise, South Korea's Four Major Rivers Restoration Project involved significant investments to prevent flooding and improve water management (Lah et al. 2015). Beyond these illustrative cases, we can see a general trend of governments building capacity over the last few decades – see Figure 7.2, which shows improvements in disaster management capacity over time.[8]

Capacity building efforts should reduce MNCs' vulnerabilities to physical climate risk by helping countries absorb climate-related disturbances and adapt to changing conditions. For example, education and training programs can equip local governments, businesses, and communities with the skills to anticipate and respond to extreme weather. Likewise, the mobilization of resources and the strengthening of institutional frameworks should help ensure that effective responses are in place and that critical infrastructure is safeguarded against climate shocks. Additionally, large-scale public projects like sea walls or underground tunnels for flood diversion can safeguard physical infrastructure from rising sea levels, storm surges, and other climate impacts. Collectively, these efforts should make nations better prepared to deal with physical disruptions that stem from climate change.

While capacity building should enhance physical resilience, it may also increase transition, litigation, and reputation risks. For example, new information generated through climate risk assessments or advanced climate modeling could lead governments to introduce stricter regulations to mitigate newly identified risks. Companies would then need to adapt their operations, technologies, or business models to comply with the new standards or face legal consequences. By the same token, if people become more knowledgeable about climate risk through public education or outreach campaigns, scrutiny and pressure on companies may grow.

[8] This data is drawn from ND-GAIN, which in turn obtained it from the United Nations Sustainable Development Goals (SDG) Indicators database. It should be acknowledged that disaster preparedness is not a perfect measure of capacity building, both because not all climate-related capacity building is about disaster management and because not all disaster management is related to climate change. Nevertheless, it does in part reflect a policy reaction to the effects of climate change on natural disasters (see Van Aalst 2006).

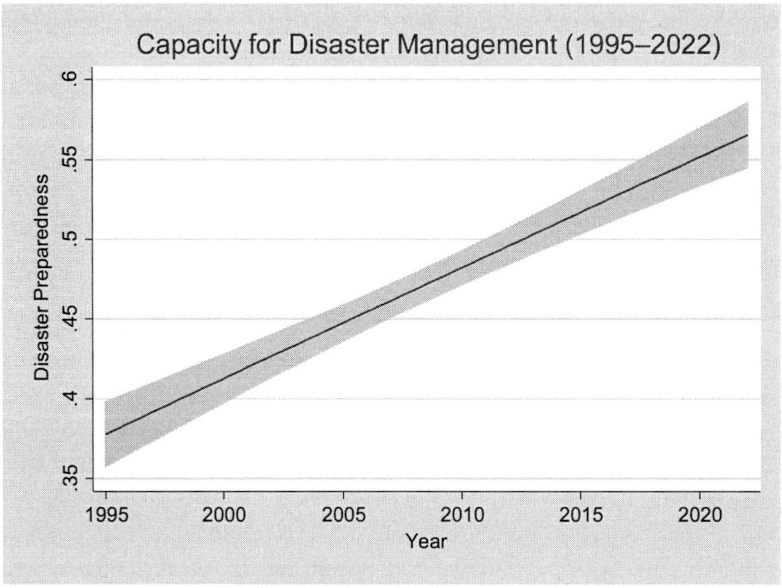

Figure 7.2 Disaster preparedness trend.
A positive trend in disaster preparedness is evident across 184 countries from 1995 to 2022. The trendline is presented with 95 percent confidence intervals. Disaster preparedness data is drawn from ND-GAIN, which obtained it from the United Nations SDG Indicators database.

7.2.3 Incentives and Regulations

Incentives are financial or other benefits that encourage private-sector actors to support national policy goals. These might include tax credits for investments in renewable energy, subsidies for retrofitting buildings to improve energy efficiency, and grants for R&D in climate technologies. For example, Germany's Renewable Energy Sources Act provides financial incentives for companies to invest in renewable energy (Böhringer et al. 2017). Likewise, the US offers a tax credit for renewable energy projects through its Residential Clean Energy Credit.[9] Incentives across countries have increased sharply since the early

[9] More information about the Residential Clean Energy Credit can be found here: https://irs.gov/credits-deductions/residential-clean-energy-credit.

1990s, including environmentally beneficial subsidies and payments, tradable permits and offsets, and deposit refunds.[10]

Regulations, which require private-sector actors to abide by national policy guidelines, can include mandatory energy efficiency standards for buildings, limitations on water usage in drought-prone areas, and requirements for the use of climate-resilient materials in construction. For example, Japan's building codes have been updated to include measures for flood resilience and earthquake-proofing (Moullier and Sakoda 2018). Similarly, California's Green Building Standards Code mandates that new buildings meet strict energy efficiency and sustainability criteria.[11] Like incentives, environmental regulations around the world have increased significantly since the early 1990s, with most countries having environmental framework laws and/or environmental provisions in their constitutions. However, it is common for these regulations to be poorly designed, lacking clear benchmarks or tailoring to local contexts. Likewise, regulatory bodies are often underfunded and poorly administered, resulting in weak enforcement (United Nations Environment Programme 2019).

Incentives and regulations – if well designed and, in the case of regulations, effectively enforced – can help companies reduce some climate risks. Incentives should lessen transition risk by lowering the cost barriers associated with investing in renewable energy, energy-efficient technologies, or other climate-friendly innovations. Regulations should mitigate physical risk to the extent that they ensure that companies' infrastructure, operations, and supply chains are designed to withstand climate-related events. For example, regulations that mandate the use of resilient building materials should reduce vulnerability to extreme storms.

On the other hand, accepting incentives could open companies up to litigation risk if they fail to abide by accompanying emissions reduction targets or reporting requirements. Likewise, as governments tighten environmental standards and impose new compliance requirements, companies must adapt their operations, technologies, and business models to meet these evolving expectations, which can involve substantial costs, such as investing in new technologies, retrofitting

10 Data on incentives can be accessed here: https://oecd-main.shinyapps.io/pinedatabase.

11 Details on California's Green Building Standards Code are available here: https://hcd.ca.gov/building-standards/calgreen.

existing infrastructure, or altering supply chains. Companies that are slow to adapt to new regulations, or fail to do so altogether, may find themselves facing fines, lawsuits, and other legal penalties.

7.2.4 Policy Contradictions and Effectiveness

While there is potential for policy initiatives to promote climate resilience, there are also reasons for skepticism regarding public policy solutions. Indeed, Stechemesser et al. (2024) find that a vast minority of climate policies result in significant reductions in GHG emissions. Two impediments to policy success stand out, with the first centering on the policy contradictions that often dilute sustainability initiatives and the second corresponding to a host of factors that can hobble policy effectiveness.

In many cases, contradictions characterize environmental policies, such that efforts to promote sustainability are undermined by simultaneous support for pollution-intensive industries. For example, a government might invest heavily in renewable energy infrastructure while at the same time providing subsidies or tax breaks to the fossil fuel industry. We saw this in Chapter 6, in the context of Saudi Arabia, which is directing Aramco to invest in renewable energy resources and technologies while simultaneously discouraging a global shift away from fossil fuels. Similar contradictions are evident in the approaches of Canada and Norway, among others (see Cecco 2024; Gross 2020; Grunstein 2023; Niranjan 2024b). These examples speak to the competing pressures that face governments, leading them to attempt both to address climate change and to support key industries.

Even when governments are fully committed to environmental betterment, the effectiveness of their policies is not assured. Miscoordination between policymakers or poor policy design can lead to limited adoption and compliance (Ran 2013) or unintended consequences that undermine climate goals (Belaïd 2022). Implementation challenges, such as inadequate funding, lack of technical expertise, or insufficient enforcement mechanisms, can also undermine the effectiveness of well-intentioned policies (see Oberthür and Kelly 2008).

Given these challenges, policy effectiveness is likely to vary significantly across countries (Steinebach 2022). Those with strong political institutions should be relatively able to overcome contradictions and hurdles, although the role of institutions is less clear-cut than has often been assumed (Dellepiane-Avellaneda 2010; Roller 2005). Other factors related to culture, historical legacies, and public support may also be significant (Anderson et al. 2017; d'Adda and de Blasio 2017; Evan and Holý 2023).

It is also important to emphasize that individual policies may not be sufficient, even when countries have the right mix of institutions to avoid the previously mentioned pitfalls. Instead, the complex and interconnected nature of climate risks will often require a holistic policy approach that integrates multiple strategies. For example, while regulations can set necessary standards for climate resilience, companies will be more readily able to adhere to them when capacity building efforts have equipped them with the knowledge and tools needed to comply. Similarly, direct government investments in infrastructure can mitigate physical risk, but those investments are likely to be more effectively channeled when proper planning has been carried out. Thus, by coordinating and combining various strategies, governments may be successful in addressing the immediate risks posed by climate change, while building a resilient and sustainable economic future for companies.

7.3 How Do MNCs React to Climate Policies?

Putting aside concerns about policy effectiveness for now, we can investigate how MNCs are responding to public policy efforts. As established in Chapter 4, some global companies appear to be systematically avoiding the countries that are most exposed to climate risks – particularly physical climate risk. This probably reflects, at least in part, MNCs' concerns that they will be left to bear the costs of adaptation if governments are incapable or unwilling to do so.

In this context, companies are likely to look for signals about the policy environment in countries that they are considering for investments (Bussy and Zheng 2023). Their concerns about adaptation costs may be assuaged where governments are (or appear to be) well prepared to manage climate change. It follows that MNCs will cease to avoid climate-vulnerable countries when the policy environment seems up to the task of climate risk management. That said, things might not be so straightforward, as active policy efforts to tackle climate change may scare off MNCs wary of transition, litigation, and reputation risks (see Xing and Kolstad 2002).

The relationship between climate risk, public policy, and the investment activities of MNCs can be clarified through data analysis. To do so, I analyze statistical models to assess whether key policy variables moderate the relationship between climate vulnerability and FDI inflows. Once again, I measure governance and planning as governance readiness and capacity building as disaster preparedness. To measure the third policy category, incentives and regulations, I use the World Bank's Country Policy and Institutional Assessment (CPIA) Policy and Institutions for Environmental Sustainability rating, which assesses "the extent to which environmental policies foster the protection and sustainable use of natural resources and the management of pollution."[12] The statistical models include the same control variables and model specifications that were used in Chapter 4. Likewise, climate vulnerability is again measured using the Vulnerability Index from ND-GAIN, while FDI inflows are measured using data from the World Bank's WDIs.

The results are presented in Table 7.2. We can begin by looking at the main effects for climate vulnerability, which are negative and significant across models. This means that climate vulnerability is negatively related to FDI inflows when each of the policy variables is at its lowest level – meaning policy support for climate resilience is essentially nonexistent. The interaction terms are positive across models, which indicates that the relationship between climate vulnerability and FDI becomes less negative as each type of policy support increases. Yet only the interaction that includes governance readiness is statistically significant, indicating that this is the strongest moderating factor (see Model 7.1).

To clarify the nature of the significant interaction term, a marginal effects plot is presented in Figure 7.3. This figure shows that the relationship between climate vulnerability and FDI inflows is negative and significant where governance readiness is low, indicating that foreign investors are warded off by climate risk concerns in settings such as these. Yet the relationship ceases to be significant as governance readiness increases, suggesting that investors' concerns are assuaged by political institutions that signal preparedness to manage climate-related disruptions.

[12] A full description of the variable can be found here: https://databank.worldbank.org/metadataglossary/world-development-indicators/series/IQ.CPA.ENVR.XQ.

Table 7.2 ***Climate risk and Foreign Direct Investment (FDI), by governance indicators.***

Dependent Variable: FDI Inflows	Model 7.1	Model 7.2	Model 7.3
Climate Vulnerability	-21.68***	-12.51**	-23.61**
	(5.344)	(5.140)	(10.77)
Governance Readiness	-7.146	N/A	N/A
	(4.497)	N/A	N/A
Climate Vulnerability * Governance Readiness	22.42**	N/A	N/A
	(8.932)	N/A	N/A
Disaster Preparedness	N/A	-1.618	N/A
	N/A	(1.732)	N/A
Climate Vulnerability * Disaster Preparedness	N/A	4.541	N/A
	N/A	(3.990)	N/A
CPIA	N/A	N/A	-1.667
	N/A	N/A	(1.037)
Climate Vulnerability * CPIA	N/A	N/A	3.239
	N/A	N/A	(1.944)
GDP	1.646***	1.393***	1.935
	(0.468)	(0.479)	(1.268)
Per Capita GDP	-1.308***	-0.408	-0.802
	(0.450)	(0.452)	(1.176)
Annual GDP Growth	0.0161***	0.0239***	0.0168**
	(0.00470)	(0.00719)	(0.00706)
Regime Type	0.0127	0.0360**	0.00197
	(0.0132)	(0.0159)	(0.0251)
High Intensity Conflict	0.0290	-0.0395	-0.211
	(0.125)	(0.137)	(0.157)
Oil Rents	0.0205**	0.0264*	0.0160
	(0.00826)	(0.0141)	(0.0109)
BITs	-0.00361	-0.00306	-0.00552
	(0.00257)	(0.00270)	(0.00423)
Observations	3,281	2,511	767
R-squared	0.448	0.441	0.158
Number of Countries	156	118	69
Country Fixed Effects	Yes	Yes	Yes
Year Fixed Effects	Yes	Yes	Yes

Linear panel data models. Robust standard errors in parentheses, clustered by country; independent and control variables lagged one year; ***$p < 0.01$, **$p < 0.05$, *$p < 0.1$.

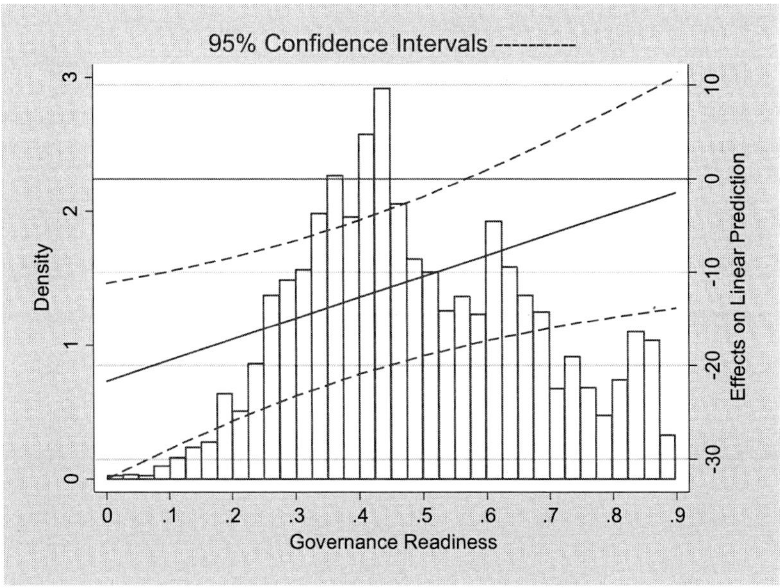

Figure 7.3 Climate risk and FDI, by governance readiness.
Marginal effects plot showing the relationship between climate risk and FDI at different values of governance readiness – which proxies governance and planning.

Although the other interaction terms are not significant, it is still important to scrutinize their marginal effects, as a focus solely on statistical significance may overlook meaningful interactions (Brambor et al. 2006). Indeed, Figure 7.4 provides evidence that both disaster preparedness (a proxy for capacity building) and CPIA (my chosen measure of incentives and regulations) moderate the relationship between climate vulnerability and FDI. Specifically, investors appear to avoid climate-vulnerable countries that are weak in either policy area, but not those that are strong.

It seems, then, that public policy assures MNCs that their business operations are safe in countries where climate risk would otherwise be a concern. This speaks to the signaling effect that policy can have on companies, giving them confidence that governments are ready and able to prevent climate-related damages to their business operations.

I also analyze models in which FDI inflows are disaggregated to differentiate primary, secondary, and tertiary investments. These results – which are featured in the Appendix, in Tables A.5, A.6,

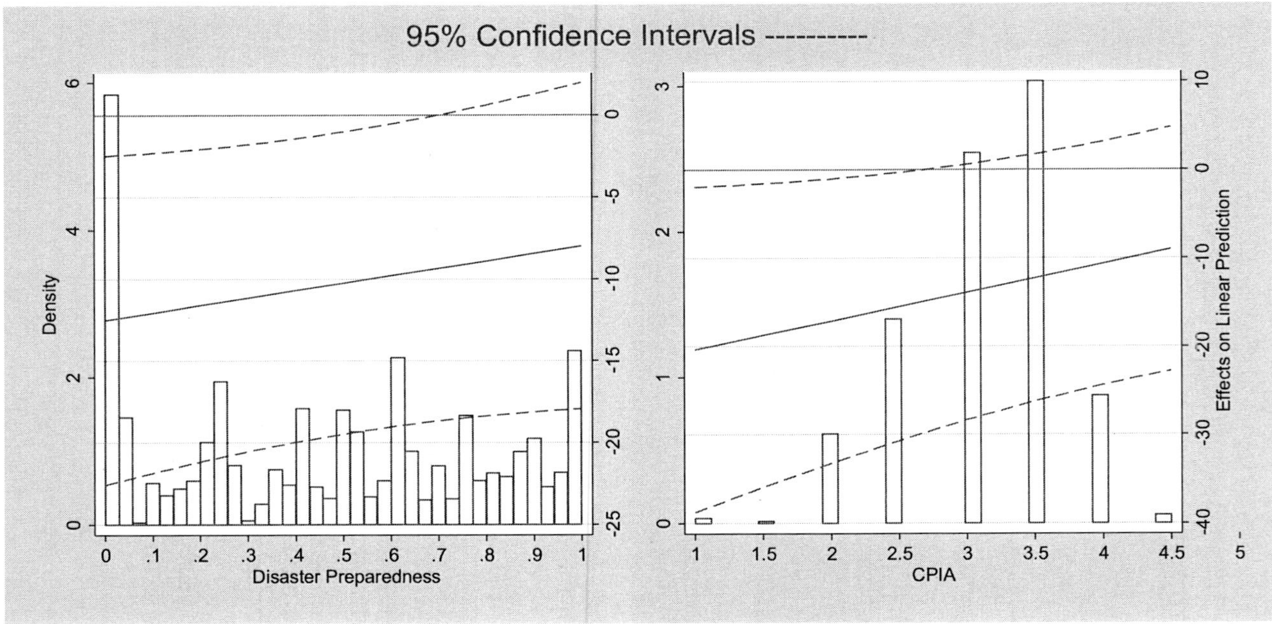

Figure 7.4 Climate risk and FDI, by disaster preparedness and CPIA.
Marginal effects plots showing the relationships between climate risk and FDI at different levels of disaster preparedness (which proxies for capacity building) and CPIA (which proxies for incentives and regulations).

and A.7 – offer one additional point of insight: tertiary-sector investors appear to be especially reassured by incentives and regulations. A few potential explanations stand out. First, these firms often rely on intangible assets like IP and branding, which align more easily with incentives to promote innovation or sustainability. The sector's consumer-facing nature further heightens its responsiveness, as these firms may be especially sensitive to public and investor expectations surrounding ESG. Finally, the shorter investment horizons typical of tertiary-sector firms mean that incentives offering immediate or near-term benefits, such as tax breaks or subsidies, may be particularly impactful in shaping investment decisions.

Next, I consider models that distinguish the elements of climate risk that contribute to the Vulnerability Index. These results – presented in Tables A.8, A.9, and A.10 in the Appendix – show distinct moderation dynamics. While all interactions between climate risk variables and governance readiness are positive, only those with health and water vulnerability are significant. Of the interactions with disaster preparedness, only ecosystem and health vulnerability are significant. Finally, the interaction between CPIA and habitat vulnerability is negative and significant, while all other CPIA interactions are positive but not significant. Collectively, these results speak to the complex ways in which climate vulnerability and policy intersect.

7.4 Policy Implications and Complexities

Cumulatively, these results suggest that MNCs are positively persuaded by governments that appear ready and able to manage the effects of climate change. The signal these MNCs are being sent via public policy stops them from systematically avoiding climate-vulnerable countries. This finding supports earlier work attesting to the role that good governance can play in addressing business risk (Ngobo and Fouda 2012), while also calling into question claims that robust climate policies will be detrimental to business activity (see Bialek and Weichenrieder 2021). Instead, it appears that policies in support of environmental sustainability are reassuring to the international business community. These findings also suggest that whatever worries about transition or litigation risks are generated by strong policies are offset by perceived reductions in physical risk.

The policy implications are fairly straightforward: if the goal is to attract FDI, then governments representing climate-vulnerable nations should invest in the sorts of policies that MNCs find comforting: governance and planning, capacity building, and incentives and regulations. Of course, policies should not be implemented exclusively for the benefit of foreign investors.[13] Climate change has significant human development implications that should take priority over the interests of MNCs or companies more generally (Adger et al. 2022; Malpede and Percoco 2024). Moreover, there is a case to be made that policies implemented for private-sector benefit effectively privatize gains while socializing losses. In this scenario, a government implements costly policies in hopes of reducing risks to private companies, thereby ensuring ongoing business activities such as foreign investment. If these policies are effective, then business will continue or even accelerate, with corporations enjoying much of the benefit. But if they fail, then taxpayers will have paid the cost with little to show for it. Such policies could also ultimately be to the detriment of MNCs if the signal that they send encourages firms to invest in risky environments that they would be better off avoiding.

That having been said, a country's human development cannot be disentangled from its engagement with the global economy. Countries that conduct extensive international trade and attract high levels of FDI often fare better than those that do not in terms of economic, social, and political development (Dollar 2001; Rudra 2005; Sachs 2000). Thus, government policies that encourage global business by building climate resilience may have second-order benefits for residents. Moreover, encouraging climate resilience should benefit a country's population directly by protecting them from the damaging impacts of changing temperatures (Dicker et al. 2021). With all of this in mind, governments should allocate resources in a manner that simultaneously maximizes human well-being while also providing at least some assurances to MNCs.

There are two additional caveats to note. First, while this chapter has centered on governments' roles in managing climate risk to reassure

[13] Policymakers may not be thinking about the business risks associated with climate change when they craft or implement environmental policies. For example, a public sector manager that I interviewed from a Caribbean nation explained that environmental policy is rarely informed by concerns about attracting foreign investment or engaging in international commerce.

investors, public policy can also lay the groundwork for corporate innovations that advance climate solutions. Indeed, some of the same policies discussed in this chapter as risk mitigators could help generate sustainable business opportunities for forward-thinking companies. This is explored further in Chapter 8.

Second, while some national governments can assure MNCs through fostering climate resilience, others lack the resources to do so. Governments representing less developed countries will face particular challenges in carrying out large-scale policy projects. There should also be concerns about whether these developing countries, which are often the most vulnerable to climate change even as they have contributed very little of the emissions that are exacerbating it, should bear the costs of climate adaptation (Füssel 2010). For these countries, foreign assistance from the international community could provide key resources, although this is not entirely assured given the complex effects of foreign aid (Dalgaard et al. 2004; Ferro and Wilson 2011). I will revisit this issue in Chapter 9.

8 *Public Policy and Climate Opportunities*

In addition to helping MNCs manage climate risk, national governments can help them realize opportunities within the green economy. Governments shape the landscape in which MNCs operate (Kostova et al. 2008; Pinkse and Kolk 2012), often providing resources, incentives, and infrastructure that create favorable conditions for companies to develop eco-oriented business models, enter green sectors, and pioneer sustainable technologies (e.g., see Wu et al. 2022). Companies can also help governments to achieve policy goals, including through PPPs, which allow governments to leverage the unique expertise, technology, and resources of the private sector to address complex challenges (see Casady et al. 2024). By pooling resources and aligning business goals with national climate objectives, PPPs can potentially produce transformative impacts that neither sector could achieve independently, accelerating decarbonization and advancing sustainability on a large scale.

This chapter explores these intersections between government policies, business opportunities, and climate solutions, highlighting how public policies and PPPs can create an environment conducive to climate-focused innovation and growth. These policies and partnerships intersect with the three pillars of sustainable business opportunity introduced in Chapter 5, creating a foundation upon which MNCs can lead as early adopters, explore emerging green markets, and develop climate technologies. Whether building renewable energy infrastructure, incentivizing the formation of resilient supply chains, or cocreating carbon mitigation technologies, government efforts can offer sustainable business opportunities to MNCs while also allowing them to engage meaningfully in climate action.

Before delving into the analysis, we should note that government support is not always aimed at encouraging green business. To the contrary, governments frequently provide tax breaks, direct subsidies, and regulatory advantages to industries that generate significant GHG emissions (Lin 2014). For example, governments spend hundreds of billions of dollars annually on subsidies that support the oil, gas, and coal industries (Skovgaard and van Asselt 2019).[1]

8.1 Leveraging Public Policy to Open Climate Opportunities

Support for fossil fuels notwithstanding, many governments around the world have been implementing policies aimed at adapting to and mitigating the effects of climate change. As was discussed in Chapter 7, these policies fall broadly into three categories: governance and planning, capacity building, and incentives and regulations. Table 8.1 offers a brief explanation as to how policies in each category can contribute to sustainable business. This is discussed further in the sections that follow.

8.1.1 Governance and Planning

Broadly speaking, governance and planning policies lay the groundwork for climate adaptation and mitigation through the formation of plans of action and the establishment of institutions dedicated to implementing them. These sorts of initiatives can stimulate sustainable business in at least two ways. First, climate-oriented plans provide predictability for companies by signaling long-term government commitment to climate goals. This offers firms confidence to invest in sustainable practices and innovations, knowing that the products they produce will align with public policies (see Yang et al. 2023). For example, the EU Climate Law establishes legally binding targets for the EU to become climate-neutral by 2050 and reduce GHG emissions by at least 55 percent, relative to 1990 levels, by 2030.[2] This law creates a stable policy environment that supports existing green markets and encourages companies in sectors like renewable energy,

[1] Subsidies can become embedded in the social and economic fabric of countries that rely on fossil fuel production, creating a political calculus where subsidy reduction risks backlash from local communities and industries (Urpelainen and George 2021). Additionally, fossil fuel companies often use their influence and networks to resist subsidy removal efforts.

[2] More information on the EU's Climate Law can be found here: https://climate.ec.europa.eu/eu-action/european-climate-law_en.

Table 8.1 *Public policy strategies and the three pillars of sustainable business opportunity.*

Policy strategy	Example	Contribution to sustainable business opportunity
Governance and Planning	EU Climate Law	**Green markets:** A stable policy framework allows firms to invest in green markets and align with the country's long-term climate goals and standards. Structured markets for sustainable products and services incentivize renewable energy, sustainable transport, and eco-friendly goods. **Climate solutions:** Creates demand for innovations and technologies to decelerate global warming.
Capacity Building	Netherlands' Room for the River project	**Green markets:** Companies can develop new product offerings based on knowledge derived from capacity-building initiatives. Companies may be contracted to build, maintain, or manage government-funded green infrastructure projects.
Incentives and Regulations	US Production Tax Credit for Renewable Energy	**Early adopters:** Incentivizes companies to adopt sustainable practices early, giving them competitive advantages and establishing them as industry leaders. **Green markets:** Creates demand for green products and services that align with regulatory guidelines. **Climate solutions:** Lowers financial barriers to investing in breakthrough technologies and innovations.

energy efficiency, and low-emission transportation to make long-term investments aligned with EU goals.

Second, by identifying specific targets, such as flood resilience, sustainable agriculture, and water conservation, governments actively create market needs that companies can fill, often with additional government support via demand-side policy instruments (Mundaca et al. 2019). This targeted demand allows MNCs to enter and expand in green markets with an assurance that their products and services will meet real and sustained demand created by government policy. For example, the EU's Fit for 55 Package sets various decarbonization benchmarks in pursuit of carbon neutrality by 2050, thereby creating structured demand for alternative fuels, sustainable building materials, and EVs.[3] Moreover, since reaching government-imposed benchmarks will require the deceleration of global warming, companies focused on developing climate solutions, such as CDR, should find a demand structure for the climate solutions that they successfully develop (see Rode et al. 2023).

8.1.2 Capacity Building

We can next turn to capacity building, which generates essential climate knowledge and infrastructure. By conducting climate risk assessments, developing best practices for resilience, and improving data collection on climate vulnerabilities, governments produce key knowledge as a public good. This knowledge can be used by companies to develop green products and services that can then be brought to market (Shi and Zhou 2024).

Firms can also contribute to the financing, construction, and operation of government-funded infrastructure projects. Private capital can support public works projects, while public initiatives to build flood defenses, sustainable water systems, and green urban infrastructure often contract to firms with expertise in climate-resilient materials, eco-friendly construction techniques, and sustainable energy solutions. For example, the Boston Government Center transit station renovation was financed in part by private-sector lenders via tax-exempt sustainability bonds (Coffee 2020), while the Netherlands' Room for the

[3] Details on *Fit for 55* are available here: https://consilium.europa.eu/en/policies/fit-for-55.

River project brought in private companies to assist with flood defenses and water management (Verweij et al. 2021).

8.1.3 Incentives and Regulations

Financial incentives like tax credits, subsidies, and grants reduce initial investment barriers, enabling companies with a forward-looking approach to explore green technologies and sustainable practices ahead of competitors. For early adopters, these incentives make it more feasible to experiment with and integrate cutting-edge solutions (Ashton et al. 2017), potentially allowing them to set industry standards, attract sustainability-focused consumers, and build reputational advantages. Additionally, by encouraging R&D in climate technology, incentives can reduce financial barriers to the companies that are developing breakthrough products, such as advanced energy storage solutions, climate-resilient materials, or CCS technologies (Comello and Reichelstein 2014). For instance, the US Production Tax Credit for Renewable Energy incentivizes companies to invest in large-scale renewable energy projects.[4]

Regulations set minimum requirements for climate-aligned practices across various industries, which effectively raise the baseline for sustainability. By establishing mandatory standards for energy efficiency, water usage, or climate-resilient materials, regulations promote innovation (Lin et al. 2024; Zhou et al. 2023) and drive demand for products and services that align with these guidelines (see Dassu and Mena 2025). MNCs that specialize in sustainable materials, green construction techniques, or efficient energy systems can capitalize on this regulated demand by positioning themselves as leaders in compliance-driven sectors. Regulations can also benefit early adopters that align their practices with emerging standards before they become widespread, thereby establishing competitive advantages in sectors that are still adjusting to new requirements.

8.2 Unlocking Innovation Through Policy

While governance and planning, capacity building, and incentives and regulations provide the groundwork for a stable and sustainable

[4] Details on the Production Tax Credit can be found here: https://epa.gov/lmop/renewable-electricity-production-tax-credit-information.

business environment, proactive policy initiatives serve as amplifiers of these efforts, creating direct and targeted pathways for innovation. Three such efforts stand out: (1) climate-focused economic zones (CFEZs), which enhance governance and planning policies and stand to be particularly effective at stimulating green markets, (2) green technology and innovation funds, which leverage capacity-building efforts and offer value to early adopters, and (3) public procurement and regulatory sandboxes, which provide incentives and regulatory support to companies and are likely to be of special benefit to those working on climate solutions. These policy efforts are briefly summarized in Table 8.2 and then detailed in the paragraphs that follow.

8.2.1 Climate-Focused Economic Zones (CFEZs)

CFEZs, which may take the specific form of low-carbon zones, eco-industrial parks, or green special economic zones, are designated areas where governments provide regulatory, financial, and infrastructural advantages to attract businesses committed to environmentally sustainable practices. Unlike general economic zones, which promote broad industrial growth, CFEZs are dedicated specifically to climate-aligned industries, such as renewable energy production, sustainable manufacturing, and eco-friendly urban infrastructure. Companies operating within these zones benefit from a variety of incentives, including tax breaks, streamlined permitting, reduced energy costs, access to climate-resilient infrastructure, and dedicated resources for R&D in climate-related fields (Yeo and Akinci 2011).

CFEZs are often situated in strategic locations that align with national or regional climate goals, such as areas with abundant renewable resources like solar or wind, regions vulnerable to climate impacts (e.g., coastal areas needing flood-resistant infrastructure), or urban areas focused on green technology and sustainable development (see Nuhu et al. 2021). Physical concentration within a zone allows businesses to benefit from shared infrastructure, proximity to suppliers and collaborators, and a streamlined institutional environment tailored to climate-focused economic activities (Bellantuono et al. 2017). Ideally, governments that plan for CFEZs start by conducting stakeholder analysis, undertaking technical diagnostics, and setting clear targets, and then implement policies to create structural clarity and stability. This can include strengthening key infrastructure, setting region-

Table 8.2 *Public policies to unlock corporate innovation.*

	Description	Connection to foundational policies	Contributions to sustainable business opportunity
Climate-Focused Economic Zones	Designated areas providing regulatory, financial, and infrastructural support for climate-aligned industries.	Builds on governance and planning initiatives, aligning with national climate strategies.	**Green markets:** Reduce operational costs and drives innovation by clustering climate-aligned firms.
Green Technology and Innovation Funds	Government funding aimed at advancing R&D and commercializing climate-focused technologies.	Expands capacity-building efforts by allocating resources for developing market-ready climate solutions.	**Early adopters:** Lower costs for integrating green technologies and sustainable practices. **Climate solutions:** Support R&D for transformative technologies.
Public Procurement and Regulatory Sandboxes	Government purchasing of sustainable goods and flexible testing grounds for green tech innovation.	Extends incentives and regulatory frameworks, using procurement to create demand and sandboxes to foster innovation.	**Green markets:** Procurement creates demand for eco-friendly products. **Climate solutions:** Sandboxes facilitate R&D and offer regulatory feedback for emerging technologies.

specific climate adaptation goals, and creating an institutional environment that ensures long-term policy consistency (World Bank Group 2014). In practice, CFEZs have often been built over traditional economic or industrial zones (see Park et al. 2008), and their operations have evolved through trial and error (Gibbs and Deutz 2005).

CFEZs are likely to be particularly useful for companies operating in green markets such as renewable energy, sustainable products, and eco-friendly services. These firms often face high initial costs and logistical challenges, such that they stand to benefit from integrated ecosystems where they can collaborate and share resources. CFEZs create this environment by clustering climate-aligned businesses and providing specialized infrastructure, which reduces entry barriers and operational costs (see Wu and Gao 2022). CFEZs are less critical for early adopters because their focus is typically on integrating sustainable practices into existing operations, not developing new products or services. Companies developing transformative climate solutions, for their part, often rely on niche R&D or specialized technologies that do not depend as heavily on collaborative networks.

8.2.2 Green Technology and Innovation Funds

Green technology and innovation funds support the development and commercialization of climate-focused technologies and techniques. These funds are often structured as grants, low-interest loans, or equity investments provided directly to firms working on renewable energy, energy efficiency, sustainable agriculture, CCS, and other climate-related innovations (Shao and Chen 2022). For instance, Germany's National Hydrogen Strategy funds companies that aim to scale up green hydrogen to support the country's decarbonization goals.[5] Likewise, the UK invested over £116 million in 2021 in private companies to support green initiatives such as CCS.[6] By lowering financial barriers associated with developing and scaling, these funds enable companies to pursue projects that would otherwise be cost-prohibitive

[5] More information about Germany's National Hydrogen Strategy can be found here: https://bmwk.de/Redaktion/EN/Hydrogen/Dossiers/national-hydrogen-strategy.html.

[6] The UK's investment is detailed here: https://gov.uk/government/news/government-invests-over-116-million-to-drive-forward-green-innovation-in-the-uk.

(Acemoglu et al. 2016). They are particularly valuable in the early stages of climate innovation, where high R&D costs, market uncertainties, and long timelines often deter private investment (see Shao and Chen 2022; Wang et al. 2022).

While foundational capacity-building efforts establish general knowledge bases, technology and innovation funds take this further by channeling financial support for the creation of market-ready solutions. For example, capacity-building programs might support climate modeling or develop best practices for resilience, creating a foundation of knowledge and technical expertise. Green technology and innovation funds then invest in companies that can turn this knowledge into viable products and technologies. For example, the US Department of Energy's (DOE) Technology Commercialization Fund has allocated billions of dollars to clean energy projects in hopes that they will ultimately be brought to market.[7]

These funds can provide significant benefits to companies engaged in large-scale climate solutions like green hydrogen production and CCS because these projects frequently involve extended R&D phases, regulatory hurdles, and significant scaling costs that private investors may find too risky. Public sector support allows firms to focus on developing technologies with long-term environmental benefits, even if commercial returns are uncertain in the near term.[8] Public funds can also reduce the financial risks to early adopters integrating sustainable practices or new technologies into existing business operations, as subsidies offset initial costs (Lin and Ho 2011; Xie et al. 2019).

8.2.3 Public Procurement and Regulatory Sandboxes

Green public procurement (GPP) involves governments directly purchasing goods and services that align with sustainability and climate goals. By doing so, they create steady demand for eco-friendly products like renewable energy, EVs, sustainable construction materials, and energy-efficient technologies (see Cheng et al. 2018). For instance, local governments in Sweden used GPP to convert their fleets of public buses

[7] More information about the DOE's Technology Commercialization Fund is available here: https://energy.gov/technologytransitions/articles/doe-announces-over-41m-funding-deliver-clean-energy-solutions-market.

[8] Public funding can also encourage engagement from private investors (Deleidi et al. 2020).

to renewable fuels, thereby creating demand for biofuels (Aldenius and Khan 2017). Regulatory sandboxes, on the other hand, offer a flexible, low-risk testing environment where businesses can experiment with new technologies, products, or business models without being fully subject to conventional regulations – even as regulators oversee their trials (Aydın and Yardımcı 2024). For example, the UK's Financial Conduct Authority has allowed green finance firms to test new sustainable investment products, helping them address compliance issues before full-scale market entry.[9]

GPP and regulatory sandboxes extend the reach of government incentives and regulations in unique ways. While regulations set baseline standards that all companies must meet, GPP creates additional demand for products that go beyond compliance. For example, when governments require ultra-low-carbon materials for public infrastructure or mandate zero-emission vehicles for government fleets, they set a higher standard that incentivizes companies to exceed baseline regulatory requirements in order to meet this demand.

While GPP effectively rewards companies that go beyond regulations, regulatory sandboxes provide a controlled environment in which regulations are temporarily relaxed. In this setting, firms can develop new innovations and technologies without being held back by burdensome regulations (Beckstedde et al. 2023). Moreover, this environment provides a forum for policymakers to work together with innovators to identify regulatory frameworks that might apply to new technologies once they mature (Aydın and Yardımcı 2024).

GPP is most impactful for green market firms. By committing to purchase sustainable goods and services, governments create predictable demand that incentivizes companies to enter or expand in green sectors. This produces a steady revenue stream that reduces market risk, enabling firms to scale faster. Public contracts for electric buses, renewable energy installations, or eco-friendly construction materials, for example, give companies the confidence to invest in production and technology, knowing that there is a buyer (Kou et al. 2024).

Regulatory sandboxes are especially impactful for companies developing innovative climate solutions, where technologies are still

[9] More information about the UK's Financial Conduct Authority, including a list of firms that have been accepted, can be found here: https://fca.org.uk/firms/innovation/regulatory-sandbox/accepted-firms.

evolving (Aydın and Yardımcı 2024). These solutions often require significant testing and optimization to achieve regulatory approval and meet performance standards, and sandboxes provide a controlled, collaborative environment for this process. This should increase the probability of success and speed up market entry. GPP can also benefit companies operating in this opportunity pillar by creating demand for large-scale climate solutions once they reach maturity, but it has limited utility at the early stages of development.

8.3 PPPs for Generating Climate Solutions

While our attention so far has focused on how governments can foster opportunities for companies, there is also potential for companies to help governments accomplish their goals, particularly through PPPs that leverage the strengths of both sectors to drive forward sustainability initiatives that would be challenging for either to accomplish independently (Buso and Stenger 2018). Governments often initiate these partnerships to reach specific sustainability targets, such as achieving a certain percentage of renewable energy,[10] improving urban resilience against climate impacts,[11] or creating green infrastructure that aligns with national climate plans (Casady et al. 2024). There are potential benefits to companies that partner with governments, such as regulatory support, public funding, and infrastructure, as well as the credibility and brand value that come with contributing to recognized public initiatives (see Xu 2023). On the other hand, misalignment between public- and private-sector partners can occur, as governments have broad societal mandates that go beyond the profit-seeking motives of firms (Beckers and Stegemann 2021). I briefly review three PPPs in the pages that follow to illustrate how these dynamics have played out in practice.

8.3.1 Japan's Fujisawa Sustainable Smart Town (Fujisawa SST)

Fujisawa SST was introduced in 2010, when Panasonic Corporation, aiming to repurpose a former factory site in Fujisawa City, proposed a

[10] Information about PPPs related to renewable energy can be found here: https://ppp.worldbank.org/public-private-partnership/energy-and-power/renewable-energy.

[11] Information about PPPs for climate-resilient cities is available here: https://ppp.worldbank.org/public-private-partnership/library/climate-resilient-city.

"smart town" model. Recognizing the potential to showcase sustainable urban living, the Fujisawa municipal government joined forces with Panasonic and several other private companies. Together, they undertook a collaborative effort to develop an eco-friendly town, emphasizing energy efficiency, environmental sustainability, and community well-being (Euklidiadas 2024; Wang 2024).

Panasonic provided the bulk of the technological expertise and financial investment, fitting each residence with solar panels and equipping the community with charging stations for electric cars and bikes. Additional private partners such as Tokyo Gas, Mitsui & Co., and PanaHome Corporation also contributed various specialized services (Euklidiadas 2024). The project has not featured much local government involvement, in contrast to some other Japanese smart cities, but regulatory approvals and support for infrastructural development were necessary to ensure that municipal policies were aligned with the project's goals and to create an enabling environment for the town's sustainable features (Pianezzi et al. 2023).

Fujisawa SST aspires to reduce CO_2 emissions by approximately 70 percent compared to 1990 levels. Beyond environmental impact, the town is designed to foster social interaction, building a strong sense of community and supporting resident well-being (Euklidiadas 2024). Crucially, from Panasonic's perspective, the project has proven economically viable, generating revenue from local businesses and residents (Wang 2024). That said, the community has been criticized for aspects of its design, and concerns have been raised about the ethics of turning significant amounts of personal data over to Panasonic (Euklidiadas 2024).

These criticisms notwithstanding, the Fujisawa SST project illustrates how public- and private-sector collaboration can yield innovative and sustainable urban development. Buy-in from local authorities and the technological prowess and financial resources of Panasonic were essential. Yet Japan's unique characteristics were also crucial, as a culturally embedded synergy between government and business facilitated the creation of a collaborative model that prioritizes collective well-being alongside innovation. In other settings where neoliberal logic pervades, commercial interests would perhaps overshadow broader civic goals (Pianezzi et al. 2023). Additionally, there were purposeful efforts to fit the smart city to the local context and attend to the needs of citizens (Wang 2024). Without these characteristics and efforts, the project may not have been successful.

8.3.2 Northern Lights Carbon Capture and Storage (CSS) Project

Born out of Norway's broader Longship initiative, the Northern Lights CCS project was launched in 2024 to reduce atmospheric CO_2 levels. This partnership brought together the Norwegian government, Equinor (Norway's state-owned energy company), and private-sector partners Shell and TotalEnergies. The project's design allowed each partner to address specific risks independently and operate with clear, upfront requirements, helping to mitigate the technical and financial complexities often associated with large-scale CCS projects (Pallanich 2024). The Norwegian government provided substantial financial backing, covering 80 percent of the project's initial costs, while Equinor led the development and operation of the CO_2 transport and storage infrastructure. Shell and TotalEnergies contributed specialized expertise and additional financial resources (Pallanich 2024).

As of September 2024, Northern Lights had completed its onshore CO_2 receiving facilities in Øygarden, Norway, and was set to begin receiving CO_2 shipments from industrial sources (Wettestad et al. 2024). Initially aiming to store 1.5 million tons of CO_2 annually, Northern Lights plans to ultimately expand to over 5 million tons per year (Wettestad et al. 2024).

This initiative was shaped by lessons learned from the Mongstad project, an earlier state-backed Norwegian CCS effort that failed due to a top-down design that placed a single company in control and did not adequately coordinate with stakeholders. Norway used this experience to reshape its approach, resulting in the more inclusive and risk-managed structure of the Longship initiative, with Northern Lights as its core component (Wettestad et al. 2024). The shift in approach underscores a policy-learning perspective that has allowed for adjustments. This more gradual, bottom-up strategy, linking project responsibilities to stakeholder strengths, has made the Northern Lights project more resilient and adaptable to changing conditions and expectations. However, Northern Lights still faces challenges, including high costs, evolving regulatory frameworks, and the still-developing market for CCS services.

8.3.3 The Alliance for Renewable Clean Hydrogen Energy Systems (ARCHES)

With a goal to produce, distribute, and utilize hydrogen fuel on a large scale, ARCHES aims to leverage California's abundant solar and wind resources to produce green hydrogen, targeting hard-to-electrify sectors such as transportation and heavy industry. In doing so, it seeks to significantly reduce GHG emissions, improve air quality, and foster economic growth through the development of a clean energy industry, with an added emphasis on environmental justice and providing opportunities for underserved communities.[12] In pursuit of these objectives, the California state government has enacted policies that promote hydrogen and committed funds to develop the necessary infrastructure. It has also worked to streamline regulatory processes for hydrogen production, storage, and distribution, and to align ARCHES with the state's long-term clean energy goals.[13] In addition to governmental support, ARCHES has mobilized over 400 partners, including companies,[14] labor unions, and community groups. Private-sector partners have taken on the technical challenges of implementing hydrogen projects, such as constructing production facilities, fueling stations, and transportation networks.

Since its inception, ARCHES has secured $12.6 billion in funding, with $1.2 billion coming from the DOE and $11.4 billion from state and private matching funds (Razaei et al. 2025). However, the program faces notable challenges, such as high initial capital requirements and the need for expansive hydrogen infrastructure to support scalable production and distribution (see Rasul et al. 2022). The sheer size and diversity of California present logistical challenges as well as opportunities, creating a broad consortium of stakeholders with varied priorities and goals while also allowing ARCHES to test hydrogen use cases across urban, industrial, and rural settings. How well it all works in practice remains to be seen.

8.3.4 Getting Public-Private Partnerships (PPPs) Right

Several lessons emerge from these cases. First, climate-focused PPPs necessitate partnerships where business motivations and public sustainability goals operate in harmony. This balance requires governments

[12] Additional details on ARCHES can be found here: https://archesh2.org/about.

[13] More information about California's hydrogen programs is available here: https://afdc.energy.gov/fuels/laws/HY?state=CA.

[14] While many of these companies are based in the US, several are headquartered in other countries, including HPQ Silicon (Canada), Hyundai (South Korea), and Garrett (Switzerland).

to design frameworks that incentivize private companies to contribute meaningfully to climate goals without compromising their profitability. In the Northern Lights project, the Norwegian government aligned corporate interests by creating favorable conditions through substantial funding and market development that enabled private partners to see a viable business opportunity in supporting public aims. This alignment allowed companies like Shell and TotalEnergies to bring their technical expertise and financial resources into the project with confidence that their investments would generate significant returns.

Another key factor is leveraging the unique strengths of each sector. Public entities typically contribute regulatory support, funding, and policy frameworks, while the private sector adds expertise in technology, operational efficiency, and project management. For instance, Northern Lights capitalized on Equinor's CO_2 transport and storage expertise while benefiting from Shell and TotalEnergies' technical resources. Similarly, the Fujisawa project relied on Panasonic's technological strengths alongside regulatory and financial support from the government. Where gaps or misalignments do exist, civil society groups can play a key role in mediating, although they are all too often excluded from decision-making processes (Storeng and Puyvallée 2018).

Cultural and contextual factors further influence the design and implementation of PPPs. Japan's smart city partnerships thrive due to a cultural norm of state-market collaboration. This contrasts with regions where a more market-driven approach might necessitate structured agreements to formally balance public and commercial interests. Contextual awareness is therefore crucial in shaping successful PPP structures, along with an understanding that one model may not be applicable in all settings.

Finally, adaptability and policy learning play important roles in achieving positive outcomes in climate-focused PPPs. Drawing insights from previous projects and adjusting based on those insights increases a partnership's likelihood of success. Northern Lights drew lessons from the Mongstad CCS project, establishing a more inclusive, bottom-up approach that better aligns partner competencies with responsibilities. More generally, adaptability allows PPPs to evolve with changing conditions, regulatory shifts, and market dynamics, ultimately helping to achieve project objectives in the long term.

Together, these principles – goal alignment, leveraging sector strengths, cultural awareness, and adaptability – offer a comprehensive framework for designing effective PPPs. As climate-focused PPPs grow, these factors form the contours of a replicable model for advancing public sustainability goals while creating profitable opportunities for private-sector actors.

8.4 Government Policies and RDT

As we have seen, governments provide key resources that firms depend on as they move into new and emerging markets. Knowing that their access to government resources is linked to their alignment with national climate objectives, companies may adjust their business practices to incorporate climate-friendly innovations that resonate with policy expectations (see Shinkle et al. 2021). This alignment is not just about meeting regulatory requirements, as it often extends to building strategic initiatives that capitalize on government-supported market trends, such as renewable energy or low-emission technologies. Within this context, MNCs become key players in climate-positive sectors that would be less accessible or profitable without state support (e.g., see Lewis 2013).

PPPs introduce a more complex dynamic within RDT – one of mutual dependence. Through these partnerships, governments and firms become interdependent, as both require resources that the other controls. Governments rely on private-sector expertise, capital, and innovation to develop climate infrastructure, clean energy projects, and adaptation solutions. At the same time, firms depend on governments to provide the regulatory approvals, funding mechanisms, and long-term policy commitments that make PPP investments feasible. If governments fail to offer clear regulatory frameworks, stable funding, or political support, then firms may hesitate to engage. Likewise, if firms do not deliver on promised innovations or cost efficiencies, then governments may reconsider future partnerships. Thus, PPPs illustrate a more complex form of dependency management, where neither the public nor private sector is fully in control and both must strategically manage their reliance on the other.

While national governments play a pivotal role in shaping business opportunities and managing corporate dependencies, they are not the only actors influencing how firms respond to climate change. The international community adds another layer of resource dependency that firms must navigate. Multilateral climate funds, carbon trading systems, and global supply chain regulations establish cross-border conditions that firms must integrate into their strategies, regardless of individual government policies. Similarly, participation in international agreements can determine access to financing, trade opportunities, and capital. As we will see in Chapters 9 and 10, understanding how international factors shape corporate resource dependencies is essential for firms seeking to manage risks and reap rewards in a warming world.

9 *International Public Policy and Climate Risk Management*

Many of the climate risks facing MNCs cannot be addressed solely by their home or host country governments. Climate change transcends national borders, such that GHG emissions from one country affect other nations, as do that country's climate management policies. For this reason, policy analysis must look beyond the nation-state to the regional and global levels. As we will see, members of the international community have taken steps to address climate change, whether through the formation of multilateral agreements or via the provision of climate-oriented foreign assistance.

The pages that follow explore these international policy efforts and their effects on corporate climate risks. The chapter provides overviews and discussions of international climate agreements (ICAs) and climate aid, accompanied by empirical analyses that assess how MNCs respond to these policies.[1] I also reflect on the challenges and controversies associated with international climate policies and offer potential solutions.

RDT provides an analytical starting point. MNCs must manage their exposure to climate risks by navigating their external resource environments, which include international governance structures and resources such as foreign aid. The presence or absence of these resources may affect MNCs' risk exposure levels, with implications for their business decisions. For example, inflows of climate aid may help host countries shore up climate resilience, giving MNCs confidence that their investments will be shielded from the physical impacts of climate change. On the other hand, when states join ICAs, they often commit to strict policy requirements that impose reporting obligations or emissions restrictions on companies. This could increase transition

[1] While these international interventions are the focus of this chapter, they do not constitute an exhaustive list of international policy efforts. For example, international courts have a role to play in determining which actors are most responsible for climate change (Quell 2024).

risk, forcing firms to either adapt or move to locations that offer a more favorable set of resources. Importantly, MNCs are not passive actors in this system. They can negotiate their resource environments by lobbying to shape ICAs or influence the distribution of aid.

Ultimately, the question is if and how these international governance mechanisms meaningfully alter climate risk exposure for MNCs: do ICAs and aid reduce the risks that would otherwise deter firms from investing in climate-vulnerable countries, or do they introduce new concerns that deter investment? By addressing this question, the chapter sheds light on the ways in which international policy efforts influence corporate resource dependencies and decision-making.

9.1 International Climate Agreements (ICAs)

We can start with ICAs, which are a subset of international environmental agreements (IEAs). IEAs are compacts between states that cover issues ranging from air pollution to biodiversity to GHG emissions and global warming. They may be bilateral, such as the Air Quality Agreement between the US and Canada, or focus on a region, like the Convention for the Protection and Development of the Marine Environment of the Wider Caribbean Region, which has been ratified by twenty-six countries. Alternatively, they may be global in membership and scope, like the Convention on International Trade in Endangered Species of Wild Flora and Fauna, which 183 countries are party to, or the Paris Agreement, which has been signed by 195 countries.

While global agreements tend to receive the most attention, they are far outnumbered by bilateral and regional IEAs (Mitchell et al. 2020). Because these agreements are negotiated between fewer and more like-minded members, they are more easily brought to fruition (Bellelli et al. 2023) and can go farther in terms of commitments (Asheim et al. 2006). For example, the EU's Green Deal set emissions reduction targets far more ambitious than what could be agreed to in the context of a global agreement.[2] While smaller-scale agreements can play a significant role in climate change mitigation, their proliferation has raised concerns about the fragmentation of global climate governance (Oh and Matsuoka 2017).

[2] Details on the EU's Green Deal can be seen here: https://commission.europa.eu/strategy-and-policy/priorities-2019-2024/european-green-deal_en.

IEAs, which vary in their bindingness (Köppel and Sprinz 2019), flexibility (Boockmann and Thurner 2006), and processes for ensuring compliance (Goeteyn and Maes 2011), have been a feature of the international landscape for decades, predating the 1972 United Nations Conference on the Human Environment, which has been cited as the launching point of international environmental law (Joyner 2005). Early on, the focus of IEAs was primarily on biodiversity, with most agreements covering concerns about animal and plant species (Mitchell et al. 2020). Pollution came to the forefront in the 1970s, with the establishment of the Convention on Long-Range Transboundary Air Pollution in 1979 and the Montreal Protocol on Substances That Deplete the Ozone Layer in 1987 (Gonzalez et al. 2015; Moses et al. 2020).

As the scientific consensus on climate change solidified in the late twentieth century, the international community turned its attention to the challenge of reducing planet-warming GHG emissions. Yet even with this shift, ICAs remain a small minority of IEAs: of the 3,766 bilateral and multilateral IEAs cataloged in the International Environmental Agreements Database Project (see Mitchell et al. 2020), only thirty-one include "climate change" in the agreement title.[3] Western European and small island developing states (SIDS) lead the way in terms of ICA membership, with France (32), Germany (29), Belize (22), Antigua and Barbuda (21), and St. Lucia (21) being party to the most agreements. Conversely, Russia (1), South Sudan (7), and Iraq (9) are among the countries that have joined the fewest.[4]

9.1.1 ICAs and Their Discontents

The United Nations Framework Convention on Climate Change (UNFCCC), established in 1992, laid the groundwork for climate-

[3] Only 24, if amendments to existing agreements are not included. To search agreements, visit the International Environmental Agreements Database Project, hosted by Université Laval, available at: https://iea.ulaval.ca/en/agreements.

[4] The proliferation of ICAs in part reflects a conventional wisdom that climate inaction reflects a free rider problem, whereby governments decline to take decarbonization steps because they prefer to free ride off the climate mitigation efforts of others (e.g., Keohane and Victor 2016). It follows that this can only be overcome through the creation of a strong centralized body with enforcement power (Bernauer 2013; Victor 2011). That said, scholars have failed to find empirical support for this free rider dynamic (Aklin and Mildenberger 2020).

focused IEAs by recognizing the global nature of climate change and emphasizing the principle of "common but differentiated responsibilities," which acknowledged the disproportionate historical contributions of developed countries to global emissions while emphasizing the need for all nations to take action (Breidenich et al. 1998). The UNFCCC led to the Kyoto Protocol in 1997, which introduced legally binding emission reduction targets for developed countries[5] but faced criticism for excluding many major emerging economies (Maamoun 2019), contributing in part to the US's refusal to ratify the agreement (Hovi et al. 2012).

While some recent appraisals have found that the Kyoto Protocol produced significant emissions reductions (Maamoun 2019; Prakash and Potoski 2017), its failure to secure US ratification prompted subsequent negotiations to seek more inclusive and flexible agreements. Within this context, the Paris Agreement, adopted in 2015, requires all participating countries to develop and submit their own targets, known as intended nationally determined contributions (INDCs). This approach allowed countries to participate in the agreement to the extent that domestic politics would allow, thereby removing a barrier to participation (Falkner 2016).

The Paris Agreement aims to limit global temperature rise to within 1.5 Celsius degrees of preindustrial levels. It also calls for industrialized countries, which are responsible for the large majority of GHG emissions, to provide financial and technical support to help developing nations adapt to climate impacts and transition to low-carbon economies (Clémençon 2016). Subsequent negotiations to advance the Paris Agreement at annual Conferences of the Parties (COP) have created new rules for carbon credit markets (Greenfield 2024) and further commitments for climate finance (Bearak 2024).

There are various criticisms of ICAs. Most saliently, concerns remain about their effectiveness (Almer and Winkler 2017), particularly in the context of collective action problems and weak enforcement (Barrett 2008). In the Paris Agreement, for example, countries voluntarily declare their own INDCs and could simply declare none at all. Moreover, even if countries commit to ambitious targets, there are no formal mechanisms to ensure compliance (Stankovic et al. 2023).

[5] During the first period, these countries were to reduce their emissions to an average of 5.2 percent below their 1990 levels.

These treaty design problems stem from conflicts over equity, domestic-level issues within member states, and geopolitical dynamics.

First, while the historical responsibility for GHG emissions lies disproportionately with developed nations, which industrialized early and contributed heavily to cumulative emissions, emerging economies such as China and India are now among the world's largest emitters. This has fostered tensions over fairness in burden sharing, with the US calling for emerging economies to adopt strict commitments and China and India arguing for the right to develop without undue constraints (Maizland 2023). Meanwhile, SIDS and many African nations, which contribute minimally to global emissions and face the brunt of climate impacts (Fonjong et al. 2024; Vousdoukas et al. 2023), have called for major emitters from both the developed and developing worlds to step up commitments (Anna 2023).

Political factors within countries add an additional set of complexities (Bang et al. 2012; Marchiori et al. 2017; Perkins and Neumayer 2007). In many nations, leaders face pressures to prioritize economic growth and protect domestic industries (Vesa et al. 2020).[6] Fossil fuel-dependent economies are particularly inclined to resist or weaken international commitments that threaten jobs or revenue streams (Tadadjeu et al. 2023). For example, Saudi Arabia was labeled a "wrecking ball" at COP29 for attempting to roll back commitments to transition away from fossil fuels (Carrington 2024b). Similarly, populist movements can shift national priorities away from global climate goals (Lockwood and Lockwood 2022). And, as was discussed in Chapter 2, corporate interests routinely lobby their governments to reject rules that challenge their business models.

Finally, geopolitical dynamics can influence the formation and ambition of ICAs (Park 2022), with the US, China, and the EU being particularly significant power players (Schreurs 2016). The US–China climate partnership was instrumental in securing the Paris Agreement, yet geopolitical tensions have hindered further collaboration (Davidson and Pearson 2024).[7] Meanwhile, the EU has come to the forefront of

6 These pressures become still more intense during economic downturns (Scruggs and Benegal 2012).

7 Indeed, geopolitical competition arguably contributed to the Trump Administration's decision to withdraw the US from the Paris Agreement. As President Trump explained: "China will be allowed to build hundreds of additional coal plants. So we can't build the plants, but they can, according to this

global climate politics, seeking to align climate governance with its values and interests, while also adapting its approach to geopolitical realities (Oberthür and Dupont 2021; Parker et al. 2017). What this means for global environmental governance going forward remains to be seen, but finding policy consensus may become more difficult in an increasingly multipolar and competitive world (Chu et al. 2024).

9.1.2 ICAs and Climate Risks

ICAs have the potential to reduce physical climate risk by establishing frameworks to decelerate the pace of global temperature rise – as well as the extreme weather events that accompany it. Additionally, agreements that channel adaptation funding to developing countries could help to reduce physical risk for companies operating in those nations. However, the effectiveness of these agreements likely depends on their implementation. The voluntary nature of commitments under frameworks like the Paris Agreement often results in significant disparities in emissions reduction targets (Flagg and Rudel 2021) and follow-through (Li et al. 2024). Funding shortfalls for adaptation initiatives in developing countries are also common, leaving vulnerable regions without the resources needed to enhance resilience (Paul 2021). As a result, the actual impact of ICAs may be insufficient to address the challenges faced by MNCs in high-risk regions.

While ICAs may help reduce physical risk, they inherently create transition risk for MNCs by compelling member nations to align with

agreement. India will be allowed to double its coal production by 2020. Think of it: India can double their coal production. We're supposed to get rid of ours. Even Europe is allowed to continue construction of coal plants. In short, the agreement doesn't eliminate coal jobs, it just transfers those jobs out of America and the United States, and ships them to foreign countries. This agreement is less about the climate and more about other countries gaining a financial advantage over the United States. The rest of the world applauded when we signed the Paris Agreement – they went wild; they were so happy – for the simple reason that it put our country, the United States of America, which we all love, at a very, very big economic disadvantage. A cynic would say the obvious reason for economic competitors and their wish to see us remain in the agreement is so that we continue to suffer this self-inflicted major economic wound. We would find it very hard to compete with other countries from other parts of the world." Trump's full comments can be read here: https://trumpwhitehouse.archives.gov/briefings-statements/statement-president-trump-paris-climate-accord.

new rules and standards. These agreements set the stage for a global shift away from carbon-intensive practices, which can be challenging and even existential for sectors like oil and gas (Halttunen et al. 2023). However, there is a layer of nuance in that ICAs are often voluntary in their commitments and lack binding enforcement mechanisms (Lawrence and Wong 2017). For MNCs operating in countries whose governments make minimal or no commitments under these agreements, the transition risk is likely to be marginal. These firms may enjoy competitive advantages if their foreign competitors must comply with stricter measures imposed by more proactive governments. The opposite is true for MNCs operating in countries that align themselves closely with international climate goals by putting ambitious measures into place. Things may become still more complicated for MNCs when governments commit to ambitious targets under ICAs but fail to follow through with the necessary policy steps to achieve them or reverse course altogether.[8]

Similar dynamics apply to litigation risk. In countries where governments make strong commitments under ICAs, companies may face heightened litigation if they fail to comply with new regulations or fall short of targets (Preston 2021). Conversely, in jurisdictions with weak commitments or limited enforcement, litigation risk will remain low due to the absence of robust legal pressures. This variability across countries creates an uneven legal landscape for MNCs, with firms operating in highly regulated markets or under active civil society scrutiny more likely to encounter lawsuits tied to climate obligations. Adding to this complexity, cross-border risks emerge as ICAs influence court rulings globally (Voigt 2023).

Reputation risk is also likely to grow. As ICAs garner widespread attention from governments, media, and civil society, they help shape public and stakeholder expectations around what constitutes responsible corporate behavior (see Tingley and Tomz 2020). Within this context, companies may be judged against global standards by consumers, investors, advocacy groups, and others who expect them to align with international norms (see Bechtel et al. 2022). Companies perceived as falling short could lose consumer trust, find themselves excluded from green investment funds, or experience shareholder activism.

[8] This is exemplified in dramatic fashion by the US, which signed the Paris Agreement in 2015, then left it in 2020, then rejoined in 2021, then left once again in 2025.

9.1.3 Empirical Analysis

Given ambiguity about the effects of ICAs on MNCs' net climate risks, we can turn to empirical analysis to see whether MNCs are enticed or deterred from investing in countries that are members of ICAs – especially countries characterized by high levels of climate vulnerability. As discussed in Chapters 4 and 7, an overarching expectation in this analysis is that MNCs avoid climate-vulnerable countries because they fear that adaptation costs will fall on them. If would-be host governments can effectively signal that they are well positioned to manage climate change, then MNCs will be less concerned about bearing the burdens of adaptation and, therefore, more willing to move forward with investments. That signal can come through domestic policy efforts, as discussed in Chapter 7, but it may also come from foreign sources (see Gamso 2025a) – including membership in ICAs. On the other hand, ICA membership typically requires states to adopt certain policies or norms, which generate transition, litigation, or reputation risks for companies. If these latter risks outweigh the perceived benefits of ICAs, then MNCs may shy away.

To assess this empirically, I analyze statistical models that evaluate the relationship between climate vulnerability and FDI inflows when host countries are party to few or many ICAs. I do so by interacting climate vulnerability with the total number of ICAs to which countries are members.[9] Model specifications in this chapter follow those used in Chapters 4 and 7, with one key addition: a control variable for climate aid, drawn from the Organisation for Economic Co-operation and Development (OECD).[10] Climate aid is included because of its likely correlation with ICAs (it also serves as the moderation variable in the next set of models presented later in the chapter).[11]

[9] I draw ICA data from the International Environmental Agreements Database Project (Mitchell et al. 2020). This data is available here: https://iea.ulaval.ca/en/agreements.

[10] This data is available here: https://web-archive.oecd.org/2024-06-04/315401-climate-change.htm.

[11] By contrast, the models in Chapter 7 did not include domestic policy controls beyond the moderation variable (e.g., the governance readiness models did not include disaster preparedness or CPIA scores) because doing so substantially reduced the sample size. For consistency and robustness, it is worth noting that the results presented here remain substantively unchanged even when the additional international policy variable is excluded. These models are available from the author on request.

Table 9.1 *Climate risk and FDI, by ICAs.*

Dependent Variable: FDI Inflows	Model 9.1
Climate Vulnerability	-13.47***
	(5.112)
ICAs	-0.224***
	(0.0836)
Climate Vulnerability * ICAs	0.476***
	(0.180)
Climate Aid	0.0107
	(0.0130)
GDP	0.813
	(0.694)
Per Capita GDP	0.0503
	(0.601)
Annual GDP Growth	0.0161*
	(0.00957)
Regime Type	0.0223
	(0.0155)
High Intensity Conflict	0.0613
	(0.158)
Oil Rents	0.00352
	(0.0101)
BITs	-0.00333
	(0.00229)
Observations	1,762
R-squared	0.402
Number of Countries	120
Country Fixed Effects	Yes
Year Fixed Effects	Yes

Linear panel data models. Country and year fixed effects; robust standard errors in parentheses, clustered by country; independent and control variables lagged one year; $^{***}p < 0.01$, $^{**}p < 0.05$, $^{*}p < 0.1$.

The results are presented in Table 9.1. I begin by explaining the main effect coefficients for climate vulnerability and ICAs, which are negative and significant. The main effect for climate vulnerability tells us that less FDI flows into risky countries when they are not members of any ICAs. Likewise, ICAs are negatively related to FDI inflows when

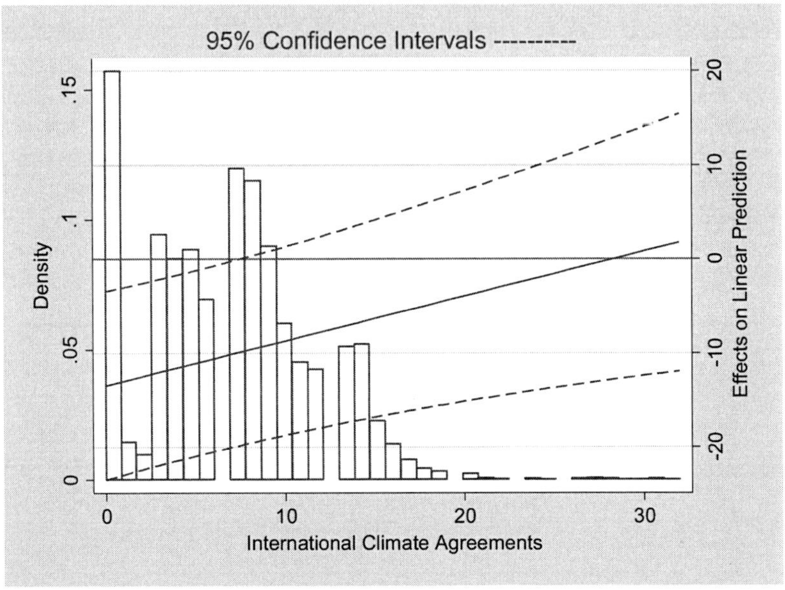

Figure 9.1 Climate risk and FDI, by ICAs.
Marginal effects plot showing the relationships between climate vulnerability and FDI inflows when states are members of various numbers of ICAs.

climate risk is very low, perhaps because companies believe that ICAs will impose constraints on their operations in host countries without meaningfully reducing their exposure to already low physical climate risk.

Next, we can turn to the positive and significant interaction term, which indicates that the presence of ICAs lessens the negative relationship between climate vulnerability and FDI. In other words, investors avoid climate-vulnerable countries at lower rates as those countries join more ICAs. To get a clearer sense of this moderation effect, I plot the marginal effects in Figure 9.1. The result shows that the relationship between climate vulnerability and FDI inflows is negative and statistically significant when states are party to few agreements, but it ceases to be significant when the number of ICAs rises to around ten. This suggests that MNCs are deterred by physical climate risk when ICA membership is low but reassured as states join more agreements.

Disaggregating the dependent and independent variables adds additional nuance. First, I distinguish primary, secondary, and tertiary sector FDI inflows (see Table A.11 in the Appendix). The only significant interaction term is in the secondary FDI model, but the interaction term is negative, unlike the model analyzing FDI in the aggregate. This result suggests that secondary-sector investors fear that ICAs lead to a ramping up of transition, litigation, or reputational pressures, which collectively outweigh any reductions in physical risk. Perhaps this reflects the unique degree to which these types of risks affect manufacturers, because of their relatively high energy use, low capacity for rapid adaptation, and complex supply chain pressures.[12]

Next, I disaggregate climate vulnerability to see which facets of climate risk are affected by ICA membership. The outputs, which are presented in Table A.12 in the Appendix, show significant and positive interactions for ecosystem, food, health, and habitat vulnerability. It appears that investors facing these sorts of risks find ICA membership reassuring, while no such significant effect is evident for infrastructure or water vulnerability (even though these interaction terms are positive).

9.1.4 The Roles of Non- and Sub-State Actors in Global Climate Governance

While ICAs are central to global efforts to address climate change, they are increasingly complemented by the actions of cities, businesses, civil society organizations, and other sub- and non-state entities, which have emerged as key players in what is often referred to as transnational climate governance. These actors have been able to form networks and coalitions that contribute to climate action without the same constraints faced by intergovernmental agreements (see Andonova et al. 2017).

Sub- and non-state initiatives vary widely in scope and function. For instance, city networks like C40 Cities[13] and the Global Covenant of Mayors for Climate & Energy[14] bring together municipalities to share

[12] The marginal effects show that the relationship between climate vulnerability and secondary sector FDI inflows is negative when ICAs are low in number, becoming still more negative as the number of ICAs increases. This plot is available from the author on request.

[13] More information about C40 Cities is available here: https://c40.org.

[14] Details on the Global Covenant of Mayors can be found here: https://globalcovenantofmayors.org.

best practices, set emissions reduction targets, and implement local climate policies. Businesses participate through initiatives such as the SBTi. Civil society organizations and advocacy groups contribute by monitoring compliance, raising public awareness, and pressuring governments and corporations to take more ambitious actions. These non-state arrangements often include partnerships across sectors, such as the We Mean Business coalition between businesses and NGOs, which seeks to accelerate corporate action on climate change.[15]

The emergence of transnational governance can be traced in part to the limitations of intergovernmental efforts (Green 2014; Hoffmann 2011). Unlike coalitions of national governments, non-state actors are not bound by the constraints of international diplomacy, such as the need for consensus among diverse and competing national interests. This allows them to set more ambitious goals and, in many cases, achieve greater progress in shorter timeframes. For example, businesses may adopt climate targets that go beyond regulatory requirements, while cities can implement strong local climate policies even in the absence of national leadership.

Over time, transnational climate governance has evolved into a critical component of the global response to climate change. While initially focused on advocacy and symbolic commitments, many initiatives have transitioned toward measurable actions, accountability frameworks, and reporting mechanisms (see Zhang et al. 2024). This evolution has strengthened the legitimacy of non-state actors, enabling them to complement ICAs by playing a more direct role in shaping the trajectory of global climate efforts (Bäckstrand et al. 2017; Jernnäs and Lövbrand 2022; Kuyper et al. 2018). That said, the growing influence of non-state actors also raises questions about accountability and equity. Unlike governments, these actors are not always subject to public oversight, and their actions may prioritize certain interests or regions over others (Bernauer and Betzold 2012). Moreover, the participation of non-state actors appears to correlate with countries' political institutions, which calls into question the degree to which they can bypass the challenges faced by national governments (Andonova et al. 2017).

[15] More information about the We Mean Business coalition is available here: https://wemeanbusinesscoalition.org.

9.2 Climate-Oriented Foreign Assistance

Climate assistance offers another intervention that can help countries manage the impacts of climate change. This aid, it should be noted, is often a key component of ICAs, such as the Paris Agreement, which calls for developed nations to provide financial and technical support to developing countries (Sengupta 2021). Yet climate aid can also be provided independently of such arrangements. In either case, it is seen as essential for helping the most vulnerable countries to mitigate and adapt to climate change (Georgieva et al. 2022), while also giving wealthier nations an avenue to compensate for their disproportionate responsibility for GHG emissions (see Ledger and Klöck 2023).

Climate aid, which is just one element of the much larger foreign aid regime, encompasses loans and grants for climate mitigation and adaptation (Bayramoglu et al. 2023).[16] It is provided by a range of actors, including national governments, such as the US and the EU, as well as IGOs like the World Bank and the United Nations Green Climate Fund (Roy 2024; Weiler et al. 2018). Climate aid can extend beyond financial transfers to include technical assistance, such as sharing knowledge and expertise, and the deployment of climate scientists or engineers to build capacity in recipient countries (see Iacobuţă et al. 2022).

Donors first undertook a concerted effort to supply funds for green energy and climate management in 2001, to help developing countries participate in the Kyoto Protocol (Hicks et al. 2008). This continued under the Copenhagen Accord, as donors pledged $32 billion for the 2010–2012 period (Kono and Montinola 2019). Donors then pledged $100 billion in annual financing through the Paris Agreement (Sengupta 2021) – a number that was increased to $300 billion at COP29 in 2024 (Bearak 2024).[17] See Figure 9.2 for a snapshot of climate assistance over time.

[16] Most climate aid comes in the form of loans, often with low interest rates and long periods for repayment (Fong 2024). Mitigation aid includes funding for renewable energy projects and emissions reduction technologies, while adaptation aid includes investments in flood defenses, drought-resistant crops, and disaster preparedness.

[17] This number falls far short of what most experts believe will be necessary to reach net-zero emissions by 2050, or to keep global temperatures from rising beyond the threshold set by the Paris Agreement (Fong 2024).

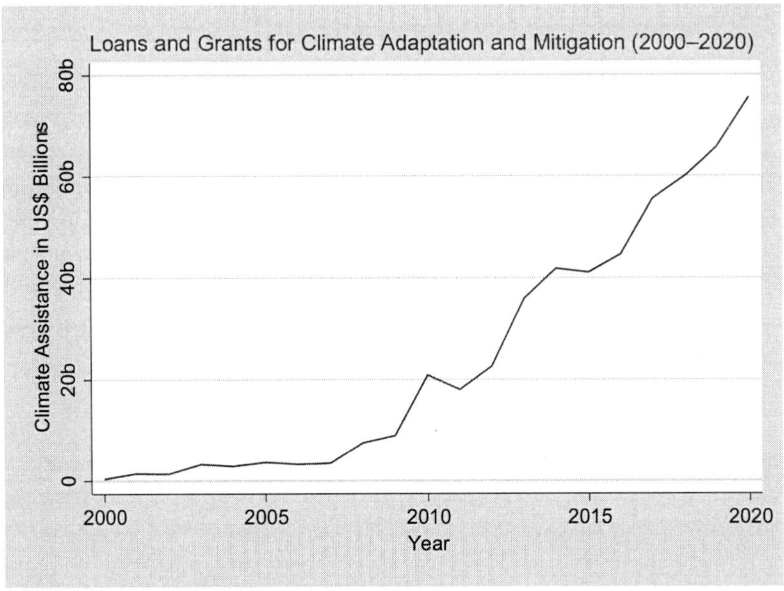

Figure 9.2 Climate assistance from 2000 to 2020.

The effectiveness of climate aid has been a subject of debate (see Bayramoglu et al. 2023). On one hand, successful programs can produce tangible benefits, such as improved disaster preparedness, reduced emissions, and enhanced resilience in vulnerable communities (Carfora and Scandurra 2019; Wu et al. 2016, 2021). On the other hand, implementation challenges and politics may limit its impact (Bayramoglu et al. 2023; Skovgaard et al. 2023). For instance, the Paris Agreement's financing goal was not met by its initial deadline (Timperley 2021), undermining trust between donor and recipient countries and calling into question the significance of subsequent pledges (Noor and Carrington 2024). Moreover, pledged funds fall short of what is needed to address the scale of the climate crisis (Fong 2024).

Criticisms of climate assistance reflect broader concerns about foreign aid (Easterly 2007; Moyo 2009). Aid flows, including those earmarked for climate purposes, are often shaped by political and geopolitical priorities rather than by the needs of vulnerable populations (see Gamso 2025b), potentially leaving less geopolitically important nations underfunded (Bayramoglu et al. 2023).[18] Disagreements between donors and recipients over the amount of aid needed, as well as over who should bear the burden of providing it, add further complexity. Developing nations often argue that wealthy countries are not contributing enough, while some donor governments emphasize fiscal constraints or point to emerging economies, like China and India, as potential contributors (see Bearak 2024).[19]

9.2.1 Climate Aid and Climate Risks

Like ICAs, climate aid seems likely to decrease some risks to MNCs while exacerbating others. It should have positive effects in terms of physical risk, to the extent that it provides recipient countries with resources to enhance climate resilience. For instance, aid that supports disaster preparedness, flood defenses, or sustainable agriculture could reduce the likelihood of disruptions to supply chains or other business operations. However, if aid is used to support recipient governments in decarbonizing their economies or adopting stricter environmental policies, then MNCs operating in aid-recipient nations could face increased transition risk.

The impacts of climate aid on litigation and reputation risks are less clear. On the one hand, aid that helps recipient governments strengthen their legal capacity could increase litigation against MNCs. On the other hand, effective climate aid could reduce litigation risk by addressing the root causes of climate-related harm, such as improving resilience to extreme weather. The reputational impacts of climate aid are similarly ambiguous: MNCs that align themselves with donor-driven projects or adopt practices in line with the goals of climate aid might see their reputations bolstered; conversely, if aid puts international attention on climate-vulnerable countries, then companies operating

[18] Private aid and financing from philanthropy, corporations, or NGOs can help fill the void (Barrett and Chaitanya 2023). These private flows may be less constrained by political considerations, though they bring their own challenges, such as lack of transparency and an overfocus on mitigation relative to adaptation (Kalinowski 2024).

[19] This point was echoed by an aid specialist I spoke with from the UNEP, who noted that China receives climate aid that it does not need (by his estimation) from the World Bank's Global Environmental Fund, when it should really be stepping up as a donor.

in these nations could face criticism for profiting in areas where local populations face severe climate impacts.

9.2.2 *Empirical Analysis*

While the previous paragraphs offer speculative insights as to how MNCs perceive climate aid, we can turn to empirical analysis for a more systematic assessment.[20] My expectation is that climate aid will send a positive signal to MNCs, because it provides recipient countries with resources that they can use to manage climate change. By signaling that host states are equipped for this task, aid should give MNCs confidence that adaptation costs will not fall on them, making them more inclined to follow through on investments. This is especially important because aid-recipient countries tend to be low- or middle-income nations that would lack these resources otherwise. Alternatively, aid could send a negative signal to investors if they expect it to be accompanied by policy conditions that speed along decarbonization or create new legal burdens.

I conduct statistical analysis by interacting climate vulnerability with climate aid.[21] In interpreting the results, which are presented in Table 9.2, it is useful to once again begin with a brief discussion of the negative and significant main effect coefficients. The main effect for climate vulnerability tells us that this variable is negatively related to FDI when climate aid inflows are at their lowest, suggesting that investors prefer to avoid risky countries that receive little to no climate aid. Likewise, the significant and negative main effect for climate aid indicates that aid inflows deter investors where climate risk is very low, perhaps reflecting concerns that climate aid will exacerbate transition risk in these scenarios while serving little benefit in terms of reducing marginal physical risk.

[20] I carried out similar analysis in an article published in *Climate and Development* (Gamso 2025a). Table 9.2 and Figure 9.3 are adapted from that article.

[21] As noted earlier, climate aid data is drawn from the OECD. The variable is logged to account for its heavy skew. 81.72 percent of this aid comes bilaterally from Development Assistance Committee (DAC) member countries, while 0.17 percent is from non-DAC donors. Multilateral assistance constitutes 15.27 percent of assistance, with the remaining 2.84 percent coming from private donors. Assistance was almost entirely targeted toward climate mitigation until 2010, with adaptation assistance increasing from this point but never exceeding mitigation aid.

Table 9.2 ***Climate risk and FDI, by climate aid.***

Dependent Variable: FDI Inflows	Model 9.2
Climate Vulnerability	-14.54***
	(5.071)
Climate Aid	-0.198***
	(0.0701)
Climate Vulnerability * Climate Aid	0.435***
	(0.143)
ICAs	-0.00264
	(0.0325)
GDP	0.932
	(0.636)
Per Capita GDP	-0.0574
	(0.566)
Annual GDP Growth	0.0158*
	(0.00942)
Regime Type	0.0229
	(0.0158)
High Intensity Conflict	0.0201
	(0.159)
Oil Rents	0.00417
	(0.0101)
BITs	-0.00343
	(0.00233)
Observations	1,762
R-squared	0.402
Number of Countries	120
Country Fixed Effects	Yes
Year Fixed Effects	Yes

Linear panel data models. Country and year fixed effects; robust standard errors in parentheses, clustered by country; independent and control variables lagged one year; $^{***}p < 0.01$, $^{**}p < 0.05$, $^{*}p < 0.1$.

The model produces a significant and positive interaction term, meaning that higher aid inflows moderate the negative relationship between climate vulnerability and FDI. This likely reflects the positive signal that climate aid sends to foreign investors worried about climate risk: access to aid offers host states resources to manage the impacts of

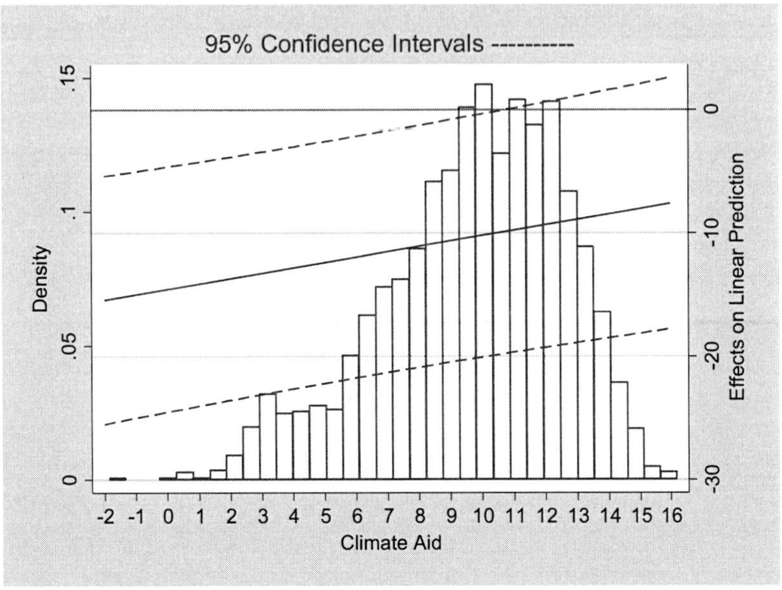

Figure 9.3 Climate risk and FDI, by climate aid.
Marginal effects plot showing the relationships between climate risk and FDI at different values of climate aid.

climate change, thereby taking the burden off MNCs; these companies, perceiving climate risk to be under control, elect to move forward with investments in risky markets that they would otherwise avoid.

I plot the marginal effects in Figure 9.3. This plot shows a negative and statistically significant relationship between climate vulnerability and FDI when climate aid is low. Yet this relationship becomes non-significant as climate aid increases. This further indicates that climate aid prevents risk-averse MNCs from avoiding climate-vulnerable countries.

We can derive further insights by disaggregating key variables, beginning with analyses in which primary, secondary, and tertiary sector FDI serve as the dependent variables – see Table A.13 in the Appendix. The interaction term is significant and positive only in the model focusing on primary sector investment. This is quite interesting given the contrast to the results in Chapters 4 and 7, as well as those presented earlier in this chapter. Collectively, these findings suggest that different sectors evaluate climate risk and climate policies through different lenses, with secondary-sector investors being concerned about risk but not finding ICAs reassuring, tertiary-sector investors caring about regulatory stability and seeing domestic policy as the strongest signal of commitment, and primary-sector investors seeing aid as a tangible tool for mitigating risk.

Climate aid, it should be noted, often funds projects that directly benefit the primary sector, such as forest conservation, irrigation, and water management (Gopalan and Rajan 2016; Hornum et al. 2024; Pascual et al. 2018). In contrast, aid projects may not target the kinds of industrial infrastructure that manufacturing firms need, such as ports, roads, and electricity grids. Likewise, since tertiary investors are more mobile and less reliant on physical resources or infrastructure, they may see little value in climate aid.

I next assess models that disaggregate the vulnerability variable into its six segments (see Table A.14 in the Appendix). Each of the corresponding interaction terms is positive, indicating that climate aid assures investors concerned about each facet of vulnerability. However, the interaction terms that include food, habitat, health, and infrastructure vulnerability are statistically significant, while those that include ecosystem and water vulnerability are not. This calls into question the perceived meaningfulness of climate aid in addressing this subset of vulnerabilities.

9.3 Policy Implications and Complexities

This chapter has provided evidence that ICAs and climate aid can prevent foreign investors from systematically avoiding climate-vulnerable countries. The surface-level policy implications are obvious: to ensure the flow of FDI, climate-vulnerable states should join ICAs, and donors should direct climate aid to these countries. However, several concerns remain about both ICAs and climate assistance. Some of these concerns were discussed earlier, but these bear repeating, and others should also be highlighted.

With regard to ICAs, a primary concern is equity and burden sharing. Climate-vulnerable countries often contribute the least to global emissions, yet bear the brunt of climate impacts (Füssel 2010).[22] Requiring these countries to join multiple agreements to

[22] According to one estimate, African countries are responsible for less than five percent of GHG emissions since the 1850s (Yimere 2025).

attract investment places an additional set of burdens on them, both in terms of the strict emissions standards that they may have to abide by and the logistical and opportunity costs of negotiating and implementing agreements. Additionally, powerful countries and interests often play an outsized role in negotiating ICAs (Brenton 2013; Hagen and Schopf 2024), leaving climate-vulnerable countries with limited influence.[23] As these countries join agreements, they might be forced to adopt policies at the behest of more powerful members that do not adequately reflect local priorities or needs, undermining sovereignty and community well-being.

The concerns about climate aid are more numerous. First, climate aid is often distributed unevenly, with strategically important nations receiving a disproportionate share compared to those that are poorer or less geopolitically significant (Bayramoglu et al. 2023). This can leave the most climate-vulnerable nations underfunded and less attractive to foreign investors. Second, once climate aid is delivered, there is no guarantee that it will be used in a way that effectively shores up climate resilience.[24] Aid is often associated with corruption and mismanagement, particularly in countries with poor governing institutions (Bethencourt and Perera-Tallo 2025). Even when this is not the case, the conditions that donors attach to aid may lead to it being allocated to projects that are less relevant to the recipient country's climate resilience (see Hennessy et al. 2023). In this context, while climate aid may send an immediate positive signal to foreign investors, the longer-term effect may be deterring as effective adaptation plans fail to materialize.

Putting aside concerns about aid allocation and utilization, the reality is that the volume of climate aid being committed by donors is insufficient to meet the needs of recipients (Fong 2024). Moreover, donors have often failed to meet these insufficient commitments in practice (e.g., see Harvey 2023). This shortfall leaves recipient nations without the resources necessary to implement the large-scale mitigation and adaptation projects required to reduce their exposure to climate

[23] See Ourbak and Magnan (2018) for a counterpoint.

[24] As an environmental aid specialist explained in an interview, aid-recipient countries often emphasize their vulnerability to climate change because they see it as a useful narrative to leverage additional aid from donors. Given the fungibility of aid, this money may ultimately go toward other priorities (see Pack and Pack 1993).

change. Donor failings also create skepticism about the reliability of future aid flows, which can deter recipients from making the policy changes necessary to align with ICAs. Furthermore, uncertainty surrounding aid makes long-term planning difficult for recipient governments, reducing their ability to implement comprehensive climate strategies. For investors, this lack of predictable funding exacerbates concerns about governance and stability, likely leading to further avoidance of climate-vulnerable regions.

These concerns suggest immediate implications for policymakers around the world. With regard to ICAs, policymakers should focus on strengthening INDCs to reflect ambitious yet realistic goals aligned with global climate targets. Commitments should be tracked with regular public reporting to ensure accountability. In doing so, equity should be top of mind, as policymakers work toward balancing the principle of common but differentiated responsibilities with the need for more ambitious action by all parties, especially major emitters – an approach consistent with the polluter-pays rule (Lange et al. 2007).

More systematic changes could include the imposition of enforcement mechanisms, such as penalties for noncompliance or benefits for achieving goals, formally integrating sub- and non-state actors into ICAs, and increasing representation of climate-vulnerable nations in decision-making processes. Stricter enforcement mechanisms should encourage wealthier nations to follow through on their commitments, thereby reducing pressure on climate-vulnerable countries to overcompensate. Likewise, integrating non-state actors like cities, businesses, and civil society groups can potentially reduce some logistical costs to climate-vulnerable countries by transferring them to non-state actors. Increasing the representation of climate-vulnerable and developing countries can amplify these nations' voices, while reducing the risks of sovereignty being undermined or local interests being sidelined in favor of the priorities of more powerful parties.

With regard to climate aid, first and foremost, donors should fulfill existing pledges and commit to increasing aid flows to meet the growing needs of vulnerable nations.[25] These countries are, by and large, victims of a climate crisis that they contributed little to, and it is only right for industrialized countries to help them adapt. Additionally,

[25] At the time of this writing, some major donors are going in the opposite direction (see Gabbatiss 2025).

donors should take steps to depoliticize climate aid so that it reaches the most climate-vulnerable countries and populations. Finally, a greater degree of monitoring and evaluation is necessary to ensure that aid is used effectively once it reaches recipients.

Reforming climate aid, even in pursuit of these fairly modest suggestions, will likely require systemic efforts. Developing countries will need well over US$1 trillion annually to effectively address the impacts of climate change (Fong 2024), and the current aid regime is simply not equipped to provide this level of funding. Integration of private financing from corporations and philanthropic organizations can help to fill the gap, but it is not sufficient (Black et al. 2023). Instead, more radical proposals, such as taxing fossil fuels, rich country citizens, or MNCs themselves, may be necessary. Suspending debt so that developing countries can refocus their interest payments on climate challenges should also be considered (see Harvey 2024). These policies would all be politically challenging to implement in practice,[26] and they would each have side effects. But the climate crisis is an extreme and even existential one, particularly for poor countries, and so drastic reforms must be on the table.

[26] Although there is some precedent: see Franczak (2024) on Unitaid, a global health program for developing countries that has been funded in large part through a tax on airline passengers.

10 *International Public Policy and Climate Opportunities*

We have seen how ICAs and climate-oriented foreign aid can affect the climate risks faced by MNCs, mitigating physical risk while potentially amplifying transition, litigation, and reputation risks. These international agreements and initiatives can also help create business opportunities, both by directly supporting companies and by fostering an ecosystem for innovation. There are also opportunities for MNCs to collaborate with international political actors in service of developing and delivering climate solutions. These collaborations can contribute to projects and innovations that help put the world on a more sustainable trajectory.

This chapter explores these opportunities over three sections. First, I examine international support for green industries. Next, I analyze avenues for collaboration between MNCs and IGOs, highlighting both the potential benefits and the unique challenges stemming from these arrangements. I conclude with a brief reflection on strategies for growing the value of international collaborations.

10.1 International Support for New and Emerging Industries

There are several ways through which ICAs, climate aid, and other international efforts can foster business opportunities for forward-thinking companies. I analyze these mechanisms through a framework that categorizes international support for green business into four areas: (1) targets and incentives, (2) signaling, (3) direct funding, and (4) enabling ecosystems. These areas are summarized in Table 10.1 and then discussed in the subsections that follow.

10.1.1 Targets and Incentives

ICAs can accelerate the development of sustainable business opportunities by establishing targets for governments to meet. For example, the

Table 10.1 *International policy support for green business.*

	Definition	Opportunities for Firms
Targets and Incentives	Setting clear goals, standards, and market mechanisms that drive ICA member countries to meet climate targets.	Firms can capitalize on government support to meet targets, as well as compliance-driven market demand.
Signaling	Creating confidence and predictability in markets through ICAs.	Firms can attract investment by aligning strategies and technologies with ICA commitments.
Direct Funding and Financial Support	Providing financial resources through climate aid to support green projects and industries.	Firms gain access to seed capital, de-risked investment opportunities, and green infrastructure.
Enabling Ecosystems	Building the foundational systems for green industries, including capacity, R&D support, and collaboration platforms.	Firms use innovation networks, knowledge sharing, and partnerships to develop and scale solutions.

Kyoto Protocol and the Paris Agreement set emission reduction targets for member countries (Maizland 2023). To achieve these goals, governments frequently turn to specific performance standards for industries and companies, such as energy efficiency requirements for vehicles and emissions limits for power plants (Nachmany and Setzer 2018). To help firms meet these standards, governments may provide them with subsidies or tax incentives. In the US, for instance, the Biden Administration sought to meet Paris Agreement commitments with investments in renewable energy and energy-saving technologies, bolstering industries such as solar and wind energy, EVs, and energy storage in the process (Bistline et al. 2023).

Complementing emissions reduction targets and performance standards are carbon trading systems, which reward businesses that adopt low-carbon technologies and practices, as well as those that help other firms reduce their carbon use. Where these systems are present, companies that reduce emissions can profit by selling surplus allowances, while producers of clean energy, carbon capture technologies, and energy-efficient solutions benefit from increased demand as industries seek to lower emissions in pursuit of cost reductions. In some cases, carbon trading is explicitly built into ICAs, such as Article 6 of the Paris Agreement.[1] Alternatively, these systems may be imposed at the national level to help countries meet their international climate commitments. For example, the EU's Emissions Trading System was initially established to meet the EU's obligations under the Kyoto Protocol.[2]

10.1.2 Signaling

Chapter 9 offered evidence that ICAs signal a low-risk investment environment to MNCs, but membership in these agreements can also signal confidence and predictability in green markets. By demonstrating member nations' long-term commitments to the green transition, ICAs make investments in sustainable industries more attractive. The Paris Agreement, for example, should send a strong signal to investors that signatories will prioritize decarbonization, ensuring likely returns on investments in renewable energy, EVs, and other low-carbon products. As confident investors channel financial support to these industries, green businesses will be afforded the resources to expand their operations to meet growing demand.

ICAs also signal policy consistency across markets. This consistency reduces the uncertainty and complexity associated with fragmented policies, simplifying firms' operations and lowering costs (Cezar and Escobar 2015). When firms see governments aligning regulatory frameworks under a shared agreement, they interpret this as a signal of predictable, long-term commitment, enabling them to standardize products, scale production, and capture global market share. For example, automakers investing in EV production gain confidence when

1 See information about Article 6 here: https://unfccc.int/process-and-meetings/the-paris-agreement/article-64-mechanism.

2 Details on the EU's Emissions Trading System are available here: https://climate.ec.europa.eu/eu-action/eu-emissions-trading-system-eu-ets_en.

governments in major markets jointly commit to phasing out internal combustion engines.

10.1.3 Direct Funding and Financial Support

Unlike the targets and signals provided through ICAs, funding and financial support flow primarily through climate aid from multilateral climate funds and bilateral assistance programs.[3] This aid creates opportunities for firms to participate in green markets, particularly in developing economies where private capital is often hesitant to invest. It does so by providing seed capital, de-risking, and funding green infrastructure.

Seed capital offers the initial investment needed to kick-start industries or projects that would otherwise struggle to attract private capital due to high perceived risk. For example, the UNEP manages a multi-donor trust fund that helps launch climate-friendly projects in African and Asian countries.[4] Early funding supports businesses developing renewable energy infrastructure, CCS, low-emission transportation systems, and other green technologies, helping them build their operations and demonstrate feasibility and profitability to private investors.

Closely related is blended finance, which combines public financing with private capital (Mutambatsere and Schellekens 2020). This approach is particularly effective in mobilizing private-sector involvement in projects with high upfront costs but significant long-term potential (Choi et al. 2023). For example, a renewable energy project in a developing country may receive concessional loans or guarantees from a multilateral climate fund, which incentivize private investors to contribute additional capital. In this scenario, private investors can enjoy the return on an investment that they would not otherwise make, while the renewable energy project has a higher probability of success thanks to the investment.

In addition to project-specific funding, climate assistance often supports broader green infrastructure development. Investments in

[3] Although, as noted in Chapter 9, climate assistance commitments have often been a component of ICAs.

[4] Information about the UNEP's donor trust fund can be found here: https://unep.org/topics/energy/energy-finance/seed-capital-assistance-facility-scaf.

modernized electricity grids[5] and expanded public transportation networks,[6] among other things, create the infrastructure needed for low-carbon industries to operate and scale. These infrastructure projects create direct opportunities for firms in sectors like construction, engineering, and energy, while also enabling the growth of downstream industries that use green infrastructure to deliver their products and services.

10.1.4 *Enabling Ecosystems*

While less tangible on its face, a fourth contribution that the international community can offer is to help foster an enabling ecosystem. This refers to the softer, systemic conditions essential for green industries to thrive, including capacity, collaboration platforms, and innovation acceleration mechanisms. Together, these conditions foster environments where green businesses can innovate, build partnerships, and scale.

The first component of this ecosystem is capacity. IGOs support programs to train local workers in renewable energy installation, maintenance, and advanced manufacturing techniques in an effort to ensure that key industries have access to skilled labor. For example, the Green Jobs for Youth Pact is a combined effort from the ILO, the UNEP, and the United Nations Children's Fund, which intends to create new green jobs, green existing jobs, and support entrepreneurs in establishing or expanding green businesses.[7]

Collaboration platforms also contribute to enabling ecosystems, providing spaces for governments, businesses, and civil society to come together to share ideas, resources, and best practices. For instance, the Green Growth Knowledge Partnership, established in 2012 by the Global Green Growth Institute, the OECD, the UNEP, and the World Bank, brings together experts and organizations to share key

[5] For example: https://worldbank.org/en/news/press-release/2021/12/21/world-bank-helps-bangladesh-build-modern-reliable-and-sustainable-electricity-supply-system.

[6] For example: https://worldbank.org/en/news/press-release/2022/06/01/el-banco-mundial-invierte-600-millones-para-modernizar-el-ferrocarril-belgrano-sur.

[7] Details on the Green Jobs for Youth Pact are available here: https://unep.org/explore-topics/education-environment/what-we-do/green-jobs-youth-pact.

insights and practices to facilitate the green transition.[8] Likewise, the United Nations hosts various events to promote joint action on topics such as the sustainable use of oceans, challenges specific to SIDS, and aligning the management of climate change with broader sustainability goals.[9] These forums create opportunities for companies to collaborate on ambitious projects, from decarbonizing supply chains to codeveloping new technologies.

IGOs have also supported the formation of innovation clusters that bring together universities, private firms, and government agencies to focus on solutions like advanced energy storage, CDR, or next-generation renewable technologies. For example, Mission Innovation, launched at COP21 to support innovation in clean energy, includes an initiative that brings together key stakeholders to identify opportunities and work toward solutions.[10] Hubs such as these promise to accelerate the pace of technological breakthroughs, while also providing firms with access to shared infrastructure, research expertise, and early-stage funding. Businesses participating in these networks can gain competitive advantages by staying at the forefront of innovation and positioning themselves as leaders in emerging markets.

10.1.5 The Role of Independent International Organizations

Independent international organizations also play a role in fostering green markets and creating business opportunities. These organizations, which include bodies like the International Organization for Standardization (ISO) and entities that oversee voluntary carbon markets, provide tools and platforms that help firms compete, innovate, and differentiate themselves in the global transition to sustainability. Additionally, bodies such as the WEF offer initiatives for innovative climate solutions.[11]

[8] More information on the Green Growth Knowledge Partnership is available here: https://greengrowthknowledge.org.

[9] See a list of recent conferences here: https://sdgs.un.org/conferences/climate-sdgs-conference-2024.

[10] More information about Mission Innovation can be found here: https://mission-innovation.net/innovation-platform-collaborate.

[11] For example, information about the WEF's clean energy initiatives is available here: https://centres.weforum.org/centre-for-energy-and-materials/home.

ISO certifications, such as ISO 14001 for environmental management systems, establish globally recognized standards that help firms demonstrate their commitment to sustainability and environmental stewardship.[12] Achieving these certifications can provide firms with competitive advantages, as many customers, investors, and business partners prefer to engage with companies that adhere to widely recognized standards (Camilleri 2022). Certifications are even a prerequisite for entering some markets or winning certain contracts (Darnall 2006). Thus, ISO certifications offer a way for businesses to signal credibility and access markets where sustainability is a priority.

Independent organizations also facilitate voluntary carbon markets. Unlike compliance carbon markets tied to governmental regulations, voluntary markets operate through frameworks established by independent standard-setting bodies such as Verra or the Gold Standard (see Kreibich and Hermwille 2021). These organizations certify carbon offset projects, ensuring that credits represent real, additional, and verifiable emissions reductions. Companies developing offset projects generate revenue by selling certified credits to other businesses, while the buyers, in turn, enjoy reputational benefits as they demonstrate progress toward net-zero goals.

Beyond direct differentiation, these platforms contribute to the standardization of green practices. Carbon markets and certification systems create a shared language that facilitates international trade and investment in green goods and services. By participating in these systems, firms gain access to broader markets while also improving their resilience in the face of evolving environmental expectations.

10.2 Collaborating with (Intergovernmental Organizations IGOs) for Climate Solutions

In addition to enriching themselves through engagements with the international community, MNCs can contribute to multilateral efforts to manage climate change and its impacts by working with IGOs such as the UNFCCC, the World Bank, and various regional development banks. Through these collaborations, MNCs and multilateral actors

[12] Firms that are ISO 14001 certified have agreed to comply with their countries' environmental laws and to adhere to various environmental standards (see Arimura et al. 2016). More information on ISO is available here: https://iso.org/home.html.

can pool resources, align strategies, and drive systemic changes across sectors and geographies.

These collaborations fit into three areas:

(1) Cross-sectoral alliances that bring together diverse stakeholders to address climate challenges that require coordinated action.
(2) Innovative financing mechanisms, such as blended finance or risk-sharing frameworks, that help overcome barriers to private-sector investment in high-impact climate projects.
(3) Joint research and knowledge-sharing initiatives, which allow MNCs to collaborate with IGOs on the development and deployment of cutting-edge technologies.

These areas are briefly summarized in Table 10.2 and then detailed in the subsections that follow.

Table 10.2 *Three areas of collaboration between IGOs and MNCs.*

Area	Definition	Example
Cross-Sectoral Alliances	Collaborative efforts between IGOs and MNCs, often involving additional stakeholders such as NGOs, aimed at addressing systemic challenges.	The United Nations Global Compact (UNGC) engages companies to align business strategies with sustainability.
Innovative Financing Mechanisms	Financial models that combine public and private funding to mobilize private-sector capital for high-impact climate projects.	Blended finance structures in renewable energy projects.
Research, Development, and Knowledge Sharing	Initiatives between MNCs and IGOs to advance research, develop cutting-edge climate technologies, and share knowledge to scale solutions globally.	The World Bank's Climate Innovation Centers connect MNCs, academics, and governments to develop renewable technologies.

Unlike partnerships between firms and national governments, these collaborations operate on a global or regional scale, addressing challenges that transcend national borders. For example, the World Bank has collaborated with corporations on projects to expand renewable energy access in developing countries[13] and to enhance climate resilience in urban areas.[14] While these partnerships offer significant opportunities to address climate change, they also pose unique challenges, including navigating diverse stakeholder interests, ensuring the equitable distribution of benefits, and aligning with multilateral governance structures. Brief overviews of the three areas of collaboration and the challenges accompanying them are offered over the next several pages.

10.2.1 Cross-Sectoral Alliances

Cross-sectoral alliances aim to address systemic challenges, such as decarbonization, supply chain sustainability, or global health issues, by leveraging the strengths of diverse stakeholders. For example, the UNGC encourages its members – thousands of businesses – to align their business models with the SDGs, offering a framework for corporate action across areas such as human rights, labor, the environment, and anti-corruption.[15] Similarly, the WEF's Alliance of CEO Climate Leaders brings together corporate leaders with IGOs and other stakeholders to accelerate pathways to net-zero emissions.[16]

While they provide useful forums for discussion and collaboration (Williams 2014), cross-sectoral alliances often face criticism for their limited impact on solving global challenges (e.g., see Sethi and Schepers 2014). Indeed, while engagement in these alliances appears to benefit firms in financial terms (Msiska et al. 2021; Orzes et al. 2020), it is not clear that it has led to improvements in sustainability (Berliner and Prakash 2014; Macellari et al. 2021). The effectiveness of cross-sectoral alliances is frequently undermined by misaligned priorities among participants (see Wiegant et al. 2024). Companies may join

13 For example: https://projects.worldbank.org/en/projects-operations/project-detail/P180547.

14 For example: https://gfdrr.org/en/crp.

15 More information about the UNGC is available here: https://unglobalcompact.org.

16 Details on the WEF's Alliance of CEO Climate Leaders can be found here: https://initiatives.weforum.org/alliance-of-ceo-climate-leaders/home.

these initiatives to enhance their reputations or signal their commitment to sustainability, yet the lack of binding commitments or enforcement mechanisms facilitates poor follow-through (Williams 2004). At the same time, IGO partners like the UNGC have incentives to prioritize growth and visibility by hosting high-profile events or expanding membership, which can overshadow the core mission of addressing systemic issues. These programs can consequently turn into platforms for rhetoric rather than meaningful progress (Sethi and Schepers 2014).

These challenges notwithstanding, cross-sectoral alliances do offer an important mechanism for aligning public- and private-sector actors. Organizations like the UNGC put sustainability on MNCs' agendas and offer them tools to integrate it into their core strategies and operations. Furthermore, these collaborations open the door for companies to share best practices with one another and to seek future partnerships with public- and nonprofit-sector actors on climate-focused initiatives.

10.2.2 Innovative Financing Mechanisms

Innovative financing mechanisms, such as blended finance arrangements and climate bonds, combine public- and private-sector resources to mobilize capital. These mechanisms incentivize private investment in projects that have the potential to produce significant environmental benefits but would struggle to attract market interest in their early stages because of high perceived risks or long payback periods.

Blended finance, as discussed earlier, combines concessional public funding – often from IGOs – with private investment to de-risk high-impact projects. For instance, public funds may provide guarantees or first-loss capital, reducing risks to private investors and encouraging them to participate in ventures they might otherwise avoid. While I already touched on the business benefits that these financial arrangements can create for MNCs, this approach can also be instrumental in developing climate management technologies and bringing them to market (see Bracking and Leffel 2021).

Similarly, climate bonds, a green debt instrument often provided by IGOs like the World Bank, enable governments and private companies to raise capital specifically for climate-friendly initiatives. Like traditional bonds, investors lend money in exchange for repayment with interest. However, the proceeds of green bonds are explicitly earmarked for environmentally beneficial projects such as solar farms, wind energy projects, or urban resilience programs (Bhutta et al. 2022).

While these mechanisms can benefit the planet and humanity by channeling capital into climate solutions, their success is not guaranteed, and they come with notable challenges. One concern is the potential for misaligned incentives: private firms are likely to focus on maximizing returns, while IGOs aim to prioritize long-term sustainability. This disconnect can lead to projects that elevate profitability over environmental outcomes or fail to generate returns for private-sector partners. Additionally, the efforts of IGOs may reflect the political interests of their key stakeholders. For example, the World Bank's International Finance Corporation, which frequently works with MNCs to fund climate adaptation and mitigation projects,[17] has been found to operate in alignment with the geopolitical interests of powerful governments (Dreher et al. 2019). This raises concerns about the equitable distribution of benefits and the extent to which these mechanisms address global climate challenges rather than serving corporate or political interests.

Despite these challenges, innovative financing mechanisms remain an important tool for advancing climate solutions. Green projects are often constrained by a lack of outside investment, and bringing private-sector finance into the fold is essential (Adhikari and Safaee Chalkasra 2023).

10.2.3 *Research, Development, and Knowledge Sharing*

The third area focuses on partnerships between MNCs and IGOs to facilitate the transfer of knowledge and technologies across borders, create environments where cutting-edge ideas can flourish, and foster global cooperation to address shared challenges. As discussed earlier, innovation hubs managed by IGOs can benefit companies by connecting them with one another as well as with governments, academics, and members of civil society. But these hubs can also contribute to the

[17] Information on the International Finance Corporation's blended finance for climate initiatives can be found here: https://ifc.org/en/what-we-do/sector-expertise/blended-finance/climate.

development of climate solutions. For example, World Bank-supported Climate Innovation Centers (CICs) have helped to launch startups in areas ranging from renewable energy to climate-smart agriculture to low-carbon services.[18]

IP agreements can also support climate solutions, which often require the dissemination of patented technologies that are costly or otherwise inaccessible to developing countries (Raiser et al. 2017). Efforts such as those under the Paris Agreement's Technology Mechanism aim to facilitate technology transfer while respecting IP protections, striking a balance between incentivizing innovation and ensuring equitable access to solutions (Minas 2020). Additionally, global R&D partnerships, such as the previously mentioned Mission Innovation, bring together public- and private-sector leaders to jointly fund and develop next-generation technologies in areas like green hydrogen, CCS, and advanced solar photovoltaics (Myslikova and Gallagher 2020).

These knowledge-sharing frameworks are not without challenges, as they require the proactive integration of participating countries, which can be undermined by domestic factors within those nations (Jandhyala and Phene 2015). Nevertheless, these frameworks offer pathways for the diffusion of innovations and best practices, including to countries and companies that would otherwise face significant barriers to engagement.

10.2.4 A Note on International Public–Private Collaborations

Relative to PPPs at the national level, which were covered in Chapter 8, partnerships involving IGOs present unique challenges. The first challenge is the complexity of multilateral governance structures. IGOs have to balance the interests of multiple member nations, which may be in conflict, with the goals of private sector partners seeking efficiency and profitability (Park et al. 2020). Additionally, the global or regional scope of these arrangements can complicate project implementation, as regulatory environments, infrastructure, and stakeholder capacities vary widely across countries (Beisheim et al. 2014). Moreover, the lack of direct accountability mechanisms in IGOs

[18] For example, see Lee et al. (2016) on Kenya's CIC.

compared to national governments can make it difficult to ensure that all parties deliver on their commitments (see Bäckstrand 2008).

Additionally, there is a potential for corporate influence to skew priorities in favor of profitability rather than broader climate goals, particularly in international collaborations where the complexity of multilateral governance and the absence of strong, localized accountability mechanisms can create gaps that allow corporate agendas to dominate (Utting and Zammit 2009). This dynamic is exacerbated by the asymmetry in power and resources between MNCs and some other stakeholders, such as local communities, civil society organizations, and smaller firms (see Schäferhoff et al. 2009). By favoring projects that prioritize profitability, these partnerships may overlook or marginalize interventions that would better serve vulnerable populations or address localized climate challenges. For example, projects such as utility-scale solar farms or offshore wind installations align well with corporate priorities because they are financially viable, scalable, and market-oriented. By contrast, smaller, local interventions such as decentralized microgrids or community-based reforestation efforts often yield higher localized benefits but are less attractive to investors because of their smaller scale, higher transaction costs, and limited profitability. While both types of projects carry value, there is a danger that corporate interests persistently steer collaborations toward the former and away from the latter.

Several steps can be taken to address these challenges. First, stronger accountability mechanisms are needed to ensure that all partners deliver on their commitments and that benefits are equitably distributed. These could include performance metrics tied to measurable social and environmental outcomes, along with greater transparency in decision-making processes. Second, IGOs should prioritize inclusive collaborations by creating formal spaces for smaller and less powerful stakeholders to contribute meaningfully to project design and implementation. Finally, aligning project priorities with both global climate goals and localized needs can help ensure that these partnerships address systemic challenges while maximizing their impacts on the ground. While these things are more easily said than done, there is an appetite for making PPPs and other sorts of public–private collaborations a centerpiece of global environmental change (Gasparro et al. 2022), suggesting that parties across sectors can be convinced to adopt reforms that improve effectiveness.

10.3 Enhancing International Collaboration

From an RDT perspective, this chapter crystallizes some of the themes that we have seen elsewhere in the book. MNCs can become reliant on resources from IGOs and other members of the international community, including stability brought about by ICAs and financing from climate aid. At the same time, these international-level inputs can reshape the resource landscape that firms operate within by impacting local policies and market dynamics in home and host countries. MNCs are not without agency, as they can negotiate their environments by lobbying or otherwise seeking to influence international policy actors or processes. Moreover, there is a mutual dependence between IGOs and MNCs in the context of global partnerships, as MNCs have key resources that public organizations can leverage to successfully develop and implement climate solutions.

RDT can also offer insights for designing and managing collaborations to improve their effectiveness. First, for firms to engage confidently and reliably as partners in pursuit of climate solutions, they need stable and predictable resource environments. This will require international political actors to provide greater certainty about long-term funding flows, policy commitments, and regulatory frameworks. When these resources disappear or become volatile, firms may be hesitant to engage with international initiatives, fearing that unstable conditions will undermine their ability to manage their dependencies effectively. At the time of this writing, many governments are backing away from ICAs and climate aid (Gabbatiss 2025), undermining international climate negotiations (Carrington 2024b), and failing to meet climate commitments (Kirk 2023).[19] This volatility makes it difficult for companies, likely deterring them from undertaking risky investments in climate innovation or participating in international partnerships and initiatives.

Even as stability and predictability are prioritized, it is also important that policymakers be able to adjust strategies in response to changing conditions. Well-designed adaptive frameworks can improve firms' confidence levels by signaling that policymakers are committed to creating environments where companies can innovate without

[19] Data on the sufficiency (or lack thereof) of governments' climate policies can be found here: https://climateactiontracker.org/countries.

becoming locked into rigid conditions. Given the uncertainty inherent in climate markets, firms may hesitate to invest if they perceive international frameworks to be excessively rigid or bureaucratic, fearing that they may become dependent on outdated institutions that stifle their operations (see Zheng 2011). Likewise, there is a danger that partnerships in service of innovation will fail in the absence of flexible funding mechanisms and adjustable regulatory frameworks that evolve in response to scientific advancements, market trends, and firms' operational realities.

RDT also underscores that MNCs are active participants in shaping their resource environments. For international partnerships to succeed, firms should not be seen merely as recipients of policy targets or funds. By the same token, arrangements that defer too much to corporate partners risk an overemphasis on profits relative to fostering long-term sustainability. To prevent this, policymakers should actively engage MNCs in codesigning programs that align with both corporate strategies and climate goals. For example, collaboration platforms that invite firms to share technical insights, identify emerging market needs, or suggest flexible regulatory pathways can improve the fit between international interventions and firms' strategic objectives. Likewise, establishing clear accountability frameworks that require firms to demonstrate measurable progress in exchange for continued policy support can incentivize companies to deliver on climate commitments while ensuring that public resources are spent efficiently.

11 *Rising to the Climate Challenge*

From the seemingly unending drought in the American Southwest (Williams et al. 2022) to hurricanes so strong that their winds exceed the Saffir–Simpson scale (Wehner and Kossin 2024), extreme weather is becoming the norm as the climate changes and Earth warms. Many governments have responded to rising temperatures by imposing emissions standards, establishing carbon trading schemes, and subsidizing decarbonization technologies, while some consumers and investors are turning toward sustainable goods and services and the companies that specialize in them.

These trends have significant implications for members of the business community. On the one hand, firms face growing physical, transition, litigation, and reputation risks as climate change threatens the infrastructure that they rely on and the sociopolitical ecosystems in which they are embedded. On the other hand, forward-thinking and innovative companies can carve out competitive advantages as the world changes. These effects are especially acute for MNCs, as they contend with diverse climate risks and opportunities across multiple countries.

To survive in this environment, firms must adopt risk management strategies. They can accept uncertainty, transfer risks to other parties, make adaptations, diversify their business operations to limit climate-related impacts, or avoid the riskiest environments altogether. They can also adopt some combination of strategies by, for example, diversifying into new markets while adapting to policy changes in existing locations. My empirical analysis indicates a tendency toward avoidance, such that MNCs limit their investments in the most climate-vulnerable countries. This should trouble development specialists, insomuch as the nations that MNCs are avoiding are typically low- and middle-income countries that stand to benefit greatly from deeper engagement with the global economy.

Even as climate risks are disrupting many firms' operations, they are creating opportunities for others. These opportunities are especially present for businesses in the emerging green market and for those developing climate management technologies. For example, producers of resilient building materials, renewable energy, and EVs should thrive as extreme weather events multiply and more cities, states, and countries adopt decarbonization policies. Governments can support firms at the forefront of the green marketplace through procurement, tax incentives, and regulatory sandboxes, among other things. Yet some have gone in the opposite direction, bolstering pollution-intensive industries like oil and gas. How governments proceed and the impacts of their efforts depend on various factors, including the demands of key stakeholders and exposure to economic, social, and political disruptions.

11.1 Key Themes and Implications

Several key themes emerge from this book. First, contrary to much conventional wisdom, policies that address climate change are not inherently at odds with stimulating business activity or promoting economic growth. On the contrary, climate change itself is a threat to many companies, deterring them from engaging in international business activities that would potentially yield significant returns. By implementing governance and planning policies, establishing well-designed incentives and regulations, joining ICAs, and providing climate assistance, policymakers can reduce investor avoidance, thereby bringing profits to firms and growth to nations. By the same token, policies that unlock sustainable business opportunities can help to entrench new industries in the green economy. Thus, it is policy action, not inaction, that will stimulate business expansion and economic growth.

This is not to say that all companies will benefit from climate action. In fact, the very survival of some firms and industries is threatened by decarbonization policies. These firms may opt to adapt by turning to greener business practices, investing in new technologies that can offset their carbon-intensive activities, or lobbying against climate policies. How governments balance pressures to decarbonize against counter-pressures from the losers of decarbonization will have significant impacts on our planet and our societies going forward.

It must also be said that not all climate policies will support MNCs. Governments that wish to effectively thread the needle between climate change management and support for global business must be careful to embrace mutually beneficial policies, eschewing those that stifle cross-border commerce. That having been said, businesses are just one set of stakeholders among many, and governments should not be solely concerned about the interests of firms. Climate change affects us all, and policymakers must have the courage to upset the business community in support of the greater good.

The second theme is that climate change creates both risks and opportunities for MNCs. As temperatures change globally, extreme weather is becoming more common, threatening the infrastructure that firms rely on. For example, buildings, vehicles, roads, and bridges may be damaged or flooded due to mega storms or rising sea levels, while intense heat or prolonged drought make it difficult or impossible for workers to perform their duties. Yet for many firms, the greatest near-term uncertainty stems not from physical climate risk, but rather from evolving policies and regulatory frameworks designed to address that risk. Reputational damage associated with perceived misbehavior or inaction in the face of rising temperatures can cause still further risk, as consumers and investors disengage from companies that appear to disregard the damage that climate change is causing. Collectively, this array of risks should give pause to members of the business community that dismiss climate change as an abstract or distant matter.

While climate change will affect many firms for the worse, there will be winners as well. Beneficiaries will include companies that specialize in renewable goods and services, consultants that offer climate risk management support, and firms developing climate mitigation technologies. Firms in these industries, and others, will see demand for their products grow as the climate changes. There are risks to companies pursuing a sustainable business agenda, and the return on investment is uncertain, but rewards could be considerable for early movers. This is exemplified by companies like Tesla and Ørsted that went all-in on low-carbon solutions before their peers, cornering large market shares and becoming leaders in their respective industries in the process.

The third theme relates to the changes that climate change is having on the resource dependencies of firms. This has many dimensions. The natural environment itself is a crucial resource for many companies, and these firms will be affected as climates and weather patterns around the world change. In some cases, the effects will be negative, such as for coffee producers in the tropics contending with warmer temperatures and more erratic rainfall (Richardson et al. 2023). In other cases, they will be positive, such as the emerging wine industry in the UK, which has benefited from warmer weather (Croft 2024). Beyond the natural environment, companies depend on various other resources, ranging from stable regulatory systems to key product inputs to supportive customers. Climate change stands to impact each of these resources and, just as in the context of natural resources, some firms will benefit and others will be hurt.

As resource dynamics change, MNCs with sufficient mobility may shift their operations to locations that provide the resources that they need to excel, potentially leading companies with certain resource demands to group together in geographic regions that can support their needs. As firms relocate, their presence will further shape their new environments over time. For example, policy incentives designed to encourage clean energy investment may create clusters of firms specializing in low-carbon technologies, reinforcing national advantages for green industries. Conversely, firms abandoning regions that face heightened climate risks may accelerate economic decline, making it even harder for those areas to attract FDI in the future. Yet critical resource inputs, such as infrastructure, regulatory stability, or skilled labor, can help stabilize these dynamics. My empirical analysis attests to the value of supportive policies in this regard, demonstrating how governments can reduce uncertainty and maintain conditions that encourage investment.

A fourth theme is that firms can play a role in developing, scaling, and implementing climate solutions. Firms may do this purely as business strategy, as they see opportunities in the green market. For example, most major automobile companies have released one or more lines of EVs or hybrids to capitalize on growing demand for sustainable vehicles. In these cases, firms are acting primarily in pursuit of profits, seeking to capitalize on emerging consumer markets. In other cases, companies may support policy efforts through engagement in PPPs. These firms are still advancing their business interests, but the public sector sets the agenda in accordance with public interests.

11.2 Contributions to Scholarship

The book has contributed to several bodies of scholarship, synergizing themes from various academic fields. These include International business (IB) and international political economy (IPE) and sustainable development. This speaks to the complex and multifaceted nature of climate change – a topic that cannot be understood or properly studied without a transdisciplinary lens.

The first contribution is to IB, where scholars have sought to identify the determinants of MNCs' global business strategies. While political, economic, and social factors have received considerable attention over the years (e.g., Czinkota et al. 2010; Giambona et al. 2017; Henisz et al. 2010), there has been remarkably little attention to climate change,[1] even as the scale of its potential impact matches or even exceeds those of other much-studied factors. This book has filled the void by offering a comprehensive exploration of the impacts that climate change has on global companies. In doing so, it serves to put climate change on the agenda of IB scholars, while offering frameworks and empirical findings for researchers to build on as they pursue additional lines of inquiry in this area.

In addition to IB, this book contributes to the scholarship in IPE by showing how climate change and global business intersect with policy and politics. Three points stand out. First, governments are instituting a host of policies at the domestic and international levels, ranging from regulations to rein in emissions, to incentives that encourage the expansion of green markets, to foreign assistance in support of climate adaptation. These policies are deleterious to some firms, leading to pushback, market avoidance, and adaptation. Yet for others, they provide crucial resources, including direct financial support, forums for product development, and demand stimulus.

Second, although related to the first point, robust government attention to climate change appears to assuage foreign investors' concerns about climate risk. This attention can come from domestic policy, in the form of governance and planning policies, capacity building, and incentives and regulations, or from international collaborations, such as ICA membership and climate aid. Not all such efforts are equally effective at curtailing investor avoidance, and there is variance across investor types, but in general it seems as though MNCs are reassured by active governance where climate risk is of significant concern.

Third, companies can impact climate policy outcomes, negotiating their environments by encouraging or discouraging policy changes.

[1] Notable exceptions include Arnell (2015), Hsueh (2025), Rivera et al. (2022), and Wright and Nyberg (2015).

Firms in fossil fuel industries and other carbon-intensive sectors often lobby for softer regulations or to weaken ICAs, while those in low-carbon-intensive industries or in sectors that can readily reduce emissions may lobby for funding and other support to facilitate their decarbonization efforts (see Kupzok and Nahm 2024). In this way, firms are not only policy takers but also policy shapers.

Next, this book contributes to the sustainable development literature by shedding light on two key issues: first, the role of MNCs in supporting or undermining development outcomes and, second, the effectiveness of foreign aid. MNCs have long been viewed as double-edged swords in sustainable development (see Cole et al. 2017). On the one hand, some firms contribute to environmental degradation or pressure governments to weaken environmental standards in pursuit of short-term economic gain. On the other hand, foreign investments can create jobs, transfer technology, and improve infrastructure, while encouraging the widespread adoption of voluntary and compulsory standards. This book provides insights into the conditions under which these concerns are realized, offering a framework for determining whether a given MNC will encourage environmental degradation or betterment. Additionally, the book highlights how firms that strategically align with emerging green markets adopt low-carbon technologies or engage in partnerships with public institutions can contribute productively to sustainable development outcomes.

With regard to foreign aid, the book demonstrates that donors can help to stabilize investment environments through the provision of climate assistance, thereby mitigating perceived climate vulnerabilities that would otherwise deter FDI. In this way, aid gives recipient governments resources with which to manage climate adaptation and mitigation, while preventing MNCs from avoiding the climate-vulnerable countries that stand to benefit most from their investments. This finding contributes to the long-standing debate about the effectiveness of aid (see Qian 2015), suggesting that climate aid can support sustainable economic growth through its impacts on foreign investment.

Finally, this book offers a new dimension to the emerging discussion about the state of globalization, which is increasingly said to be in retreat, owing to rising protectionism and geopolitical tensions (e.g., Kornprobst and Paul 2021; Witt 2019; Witt et al. 2021). While these factors are undoubtedly important, this book highlights a previously overlooked driver of global business retrenchment: climate risk is prompting some MNCs to systematically avoid countries they perceive to be too vulnerable to climate-related threats. Without effective risk management strategies, this avoidance trend will deprive many developing countries of much-needed investment.

Yet climate-induced deglobalization is not inevitable. Through domestic climate governance, ICAs, and targeted foreign aid, policymakers can reduce investor uncertainty and stabilize investment environments, thereby mitigating climate-driven exclusion from global commerce.

11.3 Limitations and Future Research

No single book can address every dimension of such a complex issue as climate change and global business. While this volume offers a comprehensive analysis of the risks and opportunities facing MNCs in a warming world, several limitations should be acknowledged. Each opens the door to productive avenues for future research, which could deepen and extend the insights developed here.

One limitation lies in the book's emphasis on MNCs as the primary unit of analysis. MNCs are undeniably important actors in the global economy, with the reach, resources, and strategic flexibility to navigate climate risks across borders. However, other types of firms, such as domestic companies, small and medium-sized enterprises, and state-owned enterprises, may experience climate risks in fundamentally different ways. These firms often lack the mobility or capital that allows MNCs to shift operations, and they may be more vulnerable to localized environmental disruptions. At the same time, they do not have to manage distinct climate risks in multiple countries, simplifying their responses.

Future research could explore how different types of firms respond to climate impacts and engage in climate solution-building. Comparative studies of MNCs and non-MNCs or among firms of different sizes and ownership structures could yield insights into varying levels of resilience and strategic adaptation. In particular, the behavior of domestic firms in climate-vulnerable countries remains an underexplored but highly relevant topic for both scholars and policymakers. This could be explored through various angles, including drawing distinctions between recent startups and more established companies, firms in formal and informal markets, and companies in primary, secondary, and tertiary sectors.

A second limitation concerns the level of policy analysis. This book focuses on how national-level climate policies and international agreements and assistance influence firm behavior. While this approach is appropriate for a global study, the significant role that subnational governments play in climate governance merits comparable attention. In large or federalized countries, regional and local authorities often set the regulatory tone, implement national commitments, and create specific incentives or disincentives for firms. Variation at the subnational level may thus be as important as cross-national differences in explaining business responses to climate change.

Future research should investigate the effects of subnational policy on business strategy. For example, comparing high-capacity and low-capacity regions within the same country could illustrate how climate policy fragmentation affects firm behavior. Additionally, it would be insightful to explore subnational green innovation zones or city-level climate alliances, which might be influential in attracting investment from sustainability-oriented firms.

Another methodological limitation arises from the absence of firm-level surveys. This book draws on a combination of cross-national statistical analysis and in-depth interviews to triangulate macro- and micro-level insights. Interviews provide rich detail but are limited in scope, while statistical models reveal patterns but not decision-making logics. Without survey data, it is difficult to systematically assess how widespread certain perceptions and behaviors are within and across firms.

Future work should complement this analysis with structured surveys of business leaders, risk managers, and sustainability officers. Surveys could assess how firms perceive climate risk, how they evaluate national or international policies, and what kinds of internal strategies they are pursuing in response. This would help build a more generalizable understanding of how climate risk is internalized within firms and how strategic decisions are made at scale.

11.4 Confronting the Climate Challenge: A Call to Action

Climate change is reshaping the foundations of the global economy. Firms, governments, and international institutions have been taking notice, but not nearly at the scale or speed required. The evidence presented in this book should make it clear that this is more than a distant or peripheral concern. It is a defining force for global business in the twenty-first century. Addressing it will require strategic foresight, political resolve, and global cooperation. The following three takeaways offer high-level guidance for the business and policy communities as they confront the climate challenge.

First, climate change must be moved to the center of the strategic agenda for MNCs. The risks are too significant, and the potential opportunities are too substantial for firms to treat them as merely reputational or compliance issues. Physical risk threatens infrastructure, supply chains, and human capital, while transition, litigation, and reputation risks create uncertainties around regulation, carbon pricing, and stakeholder expectations. Yet firms that align themselves with the climate agenda stand to gain: by investing in low-carbon technologies, adapting operations to evolving resource environments, and positioning themselves in markets where sustainability is highly valued, they can build competitive advantages and shape markets to their long-term benefit. In short, climate change is a source of strategic disruption, and firms that fail to treat it as such risk falling behind. Aligning corporate strategy with climate reality is no longer an optional strategy to be undertaken by a subset of niche companies; rather, it is a necessity for any firm that wishes to secure its future.

Second, policymakers must confront the costs of delay. While climate change is increasingly on the global agenda, attention is too often characterized by finger-pointing and foot-dragging. High-emitting countries blame one another for inaction, while commitments to climate finance remain unmet, and energy transitions proceed at a halting pace. Whether the cause is geopolitical mistrust, collective action problems, or the influence of carbon-intensive industries, the result is mounting risk for companies and communities alike. Policymakers must recognize that climate inaction is not a neutral or safe choice. Instead, it undermines investment, weakens economic resilience, and erodes trust. If governments want to attract sustainable investment and foster stable growth, then they must offer credible and consistent signals that climate risk is being taken seriously.

Third, bold and even radical efforts will be needed to bring climate change under control. Mitigation remains essential, and decarbonization efforts must be dramatically accelerated. But it is increasingly clear that a massive scale-up of adaptation efforts will be needed to deal with the harms already underway. This will require the mobilization of extraordinary resources – particularly for the low- and middle-income countries that have contributed the least to climate change but are bearing its greatest burdens. While politically difficult, options such as global carbon taxes, financial transfers from wealthy nations, or public–private adaptation funds must be on the table. While it is common to think of programs like these as acts of charity, MNCs should see them as investments in global stability, risk reduction, and long-term market development. Without adaptation, companies will find more and more regions effectively uninvestable, undermining economic development worldwide and depriving MNCs of investment opportunities that might yield substantial returns.

11.5 The Future Is Now

The stakes could not be higher. If firms treat climate risk as marginal, policymakers continue to defer hard decisions, and the global community fails to act boldly and collectively, the consequences will be felt in lost growth and deepening inequality. But if companies align strategy with climate goals, policymakers move from pledges to implementation, and adaptation is taken seriously, there is still a window of opportunity to contain the climate crisis and build a more sustainable global economy in the process.

In short, climate change is a present reality that demands immediate action. The business community and the policy world each have roles to play, and neither can succeed without the other. A shared commitment to climate resilience and low-carbon development will be essential both for avoiding harm and for identifying new paths to prosperity in a rapidly changing world. Strategic alignment with the climate agenda is now a practical necessity for navigating a world in flux. The decisions made today by corporate leaders, policymakers, and IGOs will shape the contours of global business and development for decades to come. Confronting the climate challenge is not optional. It is the defining strategic task of our time.

Appendix

Appendix Table A.1 ***Interview details.***

Interview Date	Sector	Industry	Area	Geographic Region of Focus	Interview Mode
July 14, 2023	Public	National government	Climate change management	Caribbean	Semi-structured via Zoom
August 4, 2023	Public	International organization	Foreign aid/environment	Caribbean	Semi-structured via Zoom
June 17, 2025	Private	Consulting	Supply chain sustainability	North America	Semi-structured via Zoom
June 18, 2025	Public	International organization	Company-facing	North America	Semi-structured via Zoom
June 26, 2025	Public	International organization	Foreign aid/environment	International	Semi-structured via Zoom
June 30, 2025	Private	Technology	Climate risk management/ decarbonization	Multinational	Semi-structured via Zoom
July 2, 2025	Nonprofit	Consulting	Local corporate engagement	North America	Semi-structured in-person
July 24, 2025	Private	Technology	Climate risk management/ decarbonization	Multinational	Semi-structured via Zoom
July 28, 2025	Private	Consumer goods	Sustainability manager	Multinational (North America focus)	Semi-structured via Zoom
August 5, 2025	Private	Sustainability ratings	Sustainability analyst	Multinational (Europe focus)	Semi-structured via Zoom

Appendix Table A.2 *Countries in quantitative analysis.*

Afghanistan, Albania, Algeria, Angola, Argentina, Armenia, Australia, Austria, Azerbaijan, Bahrain, Bangladesh, Belarus, Belgium, Benin, Bhutan, Bolivia, Botswana, Brazil, Bulgaria, Burkina Faso, Burundi, Cabo Verde, Cambodia, Cameroon, Canada, Central African Republic, Chad, Chile, China, Colombia, Comoros, Congo, Dem. Rep., Congo, Rep., Costa Rica, Côte d'Ivoire, Croatia, Cyprus, Czechia, Denmark, Djibouti, Dominican Republic, Ecuador, Egypt, Arab Rep., El Salvador, Equatorial Guinea, Eritrea, Estonia, Eswatini, Ethiopia, Fiji, Finland, France, Gabon, Gambia, The, Georgia, Germany, Ghana, Greece, Guatemala, Guinea, Guinea-Bissau, Guyana, Haiti, Honduras, Hungary, India, Indonesia, Iran, Islamic Rep., Iraq, Ireland, Israel, Italy, Jamaica, Japan, Jordan, Kazakhstan, Kenya, Korea, Rep., Kuwait, Kyrgyz Republic, Lao PDR, Latvia, Lebanon, Lesotho, Liberia, Libya, Lithuania, Luxembourg, Madagascar, Malawi, Malaysia, Mali, Mauritania, Mauritius, Mexico, Moldova, Mongolia, Montenegro, Morocco, Mozambique, Myanmar, Namibia, Nepal, Netherlands, New Zealand, Nicaragua, Niger, Nigeria, Norway, Oman, Pakistan, Panama, Papua New Guinea, Paraguay, Peru, Philippines, Poland, Portugal, Qatar, Romania, Russian Federation, Rwanda, Saudi Arabia, Senegal, Serbia, Sierra Leone, Singapore, Slovak Republic, Slovenia, Solomon Islands, Somalia, South Africa, Spain, Sri Lanka, Sudan, Suriname, Sweden, Switzerland, Syrian Arab Republic, Tajikistan, Tanzania, Thailand, Timor-Leste, Togo, Trinidad and Tobago, Tunisia, Turkiye, Turkmenistan, Uganda, Ukraine, United Arab Emirates, United Kingdom, United States, Uruguay, Uzbekistan, Vietnam, Yemen, Rep., Zambia, Zimbabwe

Appendix Table A.3 *Descriptive statistics.*

Variable	Mean	Standard Dev.	Minimum	Maximum
FDI (logged)	20.12991	2.179229	10.36072	26.39634
Primary sector FDI (logged)	5.038699	2.285976	-3.506558	9.049312
Secondary sector FDI (logged)	5.440234	2.277183	-3.912023	10.62595
Tertiary sector FDI (logged)	6.614917	1.577915	.8628899	11.50852
Climate vulnerability	.4824551	.0803439	.3186446	.7002951
Ecosystem vulnerability	.4863068	.072005	.3282665	.6800185
Food vulnerability	.524322	.1221149	.1686139	.8595071
Habitat vulnerability	.5453224	.0891968	.3280642	.8158956
Health vulnerability	.554719	.1488392	.2567193	.8663048
Infrastructure vulnerability	.3630195	.1135545	.1052998	.8128533
Water vulnerability	.3817212	.1149299	.0130368	.7795298
Governance readiness	.397423	.1196823	.0013949	.7610766
Disaster preparedness	.396344	.3121081	0	1
CPIA	3.089965	.5578359	1.5	4.5
ICAs	8.443044	3.02431	0	19
Climate Aid (logged)	9.800992	2.803139	.3140261	16.1731
GDP (logged)	23.95667	1.791168	20.30821	30.23322
Per capita GDP (logged)	7.791096	1.063571	5.555394	10.06375
Annual GDP growth	4.458761	5.448252	-50.33852	86.82675
Regime type	2.631182	6.033062	-10	10
High intensity conflict	.0448179	.2069524	0	1
Oil rents (% GDP)	5.013155	11.1307	0	66.68474
BITs	66.86084	91.08452	0	350

Appendix Table A.4 ***Climate risk and FDI, disaggregated by risk type and sector.***

	Model A1	Model A2	Model A3
Dependent Variables in Parentheses	(Primary Sector FDI Inflows)	(Secondary FDI Inflows)	(Tertiary FDI Inflows)
Ecosystem Vulnerability	-15.84	2.307	21.63**
	(16.31)	(13.98)	(9.921)
Food Vulnerability	-2.160	-2.583	-4.757
	(5.380)	(4.949)	(6.350)
Habitat Vulnerability	22.70*	-2.858	13.90*
	(11.96)	(5.009)	(8.248)
Health Vulnerability	-3.665	-5.369**	4.371*
	(4.965)	(2.577)	(2.565)
Infrastructure Vulnerability	8.911	-10.98**	-2.412
	(6.918)	(4.399)	(2.473)
Water Vulnerability	17.88	-15.47***	5.409
	(18.94)	(4.471)	(7.560)
GDP	3.073	-1.263	5.615***
	(3.403)	(1.418)	(1.614)
Per Capita GDP	-4.153	0.130	-5.725*
	(4.608)	(1.974)	(3.114)
Annual GDP Growth	0.0594***	0.0224*	0.0230**
	(0.0214)	(0.0113)	(0.0112)
Regime Type	-0.0497*	0.0155	-0.0134
	(0.0279)	(0.0172)	(0.0232)
High Intensity Conflict	0.0119	-0.120	-0.410***
	(0.285)	(0.223)	(0.153)
Oil Rents	-0.0675	0.0337	0.0340
	(0.0418)	(0.0315)	(0.0230)

BITs	0.00433	0.00671	-0.00140
	(0.00468)	(0.00450)	(0.00394)
Observations	436	515	554
R-squared	0.220	0.280	0.253
Number of Countries	64	68	68
Country Fixed Effects	Yes	Yes	Yes
Year Fixed Effects	Yes	Yes	Yes

Linear panel data models. Robust standard errors in parentheses, clustered by country; independent and control variables lagged one year; $^{***}p < 0.01$, $^{**}p < 0.05$, $^{*}p < 0.1$.

Appendix Table A.5 ***Climate risk and FDI, by governance readiness, disaggregated by sector.***

	Model A4	Model A5	Model A6
Dependent Variables in Parentheses	(Primary Sector FDI Inflows)	(Secondary FDI Inflows)	(Tertiary FDI Inflows)
Climate Vulnerability	18.41	-40.12***	11.72
	(28.75)	(9.805)	(11.65)
Governance Readiness	-12.71	-4.338	4.811
	(19.89)	(8.524)	(7.104)
Climate Vulnerability * Governance Readiness	40.63	12.44	1.448
	(42.27)	(16.91)	(15.48)
GDP	5.960*	-1.592	5.516***
	(3.387)	(1.472)	(1.810)
Per Capita GDP	-6.564	1.015	-5.051*
	(4.376)	(1.941)	(2.889)
Annual GDP Growth	0.0451**	0.0195	0.0175
	(0.0205)	(0.0129)	(0.0115)
Regime Type	-0.0697***	0.00501	-0.0349*
	(0.0217)	(0.0216)	(0.0202)
High Intensity Conflict	0.165	0.0292	-0.158
	(0.213)	(0.205)	(0.209)
Oil Rents	-0.0328	0.0433*	0.0475*
	(0.0412)	(0.0258)	(0.0250)
BITs	0.00542	0.00492	-0.00422
	(0.00484)	(0.00440)	(0.00480)

Observations	469	548	587
R-squared	0.196	0.263	0.227
Number of Countries	68	72	72
Country Fixed Effects	Yes	Yes	Yes
Year Fixed Effects	Yes	Yes	Yes

Linear panel data models. Country and year fixed effects; robust standard errors in parentheses, clustered by country; independent and control variables lagged one year; $^{***}p < 0.01$, $^{**}p < 0.05$, $^{*}p < 0.1$.

Appendix Table A.6 ***Climate risk and FDI, by disaster preparedness, disaggregated by sector.***

	Model A7	Model A8	Model A9
Dependent Variables in Parentheses	(Primary Sector FDI Inflows)	(Secondary FDI Inflows)	(Tertiary FDI Inflows)
Climate Vulnerability	44.09**	-30.28***	24.50
	(21.21)	(9.234)	(17.77)
Disaster Preparedness	13.18	4.871*	9.997
	(9.819)	(2.468)	(7.799)
Climate Vulnerability * Disaster Preparedness	-34.32	-10.26	-26.48
	(24.91)	(6.298)	(20.03)
GDP	6.898*	-0.769	6.663**
	(3.978)	(1.763)	(2.787)
Per Capita GDP	-6.473	0.481	-5.622
	(5.386)	(2.452)	(4.028)
Annual GDP Growth	0.0445*	0.0197	0.0231*
	(0.0225)	(0.0133)	(0.0128)
Regime Type	-0.0390	0.00804	-0.00907
	(0.0398)	(0.0213)	(0.0319)
High Intensity Conflict	-0.317	-0.105	-0.615***
	(0.287)	(0.256)	(0.208)
Oil Rents	-0.0793	0.0256	0.0103
	(0.0874)	(0.0460)	(0.0666)
BITs	0.00366	0.00301	-0.00640
	(0.00516)	(0.00354)	(0.00507)

Observations	413	471	496
R-squared	0.230	0.276	0.272
Number of Countries	58	61	61
Country Fixed Effects	Yes	Yes	Yes
Year Fixed Effects	Yes	Yes	Yes

Linear panel data models. Robust standard errors in parentheses, clustered by country; independent and control variables lagged one year; $^{***}p < 0.01$, $^{**}p < 0.05$, $^{*}p < 0.1$.

Appendix Table A.7 *Climate risk and FDI, by incentives and regulations, disaggregated by sector.*

	Model A10	Model A11	Model A12
Dependent Variables in Parentheses	(Primary Sector FDI Inflows)	(Secondary FDI Inflows)	(Tertiary FDI Inflows)
Climate Vulnerability	20.15	-30.02	-31.09*
	(23.35)	(18.74)	(17.70)
CPIA	-3.356	0.434	-4.829**
	(4.070)	(3.059)	(2.259)
Climate Vulnerability * CPIA	4.642	1.260	10.65**
	(7.015)	(5.269)	(4.368)
GDP	6.350	-4.227	6.975**
	(3.861)	(3.618)	(2.783)
Per Capita GDP	-1.230	2.021	-3.711
	(4.002)	(2.853)	(3.209)
Annual GDP Growth	0.0336	-0.0122	0.0132
	(0.0221)	(0.0260)	(0.0131)
Regime Type	-0.0565**	-0.0171	-0.0112
	(0.0258)	(0.0309)	(0.0222)
High Intensity Conflict	-0.0994	-0.00416	-0.177
	(0.199)	(0.227)	(0.276)
Oil Rents	-0.327	0.101	0.0459
	(0.190)	(0.0726)	(0.0568)
BITs	-0.00654	-0.00311	-0.00485
	(0.00880)	(0.00783)	(0.00670)
Observations	166	182	186
R-squared	0.324	0.327	0.413
Number of Countries	21	22	22
Country Fixed Effects	Yes	Yes	Yes
Year Fixed Effects	Yes	Yes	Yes

Linear panel data models. Robust standard errors in parentheses, clustered by country; independent and control variables lagged one year; ***$p < 0.01$, **$p < 0.05$, *$p < 0.1$.

Appendix Table A.8 ***Climate risk and FDI, by governance readiness, disaggregated by risk type.***

Dependent Variable: FDI Inflows	Model A13	Model A14	Model A15	Model A16	Model A17	Model A18
Ecosystem Vulnerability	-11.76*	-8.454***	-8.710***	-7.885***	-8.540***	-8.655***
	(5.964)	(2.492)	(2.508)	(2.494)	(2.519)	(2.497)
Food Vulnerability	-5.332***	-9.514**	-5.210**	-5.286***	-5.283**	-5.564***
	(2.013)	(3.661)	(2.003)	(1.963)	(2.042)	(1.965)
Habitat Vulnerability	-2.099	-1.893	-6.379	-1.689	-1.977	-1.569
	(1.977)	(2.051)	(4.937)	(1.994)	(2.013)	(2.021)
Health Vulnerability	-0.237	-0.292	-0.399	-5.013**	-0.352	-0.232
	(0.964)	(0.930)	(0.920)	(2.422)	(0.960)	(0.945)
Infrastructure Vulnerability	-1.106	-1.015	-1.102	-1.013	-3.212	-0.833
	(1.937)	(1.920)	(1.864)	(1.932)	(4.605)	(1.837)
Water Vulnerability	0.981	1.046	1.050	0.691	1.185	-10.33*
	(2.781)	(2.790)	(2.747)	(2.843)	(2.800)	(6.134)
Governance Readiness	-0.624	-1.626	-1.962	-1.704	1.141	-5.479
	(6.722)	(3.576)	(5.764)	(2.562)	(3.590)	(4.281)
Ecosystem * Governance Readiness	7.593	N/A	N/A	N/A	N/A	N/A
	(14.00)	N/A	N/A	N/A	N/A	N/A
Food * Governance Readiness	N/A	9.554	N/A	N/A	N/A	N/A
	N/A	(7.015)	N/A	N/A	N/A	N/A
Habitat * Governance Readiness	N/A	N/A	9.635	N/A	N/A	N/A
	N/A	N/A	(11.18)	N/A	N/A	N/A
Health * Governance Readiness	N/A	N/A	N/A	9.878**	N/A	N/A
	N/A	N/A	N/A	(4.663)	N/A	N/A

Appendix Table A.8 (*cont.*)

Dependent Variable: FDI Inflows	Model A13	Model A14	Model A15	Model A16	Model A17	Model A18
Infrastructure * Governance Readiness	N/A	N/A	N/A	N/A	4.762	N/A
	N/A	N/A	N/A	N/A	(8.624)	N/A
Water * Governance Readiness	N/A	N/A	N/A	N/A	N/A	22.53*
	N/A	N/A	N/A	N/A	N/A	(11.65)
GDP	1.618***	1.644***	1.724***	1.624***	1.649***	1.699***
	(0.546)	(0.534)	(0.530)	(0.536)	(0.544)	(0.506)
Per Capita GDP	-1.042**	-1.061**	-1.147**	-1.091**	-1.069**	-1.116**
	(0.479)	(0.465)	(0.461)	(0.466)	(0.474)	(0.443)
Annual GDP Growth	0.00760	0.00693	0.00695	0.00721	0.00713	0.00803
	(0.00655)	(0.00644)	(0.00646)	(0.00646)	(0.00678)	(0.00653)
Regime Type	-0.00565	-0.00561	-0.00433	-0.00613	-0.00451	-0.00278
	(0.0128)	(0.0134)	(0.0137)	(0.0133)	(0.0135)	(0.0133)
High Intensity Conflict	-0.0820	-0.0693	-0.0884	-0.0663	-0.0932	-0.0664
	(0.118)	(0.115)	(0.125)	(0.116)	(0.123)	(0.112)
Oil Rents	0.0319***	0.0310***	0.0318***	0.0309***	0.0315***	0.0319***
	(0.0105)	(0.0103)	(0.0104)	(0.0103)	(0.0104)	(0.0103)
BITs	-0.00173	-0.00183	-0.00210	-0.00174	-0.00178	-0.00153
	(0.00254)	(0.00253)	(0.00252)	(0.00252)	(0.00254)	(0.00248)
Observations	2,692	2,692	2,692	2,692	2,692	2,692
R-squared	0.456	0.458	0.457	0.459	0.456	0.460
Number of Countries	127	127	127	127	127	127
Country Fixed Effects	Yes	Yes	Yes	Yes	Yes	Yes
Year Fixed Effects	Yes	Yes	Yes	Yes	Yes	Yes

Linear panel data models. Robust standard errors in parentheses, clustered by country; independent and control variables lagged one year; ***$p < 0.01$, **$p < 0.05$, *$p < 0.1$.

Appendix Table A.9 ***Climate risk and FDI, by disaster preparedness, disaggregated by risk type.***

Dependent Variable: FDI Inflows	Model A19	Model A20	Model A21	Model A22	Model A23	Model A24
Ecosystem Vulnerability	-16.12***	-11.79***	-11.78***	-11.59***	-12.08***	-11.83***
	(3.338)	(3.291)	(3.307)	(3.218)	(3.254)	(3.311)
Food Vulnerability	-3.578*	-3.978	-3.455*	-3.508*	-3.265	-3.417*
	(1.945)	(2.397)	(1.982)	(1.936)	(1.967)	(1.966)
Habitat Vulnerability	-0.0673	-0.238	-1.139	0.0329	-0.435	-0.294
	(1.618)	(1.779)	(1.888)	(1.702)	(1.782)	(1.799)
Health Vulnerability	-1.399	-1.385	-1.399	-3.545***	-1.518	-1.386
	(0.981)	(1.012)	(1.022)	(1.172)	(0.989)	(1.012)
Infrastructure Vulnerability	-0.997	-1.537	-1.414	-0.854	-0.732	-1.587
	(1.981)	(2.038)	(2.075)	(2.039)	(2.228)	(2.034)
Water Vulnerability	3.326	2.111	1.828	2.140	1.760	1.654
	(3.002)	(2.992)	(2.899)	(2.944)	(2.999)	(2.971)
Disaster Preparedness	-4.326**	0.0777	-0.636	-1.515*	1.528	0.352
	(1.754)	(1.105)	(1.900)	(0.874)	(1.134)	(1.483)
Ecosystem * Disaster Preparedness	10.15***	N/A	N/A	N/A	N/A	N/A
	(3.489)	N/A	N/A	N/A	N/A	N/A
Food * Disaster Preparedness	N/A	1.253	N/A	N/A	N/A	N/A
	N/A	(2.612)	N/A	N/A	N/A	N/A
Habitat * Disaster Preparedness	N/A	N/A	2.384	N/A	N/A	N/A
	N/A	N/A	(3.608)	N/A	N/A	N/A
Health * Disaster Preparedness	N/A	N/A	N/A	4.504***	N/A	N/A
	N/A	N/A	N/A	(1.683)	N/A	N/A
Infrastructure * Disaster Preparedness	N/A	N/A	N/A	N/A	-2.611	N/A
	N/A	N/A	N/A	N/A	(3.172)	N/A

Appendix Table A.9 (*cont.*)

Dependent Variable: FDI Inflows	Model A19	Model A20	Model A21	Model A22	Model A23	Model A24
Water * Disaster Preparedness	N/A	N/A	N/A	N/A	N/A	0.779
	N/A	N/A	N/A	N/A	N/A	(3.801)
GDP	1.261**	1.348***	1.372***	1.324***	1.374***	1.358***
	(0.500)	(0.492)	(0.478)	(0.473)	(0.498)	(0.492)
Per Capita GDP	-0.121	-0.171	-0.181	-0.175	-0.180	-0.182
	(0.478)	(0.472)	(0.462)	(0.454)	(0.475)	(0.474)
Annual GDP Growth	0.0105	0.0111	0.0108	0.0109	0.0111	0.0110
	(0.00764)	(0.00764)	(0.00773)	(0.00749)	(0.00760)	(0.00778)
Regime Type	0.0151	0.0142	0.0157	0.0121	0.0170	0.0148
	(0.0144)	(0.0151)	(0.0154)	(0.0151)	(0.0158)	(0.0151)
High Intensity Conflict	-0.149	-0.154	-0.151	-0.138	-0.155	-0.159
	(0.120)	(0.121)	(0.120)	(0.122)	(0.124)	(0.123)
Oil Rents	0.0381**	0.0351**	0.0352**	0.0361**	0.0350**	0.0351**
	(0.0161)	(0.0158)	(0.0157)	(0.0159)	(0.0157)	(0.0157)
BITs	-0.00155	-0.00138	-0.00147	-0.00136	-0.00125	-0.00138
	(0.00253)	(0.00259)	(0.00258)	(0.00256)	(0.00263)	(0.00260)
Observations	2,073	2,073	2,073	2,073	2,073	2,073
R-squared	0.464	0.460	0.460	0.463	0.460	0.459
Number of Countries	96	96	96	96	96	96
Country Fixed Effects	Yes	Yes	Yes	Yes	Yes	Yes
Year Fixed Effects	Yes	Yes	Yes	Yes	Yes	Yes

Linear panel data models. Robust standard errors in parentheses, clustered by country; independent and control variables lagged one year; ***$p < 0.01$, **$p < 0.05$, *$p < 0.1$.

Appendix Table A.10 *Climate risk and FDI, by incentives and regulations, disaggregated by risk type.*

Dependent Variable: FDI Inflows	Model A25	Model A26	Model A27	Model A28	Model A29	Model A30
Ecosystem Vulnerability	5.392	17.34	12.67	15.27	13.89	21.66
	(24.32)	(26.18)	(25.48)	(25.58)	(25.03)	(26.13)
Food Vulnerability	-1.956	-9.045	-0.749	-1.651	-1.567	-0.324
	(3.238)	(6.418)	(2.960)	(3.177)	(3.395)	(3.015)
Habitat Vulnerability	0.728	0.483	13.24*	0.211	0.525	1.356
	(3.297)	(3.486)	(7.230)	(3.511)	(3.120)	(3.507)
Health Vulnerability	-4.623***	-4.457***	-3.723**	-11.06**	-4.187***	-4.662***
	(1.579)	(1.553)	(1.561)	(4.397)	(1.533)	(1.635)
Infrastructure Vulnerability	-5.480*	-6.072*	-5.247*	-5.458*	-14.75**	-5.890*
	(2.961)	(3.103)	(2.729)	(2.867)	(6.951)	(3.008)
Water Vulnerability	13.64*	14.25*	16.79*	15.14*	14.72*	7.900
	(7.762)	(8.086)	(8.767)	(7.699)	(8.355)	(9.405)
CPIA	-1.926	-1.466	2.321**	-1.148	-1.016	-0.939
	(1.273)	(1.075)	(1.118)	(0.840)	(0.821)	(0.748)
Ecosystem * CPIA	4.106	N/A	N/A	N/A	N/A	N/A
	(2.519)	N/A	N/A	N/A	N/A	N/A
Food * CPIA	N/A	2.795	N/A	N/A	N/A	N/A
	N/A	(1.827)	N/A	N/A	N/A	N/A
Habitat * CPIA	N/A	N/A	-3.742*	N/A	N/A	N/A
	N/A	N/A	(2.021)	N/A	N/A	N/A
Health * CPIA	N/A	N/A	N/A	2.132	N/A	N/A
	N/A	N/A	N/A	(1.292)	N/A	N/A
Infrastructure * CPIA	N/A	N/A	N/A	N/A	3.096	N/A
	N/A	N/A	N/A	N/A	(2.021)	N/A

Appendix Table A.10 (*cont.*)

Dependent Variable: FDI Inflows	Model A25	Model A26	Model A27	Model A28	Model A29	Model A30
Water * CPIA	N/A	N/A	N/A	N/A	N/A	2.579
	N/A	N/A	N/A	N/A	N/A	(1.624)
GDP	1.817	1.627	1.855	1.685	1.652	1.645
	(1.444)	(1.417)	(1.368)	(1.413)	(1.437)	(1.484)
Per Capita GDP	-1.607	-1.288	-1.267	-1.465	-1.249	-1.391
	(1.208)	(1.178)	(1.154)	(1.189)	(1.226)	(1.238)
Annual GDP Growth	0.00686	0.00709	0.00192	0.00834	0.00436	0.00689
	(0.0105)	(0.0102)	(0.00956)	(0.0104)	(0.00931)	(0.0104)
Regime Type	-0.0279	-0.0283	-0.0263	-0.0268	-0.0313	-0.0211
	(0.0205)	(0.0210)	(0.0164)	(0.0228)	(0.0220)	(0.0172)
High Intensity Conflict	-0.150	-0.252**	-0.203**	-0.226	-0.278**	-0.182**
	(0.113)	(0.119)	(0.0797)	(0.137)	(0.130)	(0.0740)
Oil Rents	0.0189*	0.0170	0.0153	0.0191*	0.0169	0.0174
	(0.0107)	(0.0109)	(0.0108)	(0.0107)	(0.0109)	(0.0105)
BITs	-0.00458	-0.00420	-0.00350	-0.00403	-0.00462	-0.00445
	(0.00330)	(0.00346)	(0.00360)	(0.00339)	(0.00338)	(0.00359)
Observations	493	493	493	493	493	493
R-squared	0.255	0.254	0.259	0.254	0.256	0.255
Number of Countries	45	45	45	45	45	45
Country Fixed Effects	Yes	Yes	Yes	Yes	Yes	Yes
Year Fixed Effects	Yes	Yes	Yes	Yes	Yes	Yes

Linear panel data models. Robust standard errors in parentheses, clustered by country; independent and control variables lagged one year; $^{***}p < 0.01$, $^{**}p < 0.05$, $^{*}p < 0.1$.

Appendix Table A.11 ***Climate risk and FDI, by ICAs, disaggregated by sector.***

	Model A31	Model A32	Model A33
Dependent Variables in Parentheses	(Primary Sector FDI Inflows)	(Secondary FDI Inflows)	(Tertiary FDI Inflows)
Climate Vulnerability	21.10	-36.66***	2.380
	(24.48)	(12.35)	(12.46)
ICAs	-0.268	0.594**	0.0838
	(0.400)	(0.250)	(0.282)
Climate Vulnerability * ICAs	0.0963	-1.076**	-0.332
	(0.838)	(0.444)	(0.670)
Climate Aid	0.0139	0.0688	0.0193
	(0.0636)	(0.0518)	(0.0317)
GDP	5.305	0.722	6.189*
	(4.495)	(2.073)	(3.234)
Per Capita GDP	-5.362	-0.917	-5.370
	(5.893)	(2.399)	(4.630)
Annual GDP Growth	0.0390*	0.0205	0.0295**
	(0.0226)	(0.0150)	(0.0121)
Regime Type	-0.0738**	0.00345	-0.0298
	(0.0275)	(0.0239)	(0.0268)
High Intensity Conflict	0.0585	-0.0218	-0.360
	(0.224)	(0.267)	(0.263)
Oil Rents	-0.136	-0.00181	-0.0485
	(0.0849)	(0.0444)	(0.0539)
BITs	0.00357	0.00162	-0.00679
	(0.00564)	(0.00377)	(0.00425)
Observations	354	379	399

Appendix Table A.11 (*cont.*)

	Model A31	Model A32	Model A33
Dependent Variables in Parentheses	(Primary Sector FDI Inflows)	(Secondary FDI Inflows)	(Tertiary FDI Inflows)
R-squared	0.205	0.351	0.277
Number of Countries	39	40	40
Country Fixed Effects	Yes	Yes	Yes
Year Fixed Effects	Yes	Yes	Yes

Linear panel data models. Robust standard errors in parentheses, clustered by country; independent and control variables lagged one year; $^{***}p < 0.01$, $^{**}p < 0.05$, $^{*}p < 0.1$.

Appendix Table A.12 *Climate risk and FDI, by ICAs, disaggregated by risk type.*

Dependent Variable: FDI Inflows	Model A34	Model A35	Model A36	Model A37	Model A38	Model A39
Ecosystem Vulnerability	-2.110	1.565	0.276	0.650	0.159	-0.354
	(4.245)	(4.187)	(4.239)	(4.214)	(4.265)	(4.234)
Food Vulnerability	-1.769	-4.824**	-1.775	-1.199	-1.635	-1.803
	(2.095)	(2.273)	(2.027)	(2.014)	(2.028)	(1.985)
Habitat Vulnerability	0.428	-0.0282	-3.088*	0.139	0.0695	-0.0613
	(1.481)	(1.480)	(1.701)	(1.470)	(1.453)	(1.550)
Health Vulnerability	-1.433	-2.103	-1.310	-3.576**	-1.553	-1.311
	(1.362)	(1.345)	(1.373)	(1.569)	(1.406)	(1.382)
Infrastructure Vulnerability	-1.973	-1.607	-1.625	-1.517	-2.966	-2.161
	(1.787)	(1.858)	(1.860)	(1.851)	(2.133)	(1.859)
Water Vulnerability	-0.0368	0.307	0.508	0.334	-0.162	-0.961
	(4.097)	(4.129)	(4.091)	(4.321)	(4.516)	(4.394)
ICAs	-0.188***	-0.196***	-0.189**	-0.132**	-0.0610	-0.0987
	(0.0692)	(0.0602)	(0.0757)	(0.0601)	(0.0544)	(0.0649)
Ecosystem * ICAs	0.392***	N/A	N/A	N/A	N/A	N/A
	(0.143)	N/A	N/A	N/A	N/A	N/A
Food * ICAs	N/A	0.399***	N/A	N/A	N/A	N/A
	N/A	(0.0997)	N/A	N/A	N/A	N/A
Habitat * ICAs	N/A	N/A	0.330***	N/A	N/A	N/A
	N/A	N/A	(0.123)	N/A	N/A	N/A
Health * ICAs	N/A	N/A	N/A	0.252**	N/A	N/A
	N/A	N/A	N/A	(0.0960)	N/A	N/A
Infrastructure * ICAs	N/A	N/A	N/A	N/A	0.123	N/A
	N/A	N/A	N/A	N/A	(0.136)	N/A

Appendix Table A.12 (*cont.*)

Dependent Variable: FDI Inflows	Model A34	Model A35	Model A36	Model A37	Model A38	Model A39
Water * ICAs	N/A	N/A	N/A	N/A	N/A	0.208
	N/A	N/A	N/A	N/A	N/A	(0.130)
Climate Aid	0.00679	0.00657	0.00495	0.00447	0.00854	0.00604
	(0.0147)	(0.0148)	(0.0145)	(0.0146)	(0.0148)	(0.0147)
GDP	1.934***	1.314**	1.553**	1.388**	2.016***	1.795**
	(0.639)	(0.530)	(0.629)	(0.628)	(0.693)	(0.691)
Per Capita GDP	-0.756	-0.145	-0.281	-0.205	-0.844	-0.627
	(0.598)	(0.533)	(0.597)	(0.575)	(0.675)	(0.669)
Annual GDP Growth	0.00268	0.00280	0.00279	0.00316	0.00369	0.00303
	(0.00772)	(0.00768)	(0.00782)	(0.00783)	(0.00784)	(0.00774)
Regime Type	0.0164	0.0117	0.0150	0.0139	0.0149	0.0153
	(0.0153)	(0.0148)	(0.0139)	(0.0147)	(0.0150)	(0.0166)
High Intensity Conflict	-0.107	-0.0599	-0.100	-0.0697	-0.119	-0.104
	(0.146)	(0.140)	(0.142)	(0.142)	(0.138)	(0.146)
Oil Rents	0.00577	0.00496	0.00627	0.00318	0.00181	0.00421
	(0.0112)	(0.0110)	(0.0110)	(0.0107)	(0.0108)	(0.0108)
BITs	-0.00315	-0.00334	-0.00218	-0.00296	-0.00320	-0.00337
	(0.00231)	(0.00224)	(0.00230)	(0.00224)	(0.00235)	(0.00244)
Observations	1,382	1,382	1,382	1,382	1,382	1,382
R-squared	0.461	0.466	0.460	0.461	0.456	0.458
Number of Countries	93	93	93	93	93	93
Country Fixed Effects	Yes	Yes	Yes	Yes	Yes	Yes
Year Fixed Effects	Yes	Yes	Yes	Yes	Yes	Yes

Linear panel data models. Robust standard errors in parentheses, clustered by country; independent and control variables lagged one year; $^{***}p < 0.01$, $^{**}p < 0.05$, $^{*}p < 0.1$.

Appendix Table A.13 ***Climate risk and FDI, by climate aid, disaggregated by sector.***

	Model A40	Model A41	Model A42
Dependent Variables in Parentheses	(Primary Sector FDI Inflows)	(Secondary FDI Inflows)	(Tertiary FDI Inflows)
Climate Vulnerability	9.810	-31.04**	4.242
	(24.38)	(14.81)	(11.96)
Climate Aid	-0.930**	0.348	0.106
	(0.377)	(0.311)	(0.211)
Climate Vulnerability * Climate Aid	2.099**	-0.665	-0.206
	(0.846)	(0.690)	(0.488)
ICAs	-0.251*	0.0717	-0.0764
	(0.132)	(0.111)	(0.0904)
GDP	2.902	-0.628	5.821**
	(3.681)	(2.393)	(2.292)
Per Capita GDP	-3.334	0.175	-5.087
	(4.934)	(2.467)	(3.744)
Annual GDP Growth	0.0345	0.0244	0.0310**
	(0.0231)	(0.0152)	(0.0120)
Regime Type	-0.0765***	0.00445	-0.0295
	(0.0266)	(0.0236)	(0.0267)
High Intensity Conflict	-0.182	0.0455	-0.348
	(0.204)	(0.247)	(0.242)
Oil Rents	-0.151*	0.00199	-0.0483
	(0.0841)	(0.0457)	(0.0529)

Appendix Table A.13 (*cont.*)

	Model A40	Model A41	Model A42
Dependent Variables in Parentheses	(Primary Sector FDI Inflows)	(Secondary FDI Inflows)	(Tertiary FDI Inflows)
BITs	0.00226	0.00123	-0.00692
	(0.00588)	(0.00364)	(0.00459)
Observations	354	379	399
R-squared	0.228	0.340	0.276
Number of Countries	39	40	40
Country Fixed Effects	Yes	Yes	Yes
Year Fixed Effects	Yes	Yes	Yes

Linear panel data models. Robust standard errors in parentheses, clustered by country; independent and control variables lagged one year; $^{***}p < 0.01$, $^{**}\ p < 0.05$, $^{*}\ p < 0.1$.

Appendix Table A.14 ***Climate risk and FDI, by climate aid, disaggregated by risk type.***

Dependent Variable: FDI Inflows	Model A43	Model A44	Model A45	Model A46	Model A47	Model A48
Ecosystem Vulnerability	-1.506	0.707	0.0943	0.606	-0.0187	-0.244
	(4.191)	(4.172)	(4.211)	(4.227)	(4.206)	(4.238)
Food Vulnerability	-1.879	-4.160*	-1.741	-1.319	-1.367	-1.738
	(2.102)	(2.269)	(2.050)	(2.084)	(2.037)	(2.011)
Habitat Vulnerability	0.0992	-0.255	-3.153*	-0.251	0.0117	0.0587
	(1.452)	(1.432)	(1.735)	(1.434)	(1.438)	(1.490)
Health Vulnerability	-1.432	-1.731	-1.417	-3.921**	-1.557	-1.489
	(1.374)	(1.347)	(1.376)	(1.538)	(1.388)	(1.374)
Infrastructure Vulnerability	-2.136	-1.935	-1.932	-1.787	-4.190*	-2.201
	(1.816)	(1.841)	(1.860)	(1.829)	(2.189)	(1.845)
Water Vulnerability	0.0679	0.137	-0.0814	0.0442	-0.0910	-0.663
	(4.385)	(4.340)	(4.271)	(4.326)	(4.475)	(4.427)
Climate Aid	-0.0816	-0.115**	-0.130**	-0.120**	-0.0730*	-0.0283
	(0.0703)	(0.0508)	(0.0588)	(0.0483)	(0.0439)	(0.0511)
Ecosystem * Climate Aid	0.189	N/A	N/A	N/A	N/A	N/A
	(0.149)	N/A	N/A	N/A	N/A	N/A
Food * Climate Aid	N/A	0.248**	N/A	N/A	N/A	N/A
	N/A	(0.101)	N/A	N/A	N/A	N/A
Habitat * Climate Aid	N/A	N/A	0.256**	N/A	N/A	N/A
	N/A	N/A	(0.114)	N/A	N/A	N/A
Health * Climate Aid	N/A	N/A	N/A	0.242**	N/A	N/A
	N/A	N/A	N/A	(0.0923)	N/A	N/A
Infrastructure * Climate Aid	N/A	N/A	N/A	N/A	0.228**	N/A
	N/A	N/A	N/A	N/A	(0.112)	N/A

Appendix Table A.14 (*cont.*)

Dependent Variable: FDI Inflows	Model A43	Model A44	Model A45	Model A46	Model A47	Model A48
Water * Climate Aid	N/A	N/A	N/A	N/A	N/A	0.0954
	N/A	N/A	N/A	N/A	N/A	(0.130)
ICAs	-0.0150	-0.0154	-0.0159	-0.00836	-0.0158	-0.0213
	(0.0359)	(0.0354)	(0.0355)	(0.0352)	(0.0362)	(0.0355)
GDP	1.997***	1.615**	1.758***	1.495**	1.979***	1.938***
	(0.674)	(0.638)	(0.663)	(0.654)	(0.687)	(0.696)
Per Capita GDP	-0.785	-0.420	-0.525	-0.284	-0.798	-0.745
	(0.647)	(0.612)	(0.643)	(0.617)	(0.672)	(0.679)
Annual GDP Growth	0.00277	0.00281	0.00264	0.00261	0.00400	0.00332
	(0.00776)	(0.00753)	(0.00748)	(0.00751)	(0.00770)	(0.00787)
Regime Type	0.0148	0.0128	0.0165	0.0126	0.0136	0.0151
	(0.0153)	(0.0151)	(0.0144)	(0.0151)	(0.0148)	(0.0156)
High Intensity Conflict	-0.125	-0.106	-0.102	-0.105	-0.120	-0.121
	(0.143)	(0.143)	(0.138)	(0.143)	(0.136)	(0.142)
Oil Rents	0.00477	0.00355	0.00448	0.00274	0.00112	0.00359
	(0.0108)	(0.0109)	(0.0106)	(0.0108)	(0.0105)	(0.0106)
BITs	-0.00309	-0.00312	-0.00254	-0.00289	-0.00323	-0.00313
	(0.00234)	(0.00237)	(0.00232)	(0.00232)	(0.00233)	(0.00245)
Observations	1,382	1,382	1,382	1,382	1,382	1,382
R-squared	0.456	0.460	0.458	0.461	0.459	0.456
Number of Countries	93	93	93	93	93	93
Country Fixed Effects	Yes	Yes	Yes	Yes	Yes	Yes
Year Fixed Effects	Yes	Yes	Yes	Yes	Yes	Yes

Linear panel data models. Robust standard errors in parentheses, clustered by country; independent and control variables lagged one year; $^{***}p < 0.01$, $^{**}p < 0.05$, $^{*}p < 0.1$.

References

Adegboye, F.B., R. Osabohien, F.O. Olokoyo, O. Matthew, and O. Adediran. "Institutional Quality, Foreign Direct Investment, and Economic Development in Sub-Saharan Africa." *Humanities and Social Sciences Communications* 7, no. 1 (2020): 1–9.

Abidoye, Babatunde O., and Ayodele F. Odusola. "Climate Change and Economic Growth in Africa: An Econometric Analysis." *Journal of African Economies* 24, no. 2 (2015): 277–301.

Acemoglu, Daron, Ufuk Akcigit, Douglas Hanley, and William Kerr. "Transition to Clean Energy." *Journal of Political Economy* 124, no. 1 (2016): 52–104.

Adams, Samuel, and Edem Kwame Mensah Klobodu. "Urbanization, Democracy, Bureaucratic Quality, and Environmental Degradation." *Journal of Policy Modeling* 39, no. 6 (2017): 1035–51.

Adgate, Brad. "The Impact COVID-19 Had on the Entertainment Industry in 2020." *Forbes*, April 13, 2021. https://forbes.com/sites/bradadgate/2021/04/13/the-impact-covid-19-had-on-the-entertainment-industry-in-2020/?sh=4c665d63250f.

Adger, W. Neil. "Climate Change, Human Well-Being, and Insecurity." *New Political Economy* 15, no. 2 (2010): 275–92.

Adger, W. Neil, Jon Barnett, Stacey Heath, and Sergio Jarillo. "Climate Change Affects Multiple Dimensions of Well-Being Through Impacts, Information and Policy." *Nature Human Behavior* 6, no. 11 (2022): 1465–73.

Adhikari, Bhim, and Lolita Shaila Safaee Chalkasra. "Mobilizing Private Sector Investment for Climate Action: Enhancing Ambition and Scaling Up Implementation." *Journal of Sustainable Finance & Investment* 13, no. 2 (2023): 1110–27.

Aertsens, Joris, Koen Mondelaers, Wim Verbeke, Jeroen Buysse, and Guido Van Huylenbroeck. "The Influence of Subjective and Objective Knowledge on Attitude, Motivations and Consumption of Organic Food." *British Food Journal* 113, no. 11 (2011): 1353–78.

Aeschlimann, Silvan, Charithea Charalambous, and Daniel Pike. "Reality Check: This Decade Is Make-or-Break for Direct Air Capture." *RMI*, March 30, 2023. https://rmi.org/make-or-break-for-direct-air-capture.

Afewerki, Samson, and Markus Steen. "Gaining Lead Firm Position in an Emerging Industry: A Global Production Networks Analysis of Two Scandinavian Energy Firms in Offshore Wind Power." *Competition and Change* 27, nos. 3–4 (2023): 551–74.

Ahmadi, Pouria. "Environmental Impacts and Behavioral Drivers of Deep Decarbonization for Transport through Electric Vehicles." *Journal of Cleaner Production* 225 (2019): 1209–19.

Aisbett, Emma, and Magdalene Silberberger. "Tariff Liberalization and Product Standards: Regulatory Chill and Race to the Bottom?" *Regulation & Governance* 15, no. 3 (2021): 987–1006.

Akbostancı, Elif, G. Ipek Tunç, and Serap Türüt-Aşik. "Pollution Haven Hypothesis and the Role of Dirty Industries in Turkey's Exports." *Environment and Development Economics* 12, no. 2 (2007): 297–322.

Aklin, Michaël, and Matto Mildenberger. "Prisoners of the Wrong Dilemma: Why Distributive Conflict, Not Collective Action, Characterizes the Politics of Climate Change." *Global Environmental Politics* 20, no. 4 (2020): 4–27.

Akram, Naeem. "Is Climate Change Hindering Economic Growth of Asian Economies?" *Asia-Pacific Development Journal* 19, no. 2 (2012): 1–18.

Alagidede, Paul, George Adu, and Prince Boakye Frimpong. "The Effect of Climate Change on Economic Growth: Evidence from Sub-Saharan Africa." *Environmental Economics and Policy Studies* 18, no. 3 (2016): 417–36.

Alänge, Sverker, Gunilla Clancy, and Magnus Marmgren. "Naturalizing Sustainability in Product Development: A Comparative Analysis of IKEA and SCA." *Journal of Cleaner Production* 135, no. 1 (2016): 1009–22.

Aldenius, Malin, and Jamil Khan. "Strategic Use of Green Public Procurement in the Bus Sector: Challenges and Opportunities." *Journal of Cleaner Production* 164 (2017): 250–57.

Alhouti, Sarah, and Giles D'Souza. "Benefits of Corporate Social Responsibility." *Journal of Consumer Marketing* 35, no. 3 (2018): 277–86.

Ali, Majid, Kahn Faqir, Bilal Haider, Khurram Shahzad, and Nosheen Nosheen. "Belt and Road Environmental Implications for South Asia." *Frontiers in Public Health* 10 (2022). https://doi.org/10.3389/fpubh.2022.876606.

Alifu, Haireti, Yukiko Hirabayashi, Yukiko Imada, and Hideo Shiogama. "Enhancement of River Flooding Due to Global Warming." *Scientific Reports* 12 (2022): Article 20687.

Almer, Christian, and Ralph Winkler. "Analyzing the Effectiveness of International Environmental Policies: The Case of the Kyoto Protocol." *Journal of Environmental Economics and Management* 82 (2017): 125–51.

Ambrose, Jillian. "ExxonMobil 'Tried to Get European Green Deal Watered Down.'" *The Guardian*, March 6, 2020. https://theguardian.com/business/2020/mar/06/exxonmobil-tried-to-get-european-green-deal-watered-down-claims-climate-lobbying-watchdog.

"Why Oil Giants Are Swapping Oil Rigs for Offshore Windfarms." *The Guardian*, February 10, 2021. https://theguardian.com/business/2021/feb/10/why-oil-giants-are-swapping-oil-rigs-for-offshore-windfarms.

"Big Five Oil Companies to Reward Shareholders with Record Payouts." *The Guardian*, January 1, 2024. https://theguardian.com/business/2024/jan/01/oil-companies-shareholders-payouts-bp-shell-chevron-exxonmobil-totalenergies.

An, Yao, Ning Liu, Lin Zhang, and Huanhuan Zheng. "Adapting to Climate Risks through Cross-Border Investments: Industrial Vulnerability and Smart City Resilience." *Climatic Change* 174, nos. 1–2 (2022): Article 10.

Anderson, Brilé, Tobias Böhmelt, and Hugh Ward. "Public Opinion and Environmental Policy Output: A Cross-National Analysis of Energy Policies in Europe." *Environmental Research Letters* 12, no. 11 (2017): 114001.

Andonova, Liliana B., Thomas N. Hale, and Charles B. Roger. "National Policy and Transnational Governance of Climate Change: Substitutes or Complements?" *International Studies Quarterly* 61, no. 2 (2017): 253–68.

Andrews, Talbot M., Andrew W. Delton, and Reuben Kline. "Anticipating Moral Hazard Undermines Climate Mitigation in an Experimental Geoengineering Game." *Ecological Economics* 196 (2022): 107421.

Anna, Cara. "African Climate Summit Issues Unanimous Call for World Leaders to Support Global Carbon Tax on Fossil Fuels." *PBS NewsHour*, September 6, 2023. https://pbs.org/newshour/politics/african-climate-summit-issues-unanimous-call-for-world-leaders-to-support-global-carbon-tax-on-fossil-fuels.

Arel-Bundock, Vincent, Clint Peinhardt, and Amy Pond. "Political Risk Insurance: A New Firm-Level Data Set." *Journal of Conflict Resolution* 64, no. 5 (2020): 987–1006.

Arimura, Toshi H., Nicole Darnall, Rama Ganguli, and Hajime Katayama. "The Effect of ISO 14001 on Environmental Performance: Resolving

Unequivocal Findings." *Journal of Environmental Management* 166 (2016): 556–66.

Arnell, Nigel. *A Short Guide to Climate Change Risk*. London: Routledge, 2015.

Arnell, Nigel W., Alastair L. Kay, Anna Freeman, Alison C. Rudd, and Jason A. Lowe. "Changing Climate Risk in the UK: A Multi-Sectoral Analysis Using Policy-Relevant Indicators." *Climate Risk Management* 31 (2021): 100265.

Arora, Mitali P., and Sumit Lodhia. "The BP Gulf of Mexico Oil Spill: Exploring the Link between Social and Environmental Disclosures and Reputation Risk Management." *Journal of Cleaner Production* 140, no. 3 (2017): 1287–97.

Arora, Puneet, and Alberto Chong. "Government Effectiveness in the Provision of Public Goods: The Role of Institutional Quality." *Journal of Applied Economics* 21, no. 1 (2018): 175–96.

Arvin, B. Mak, and Byron Lew. "Does Democracy Affect Environmental Quality in Developing Countries?" *Applied Economics* 43, no. 9 (2011): 1151–60.

Ascani, Andrea, Lakshmi Balachandran Nair, and Simona Iammarino. "Racing to the Bottom or Seeking Legitimacy? National Environmental Performance and the Location Strategies of Chinese MNEs." *Journal of International Management* 29, no. 2 (2023): 100993.

Asheim, Geir B., Camilla Bretteville Froyn, Jon Hovi, and Fredric C. Menz. "Regional versus Global Cooperation for Climate Control." *Journal of Environmental Economics and Management* 50, no. 1 (2006): 93–109.

Ashton, Weslynne, Suzana Russell, and Elizabeth Futch. "The Adoption of Green Business Practices Among Small US Midwestern Manufacturing Enterprises." *Journal of Environmental Planning and Management* 60, no. 12 (2017): 2133–49.

Aydın, Zühre, and Okan Yardımcı. "Regulatory Sandboxes and Pilot Projects: Trials, Regulations, and Insights in Energy Transition." *Engineering Science and Technology, an International Journal* 56 (2024): 101792.

Bäckstrand, Karin. "Accountability of Networked Climate Governance: The Rise of Transnational Climate Partnerships." *Global Environmental Politics* 8, no. 3 (2008): 74–102.

Bäckstrand, Karin, Jonathan W. Kuyper, Björn-Ola Linnér, and Eva Lövbrand. "Non-State Actors in Global Climate Governance: From Copenhagen to Paris and Beyond." *Environmental Politics* 26, no. 4 (2017): 561–79.

Baker, Rachel E., Ayesha S. Mahmud, Ian F. Miller, Malavika Rajeev, Fidisoa Rasambainarivo, Benjamin L. Rice, Saki Takahashi, Andrew J.

Tatem, Caroline E. Wagner, Lin-Fa Wang, Amy Wesolowski, and C. Jessica, E. Metcalf. "Infectious Disease in an Era of Global Change." *Nature Reviews Microbiology* 20, no. 4 (2022): 193–205.

Balsa-Barreiro, José, Aymeric Vié, Alfredo J. Morales, and Manuel Cebrián. "Deglobalization in a Hyper-Connected World." *Palgrave Communications* 6 (2020): Article 28.

Bamber, Jonathan L., Michael Oppenheimer, Robert E. Kopp, Willy P. Aspinall, and Roger M. Cooke. "Ice Sheet Contributions to Future Sea-Level Rise from Structured Expert Judgement." *Proceedings of the National Academy of Sciences of the United States of America* 116, no. 23 (2019): 11195–11200.

Bang, Guri, Jon Hovi, and Detlef F. Sprinz. "US Presidents and the Failure to Ratify Multilateral Environmental Agreements." *Climate Policy* 12, no. 6 (2012): 755–63.

Bar, Am Jordan, Laura Furstenthal, Felicitas Jorge, and Erik Roth. "Innovation in a Crisis: Why It Is More Critical than Ever." *McKinsey & Company*, April 17, 2020. https://mckinsey.com/capabilities/strategy-and-corporate-finance/our-insights/innovation-in-a-crisis-why-it-ismore-critical-than-ever.

Barboza, David. "Apple Cited as Adding to Pollution in China." *The New York Times*, September 1, 2011. https://nytimes.com/2011/09/02/technology/apple-suppliers-causing-environmental-problems-chinese-group-says.html.

Baroudi, Merli Margaret. "Innovation in Political Risk Insurance: Experience from the Multilateral Investment Guarantee Agency." *Global Policy* 8, no. 3 (2017): 406–13.

Barroso, Marta, and Juan Laborda. "Digital Transformation and the Emergence of the Fintech Sector: Systematic Literature Review." *Digital Business* 2, no. 2 (2022): 100028.

Barrett, Scott. "Climate Treaties and the Imperative of Enforcement." *Oxford Review of Economic Policy* 24, no. 2 (2008): 239–58.

Barrett, Scott, and Raghav S. K. Chaitanya. "Getting Private Investment in Adaptation to Work: Effective Adaptation, Value, and Cash Flows." *Global Environmental Change* 83 (2023): 102761.

Bartkus, Kenneth R., Cathy L. Hartman, and Roy D. Howell. "The Measurement of Consumer Environmental Knowledge: Revisions and Extensions." *Journal of Social Behavior and Personality* 14, no. 1 (1999): 129–46.

Bartley, Tim, and Curtis Child. "Movements, Markets and Fields: The Effects of Anti-Sweatshop Campaigns on U.S. Firms, 1993–2000." *Social Forces* 90, no. 2 (2011): 425–51.

Baumgarte, Felix, Matthias Kaiser, and Robert Keller. "Policy Support Measures for Widespread Expansion of Fast Charging Infrastructure for Electric Vehicles." *Energy Policy* 156 (2021): 112372.

Baur, Susanne, Alexander Nauels, Zebedee Nicholls, Benjamin M. Sanderson, and Carl-Friedrich Schleussner. "The Deployment Length of Solar Radiation Modification: An Interplay of Mitigation, Net-Negative Emissions and Climate Uncertainty." *Earth System Dynamics* 14, no. 2 (2023): 367–81.

Bayramoglu, Basak, Jean-François Jacques, Clémente Nedoncelle, and Lucille Neumann-Noel. "International Climate Aid and Trade." *Journal of Environmental Economics and Management* 117 (2023): 102748.

Bearak, Max. "Climate Talks End with a Bitter Fight and a Deal on Money." *The New York Times*, November 23, 2024. https://nytimes.com/2024/11/23/climate/cop29-climate-talks-conclusion.html.

Bechtel, Michael M., Kenneth F. Scheve, and Elisabeth van Lieshout. "Improving Public Support for Climate Action through Multilateralism." *Nature Communications* 13 (2022): Article 6441.

Beckers, Frank, and Uwe Stegemann. "A Smarter Way to Think About Public-Private Partnerships." *McKinsey & Company*, September 14, 2021. https://mckinsey.com/capabilities/risk-and-resilience/our-insights/a-smarter-way-to-think-about-public-private-partnerships.

Beckstedde, Ellen, Mauricio Correa Ramírez, Rafael Cossent, Janka Vanschoenwinke, and Leonardo Meeus. "Regulatory Sandboxes: Do They Speed Up Innovation in Energy?" *Energy Policy* 180 (2023): 113656.

Beech, Hannah. "Welcome to Nusantara." *The New York Times*, May 16, 2023. https://nytimes.com/interactive/2023/05/16/headway/indonesia-nusantara-jakarta.html.

Beer, Jeff. "Patagonia Enlists Teen Activists to Speak Out for Global Climate Strike Campaign." *Fast Company*, September 19, 2019. https://fastcompany.com/90406565/patagonia-enlists-teen-activists-to-speak-out-for-global-climate-strike-campaign.

Beisheim, Marianne, Andrea Liese, Hannah Janetschek, and Johanna Sarre. "Transnational Partnerships: Conditions for Successful Service Provision in Areas of Limited Statehood." *Governance* 27, no. 4 (2014): 655–73.

Belaïd, Fateh. "Implications of Poorly Designed Climate Policy on Energy Poverty: Global Reflections on the Current Surge in Energy Prices." *Energy Research & Social Science* 92 (2022): 102790.

Bellantuono, Nicola, Nunzia Carbonara, and Pierpaolo Pontrandolfo. "The Organization of Eco-Industrial Parks and Their Sustainable Practices." *Journal of Cleaner Production* 161 (2017): 362–75.

Bellelli, Francesco S., Riccardo Scarpa, and Ashar Aftab. "An Empirical Analysis of Participation in International Environmental Agreements." *Journal of Environmental Economics and Management* 118 (2023): 102783.

Ben-David, Itzhak, Yeejin Jang, Stefanie Kleimeier, and Michael Viehs. "Exporting Pollution: Where Do Multinational Firms Emit CO_2?" *Economic Policy* 26, no. 107 (2021): 377–437.

Berge, Tarald Laudal, and Taylor St. John. "Asymmetric Diffusion: World Bank 'Best Practice' and the Spread of Arbitration in National Investment Laws." *Review of International Political Economy* 28, no. 3 (2021): 584–610.

Bergmann, Anne, Kristin Stechemesser, and Edeltraud Guenther. "Natural Resource Dependence Theory: Impacts of Extreme Weather Events on Organizations." *Journal of Business Research* 69, no. 4 (2016): 1361–66.

Berliner, Daniel, and Aseem Prakash. "The United Nations Global Compact: An Institutionalist Perspective." *Journal of Business Ethics* 122, no. 2 (2014): 217–23.

Bernauer, Thomas. "Climate Change Politics." *Annual Review of Political Science* 16 (2013): 421–48.

Bernauer, Thomas, and Carola Betzold. "Civil Society in Global Environmental Governance." *The Journal of Environment & Development* 21, no. 1 (2012): 62–66.

Besley, Timothy, and Torsten Persson. "Why Do Developing Countries Tax So Little?" *Journal of Economic Perspectives* 28, no. 4 (2014): 99–120.

Bethencourt, Carlos, and Fernando Perera-Tallo. "Foreign Aid and Corruption: Unveiling the Obstacles to Effective Development." *Southern Economic Journal* 91, no. 3 (2025): 881–914.

Bialek, Sylwia, and Alfons J. Weichenrieder. "Do Stringent Environmental Policies Deter FDI? M&A versus Greenfield." *Environmental and Resource Economics* 80, no. 3 (2021): 603–36.

Bhutta, Umair Saeed, Adeel Tariq, Muhammad Farrukh, Ali Raza, and Muhammad Khalid Iqbal. "Green Bonds for Sustainable Development: Review of Literature on Development and Impact of Green Bonds." *Technological Forecasting and Social Change* 175 (2022): 121378.

Bird, Lori, Mark Bolinger, Troy Gagliano, Ryan Wiser, Matthew Brown, and Brian Parsons. "Policies and Market Factors Driving Wind Power Development in the United States." *Energy Policy* 33, no. 11 (2005): 1397–1407.

Bistline, John, Geoffrey Blanford, Maxwell Brown, Dallas Burtraw, Maya Domeshek, Jamil Farbes, Allen Fawcett, Anne Hamilton, Jesse Jenkins, Ryan Jones, Ben King, Hannah Kolus, John Larsen, Amanda Levin, Megan Mahajan, Cara Marcy, Erin Mayfield, James McFarland, Haewon McJeon, Robbie Orvis, Neha Patankar, Kevin Rennert, Christopher Roney, Nicholas Roy, Greg Schivley, Daniel Steinberg, Nadejda Victor, Shelley Wenzel, John Weyant, Ryan Wiser, Mei Yuan, and Alicia Zhao. "Emissions and Energy Impacts of the Inflation Reduction Act." *Science* 380, no. 6652 (2023): 1324–27.

Black, Bernard, Brian Cheffins, and Michael Klausner. "Liability Risk for Outside Directors: A Cross-Border Analysis." *European Financial Management* 11, no. 2 (2005): 153–71.

Black, Simon, Florence Jaumotte, and Prasad Ananthakrishnan. "World Needs More Policy Ambition, Private Funds, and Innovation to Meet Climate Goals." *IMF Blog*, November 27, 2023. https://imf.org/en/Blogs/Articles/2023/11/27/world-needs-more-policy-ambition-private-funds-and-innovation-to-meet-climate-goals.

Bogmans, Christian, Andrea Pescatori, and Ervin Prifti. "The Impact of Climate Policy on Oil and Gas Investment: Evidence from Firm-Level Data." *European Economic Review* 165 (2024): 104750.

Böhringer, Christoph, Alexander Cuntz, Dietmar Harhoff, and Emmanuel Asane-Otoo. "The Impact of the German Feed-in Tariff Scheme on Innovation: Evidence Based on Patent Filings in Renewable Energy Technologies." *Energy Economics* 67 (2017): 545–53.

Boockmann, B., and Paul W. Thurner. "Flexibility Provisions in Multilateral Environmental Treaties." *International Environmental Agreements: Politics, Law and Economics* 6, no. 2 (2006): 113–35.

Bortoló, Gemma Molleví, Jesús Álvarez Valdés, and Ruben Nicolas-Sans. "Sustainable, Technological, and Innovative Challenges Post Covid-19 in Health, Economy, and Education Sectors." *Technological Forecasting and Social Change* 190 (2023): 122424.

Bosello, Francesco, Robert J. Nicholls, Julie Richards, Roberto Roson, and Richard S. J. Tol. "Economic Impacts of Climate Change in Europe: Sea-Level Rise." *Climatic Change* 112, no. 1 (2012): 63–81.

Botrić, Valerija, and Lorena Ŝkuflić. "Main Determinants of Foreign Direct Investment in the Southeast European Countries." *Transnational Studies Review* 13, no. 2 (2006): 359–77.

Boudette, Neal E. "More Gas Cars and Trucks, Fewer E.V.s as Automakers Change Plans." *The New York Times*, July 18, 2024. https://nytimes.com/2024/07/18/business/ford-electric-vehicles-canada.html.

Bracking, Sarah, and Benjamin Leffel. "Climate Finance Governance: Fit for Purpose?" *WIREs Climate Change* 12, no. 4 (2021): e709.

Bradsher, Keith. "Why Heat Waves Are Deepening China's Addiction to Coal." *The New York Times*, July 20, 2023. https://nytimes.com/2023/07/20/business/china-coal-climate-change.html.

Brady, Jeff. "Exxon Climate Predictions Were Accurate Decades Ago. Still It Sowed Doubt." *NPR*, January 12, 2023. https://npr.org/2023/01/12/1148376084/exxon-climate-predictions-were-accurate-decades-ago-still-it-sowed-doubt.

Brakman, Steven, Harry Garretsen, and Arjen van Witteloostuijn. "Robots Do Not Get the Coronavirus: The COVID-19 Pandemic and the

International Division of Labor." *Journal of International Business Studies* 52, no. 6 (2021): 1215–24.

Brambor, Thomas, William Roberts Clark, and Matt Golder. "Understanding Interaction Models: Improving Empirical Analyses." *Political Analysis* 14, no. 1 (2006): 63–82.

Breidenich, Clare, Daniel Magraw, Anne Rowley, and James W. Rubin. "The Kyoto Protocol to the United Nations Framework Convention on Climate Change." *American Journal of International Law* 92, no. 2 (1998): 315–31.

Brenton, Sir Anthony. "'Great Powers' in Climate Politics." *Climate Policy* 13, no. 5 (2013): 541–46.

Bressler, R. Daniel. "The Mortality Cost of Carbon." *Nature Communications* 12 (2021): Article 4467.

Brothers, Albert, Ondrej Burkacky, Julia Dragon, Jo Kakarwada, Abhijit Mahindroo, Jwalit Patel, and Anupama Suryanarayanan. "New Silicon Carbide Prospects Emerge as Market Adapts to EV Expansion." *McKinsey & Company*, March 20, 2023. https://mckinsey.com/industries/semiconductors/our-insights/new-silicon-carbide-prospects-emerge-as-market-adapts-to-ev-expansion.

Broto, Vanesa Castán. "Urban Governance and the Politics of Climate Change." *World Development* 93 (2017): 1–15.

Brulle, Robert J. "Networks of Opposition: A Structural Analysis of U.S. Climate Change Countermovement Coalitions 1989–2015." *Sociological Inquiry* 91, no. 3 (2021): 603–24.

"Advocating Inaction: A Historical Analysis of the Global Climate Coalition." *Environmental Politics* 32, no. 2 (2023): 185–206.

Brulle, Robert J., and Christian Downie. "Following the Money: Trade Associations, Political Activity and Climate Change." *Climatic Change* 175, no. 3 (2022): Article 11.

Brunnermeier, Markus K. "Deciphering the Liquidity and Credit Crunch 2007–2008." *Journal of Economic Perspectives* 23, no. 1 (2009): 77–100.

Bu, Maoliang, and Marcus Wagner. "Racing to the Bottom and Racing to the Top: The Crucial Role of Firm Characteristics in Foreign Direct Investment Choices." *Journal of International Business Studies* 47, no. 9 (2016): 1032–57.

Buck, Holly Jean, and Simon Nicholson. "Solar Geoengineering Research in the Global Public Interest: A Proposal for How to Do It." *One Earth* 6, no. 12 (2023): 1652–64.

Buckley, Peter J. "Is the International Business Research Agenda Running Out of Steam?" *Journal of International Business Studies* 33, no. 2 (2002): 365–73.

Buckley, Peter J., and Donald R. Lessard. "Regaining the Edge for International Business Research." *Journal of International Business Studies* 36, no. 6 (2005): 595–99.

Bueno de Mesquita, Bruce, Alastair Smith, Randolph M. Silverson, and James D. Morrow. *The Logic of Political Survival.* Cambridge, MA: MIT Press, 2003.

Buitenzorgy, Meilanie, and Arthur P. J. Mol. "Does Democracy Lead to a Better Environment? Deforestation and the Democratic Transition Peak." *Environmental and Resource Economics* 48, no. 1 (2011): 59–70.

Burgess, Matthew G., Christian Suarez, Ashley Dancer, Lachlan J. Watkins, and Renae E. Marshall. *Climate Change Opinion and Recent Presidential Elections.* Center for Social and Environmental Futures Report, 2024.

Burke, Marshall B., Edward Miguel, Shanker Satyanath, John A. Dykema, and David B. Lobell. "Warming Increases the Risk of Civil War in Africa." *Proceedings of the National Academy of Sciences of the United States of America* 106, no. 49 (2009): 20670–74.

Buso, Marco, and Anne Stenger. "Public-Private Partnerships as a Policy Response to Climate Change." *Energy Policy* 119 (2018): 487–94.

Business of Fashion, and McKinsey & Company. *The State of Fashion 2020.* London: Business of Fashion and McKinsey & Company, 2020.

Bussmann, Margit. "Foreign Direct Investment and Militarized Interstate Conflict." *Journal of Peace Research* 47, no. 2 (2010): 143–53.

Bussy, Adrien, and Huanhuan Zheng. "Responses of FDI to Geopolitical Risks: The Role of Governance, Information, and Technology." *International Business Review* 32, no. 4 (2023): 102136.

Büthe, Tim, and Helen V. Milner. "The Politics of Foreign Direct Investment into Developing Countries: Increasing FDI through International Trade Agreements." *American Journal of Political Science* 52, no. 4 (2008): 741–62.

"Foreign Direct Investment and Institutional Diversity in Trade Agreements: Credibility, Commitment, and Economic Flows in the Developing World, 1979–2007." *World Politics* 66, no. 2 (2014): 88–122.

Caesar, L., G. D. McCarthy, D. J. R. Thornalley, N. Cahill, and S. Rahmstorf. "Current Atlantic Meridional Overturning Circulation Weakest in Last Millennium." *Nature Geoscience* 14 (2021): 118–20.

Caldwell, J. H. "A Moving Target: Refocusing Risk and Resiliency Amidst Continued Uncertainty." *Deloitte Insights*, 2021. www2.deloitte.com/us/en/insights/industry/financial-services/global-risk-management-survey-financial-services.html.

Camilleri, Mark Anthony. "The Rationale for ISO 14001 Certification: A Systematic Review and a Cost-Benefit Analysis." *Corporate Social*

Responsibility and Environmental Management 29, no. 4 (2022): 1067–83.

Cancherini, Laura, Joseph Lydon, Jorge Santos da Silva, and Alexandra Zemp. "What's Ahead for Biotech: Another Wave or Low Tide?" *McKinsey & Company*, 2021. https://mckinsey.com/industries/life-sciences/our-insights/whats-ahead-for-biotech-another-wave-or-low-tide.

Carfora, Alfonso, and Giuseppe Scandurra. "The Impact of Climate Funds on Economic Growth and Their Role in Substituting Fossil Energy Sources." *Energy Policy* 129 (2019): 182–92.

Carioti, Ricky. "A Rising Fortress in Sinking Land." *The Washington Post*, May 13, 2024. https://washingtonpost.com/climate-environment/interactive/2024/louisiana-sea-wall-gas-facility-flooding.

Carrington, Damian. "Most People in Petrostates Want Quick Switch to Clean Energy, UN Poll Finds." *The Guardian*, June 20, 2024a. https://theguardian.com/environment/article/2024/jun/20/most-people-in-petrostates-want-quick-switch-to-clean-energy-un-poll-finds.

"Revealed: Saudi Arabia Accused of Modifying Official COP29 Negotiating Text." *The Guardian*, November 23, 2024b. https://theguardian.com/environment/2024/nov/23/revealed-saudi-arabia-accused-of-modifying-official-cop29-negotiating-text.

"'Ironic': Climate-Driven Sea Level Rise Will Overwhelm Major Oil Ports, Study Shows." *The Guardian*, January 4, 2025. https://theguardian.com/environment/2025/jan/04/climate-driven-sea-level-rise-set-to-flood-major-oil-ports.

Casady, Carter B., Alessandra Cepparulo, and Luisa Giuriato. "Public-Private Partnerships for Low-Carbon, Climate-Resilient Infrastructure: Insights from the Literature." *Journal of Cleaner Production* 470 (2024): 143338.

Cecco, Leyland. "Canada Is Proposing to Lead on Climate – But It's Doubling Down on Oil." *The Guardian*, July 25, 2024. https://theguardian.com/environment/article/2024/jul/25/trans-mountain-pipeline-canada.

Center for Sustainable Systems, University of Michigan. *Geothermal Energy Factsheet*. Pub. No. CSS10-10. Ann Arbor: University of Michigan, 2023.

Cezar, Rafael, and Octavio R. Escobar. "Institutional Distance and Foreign Direct Investment." *Review of World Economics* 151, no. 4 (2015): 713–33.

Chan, Ricky Y. K., and Loretta B. Y. Lau. "Antecedents of Green Purchases: A Survey in China." *Journal of Consumer Marketing* 17, no. 4 (2000): 338–57.

Chen, Yingtong, Dayong Zhang, Fei Wu, and Qiang Ji. "Climate Risks and Foreign Direct Investment in Developing Countries: The Role of

National Governance." *Sustainability Science* 17, no. 5 (2022): 1723–40.

Cheng, Wenjuan, Andrea Appolloni, Alessio D'Amato, and Qinghua Zhu. "Green Public Procurement, Missing Concepts and Future Trends – A Critical Review." *Journal of Cleaner Production* 176 (2018): 770–84.

Choi, Esther, Eunkyung Jang, and Valerie Laxton. "What It Takes to Attract Private Investment to Climate Adaptation." *World Resources Institute*, 2023. https://wri.org/insights/private-sector-climate-adaptation-finance.

Christmann, Petra. "Multinational Companies and the Natural Environment: Determinants of Global Environmental Policy Standardization." *Academy of Management Journal* 47, no. 5 (2004): 747–60.

Chu, Sinan, Heike Holbig, Amrita Narlikar, and Johannes Plagemann. "In the Eyes of the Beholders: The Legitimacy of Global Governance Institutions under Multipolarity." *International Studies Quarterly* 68, no. 2 (2024): sqae034.

Claassen, Christopher, and Lauren McLaren. "Does Immigration Produce a Public Backlash or Public Acceptance? Time-Series, Cross-Sectional Evidence from Thirty European Democracies." *British Journal of Political Science* 52, no. 3 (2022): 1013–31.

Clémençon, Raymond. "The Two Sides of the Paris Climate Agreement: Dismal Failure or Historic Breakthrough?" *The Journal of Environment & Development* 25, no. 1 (2016): 3–24.

Coffee, Joyce. "Financing Resilient Infrastructure." In *Optimizing Community Infrastructure: Resilience in the Face of Shocks and Stresses*, edited by Ryan Colker, 101–21. Oxford: Elsevier, 2020.

Cole, Matthew A. "Trade, the Pollution Haven Hypothesis and the Environmental Kuznets Curve: Examining the Linkages." *Ecological Economics* 48, no. 1 (2004): 71–81.

Cole, Matthew A., Robert J. R. Elliott, and Liyun Zhang. "Foreign Direct Investment and the Environment." *Annual Review of Environment and Resources* 42 (2017): 465–87.

Colgan, Charles. "The Warming Ocean Is Leaving Coastal Economies in Hot Water." *The Conversation*, March 28, 2024. https://theconversation.com/the-warming-ocean-is-leaving-coastal-economies-in-hot-water-230088.

Colgan, Jeff D., Jessica F. Green, and Thomas N. Hale. "Asset Revaluation and the Existential Politics of Climate Change." *International Organization* 75, no. 2 (2021): 586–610.

Coll, Steve. *Private Empire: ExxonMobil and American Power*. New York: Penguin, 2012.

Comello, Stephen, and Stefan Reichelstein. "Incentives for Early Adoption of Carbon Capture Technology." *Energy Policy* 74 (2014): 579–88.

Cook, Steven A., and Christina Bouri. "Climate Change Is Making the Middle East Uninhabitable." *Foreign Policy*, August 19, 2024. https://foreignpolicy.com/2024/08/19/climate-change-is-making-the-middle-east-uninhabitable.

Copeland, Brian R., and M. Scott Taylor. "Trade, Growth, and the Environment." *Journal of Economic Literature* 42, no. 1 (2004): 7–71.

Cory, Jared, Michael Lerner, and Iain Osgood. "Supply Chain Linkages and the Extended Carbon Coalition." *American Journal of Political Science* 65, no. 1 (2021): 69–87.

Cosby, Arthur G., Viswadeep Lebakula, C. N. Smith, D. W. Wanik, Darissa D. Bergene, A. N. Rose, David A. Swanson, and D. E. Bloom. "Accelerating Growth of Human Coastal Populations at the Global and Continent Levels: 2000–2018." *Scientific Reports* 14 (2024): 22489.

Costello, Anthony, Marina Romanello, Stella Hartinger, Georgiana Gordon-Strachan, Saleemul Huq, Peng Gong, Tord Kjellstrom, Paul Ekins, and Hugh Montgomery. "Climate Change Threatens Our Health and Survival within Decades." *The Lancet* 401, no. 10371 (2023): 85–87.

Croft, Jane. "'It's a Sun Trap': Climate Crisis Brings Boomtime for British Wine." *The Guardian*, April 12, 2024. https://theguardian.com/business/2024/apr/12/its-a-sun-trap-climate-crisis-brings-boomtime-for-british-wine.

Cruz, Ana Maria, and Elisabeth Krausmann. "Vulnerability of the Oil and Gas Sector to Climate Change and Extreme Weather Events." *Climatic Change* 121, no. 1 (2013): 41–53.

Cuervo-Cazurra, Alvaro, Andrew Inkpen, Aldo Musacchio, and Kannan Ramaswamy. "Governments as Owners: State-Owned Multinational Companies." *Journal of International Business Studies* 45, no. 8 (2014): 919–42.

Cuervo-Cazurra, Alvaro, Yadong Luo, Ravi Ramamurti, and Siah Hwee Ang. "The Impact of the Home Country on Internationalization." *Journal of World Business* 53, no. 5 (2018): 593–604.

Curkovic, Sime, and Robert Sroufe. "Using ISO 14001 to Promote a Sustainable Supply Chain Strategy." *Business Strategy and the Environment* 20, no. 2 (2011): 71–93.

Czarnek, Gabriela, Malgorzata Kossowska, and Paulina Szwed. "Right-Wing Ideology Reduces the Effects of Education on Climate Change Beliefs in More Developed Countries." *Nature Climate Change* 11, no. 1 (2021): 9–13.

Czinkota, Michael R., Gary Knight, Peter W. Liesch, and John Steen. "Terrorism and International Business: A Research Agenda." *Journal of International Business Studies* 41, no. 5 (2010): 826–43.

Dardati, Evangelina, and Meryem Saygili. "Multinationals and Environmental Regulation: Are Foreign Firms Harmful?" *Environment and Development Economics* 17, no. 2 (2012): 163–86.

d'Adda, Giovanna, and Guido de Blasio. "Historical Legacy and Policy Effectiveness: The Long-Term Influence of Preunification Borders in Italy." *Journal of Regional Science* 57, no. 2 (2017): 319–41.

Dalgaard, Carl-Johan, Henrik Hansen, and Finn Tarp. "On the Empirics of Foreign Aid and Growth." *The Economic Journal* 114, no. 496 (2004): F191–F216.

Damania, Richard. "Environmental Controls with Corrupt Bureaucrats." *Environment and Development Economics* 7, no. 3 (2002): 407–27.

Dance, Scott. "Earth Is at Its Hottest in Thousands of Years. Here's How We Know." *The Washington Post*, July 8, 2023. https://washingtonpost.com/weather/2023/07/08/earth-hottest-years-thousands-climate.

Dang, Quyen Thao, Pavlina Jasovka, and Hussain Gulzar Rammal. "International Business-Government Relations: The Risk Management Strategies of MNEs in Emerging Economies." *Journal of World Business* 55, no. 1 (2020): 101042.

D'Aprile, Paolo, Thomas Geissmann, Fernando Pérez López, Jesús Rodríguez González, and Humayun Tai. "How to Increase Grid Resilience through Targeted Investments." *McKinsey & Company*, 2021. https://mckinsey.com/industries/electric-power-and-natural-gas/our-insights/how-to-increase-grid-resilience-through-targeted-investments.

Darnall, Nicole. "Why Firms Mandate ISO 14001 Certification." *Business & Society* 45, no. 3 (2006): 354–81.

Dassu, Imran, and Pelayo Gonzalez Escalada Mena. "How Governments Can Leverage Public Procurement for a Greener Future." *World Economic Forum*, January 2025. https://weforum.org/stories/2025/01/how-governments-can-leverage-public-procurement-for-a-greener-future.

Davenport, Coral. "Heat Is Costing the U.S. Economy Billions in Lost Productivity." *The New York Times*, July 31, 2023. https://nytimes.com/2023/07/31/climate/heat-labor-productivity-climate.html.

Davidson, Helen, Hibaq Farah, and Dan Milmo. "China Reportedly Extends iPhone Ban to More Workers as Tensions with the U.S. Rise." *The Guardian*, September 8, 2023. https://theguardian.com/world/2023/sep/08/china-iphone-ban-government-state-owned-firms-workers-apple-us.

Davidson, Michael R., and Margaret M. Pearson. "Where Are the U.S. and China on Addressing Climate Change?" *Brookings*, 2024. https://brookings.edu/articles/where-are-the-us-and-china-on-addressing-climate-change.

Davies, Shawn, Terése Pattersson, and Magnus Öberg. "Organized Violence 1989–2021 and Drone Warfare." *Journal of Peace Research* 59, no. 4 (2022): 593–610.

Dawson, Richard J., David Thompson, Daniel Johns, Ruth Wood, Geoff Darch, Lee Chapman, Paul N. Hughes, Geoff V. R. Watson, Kevin Paulson, Sarah Bell, Simon N. Gosling, William Powrie, and Jim W. Hall. "A Systems Framework for National Assessment of Climate Risks to Infrastructure." *Philosophical Transactions of the Royal Society A: Mathematical, Physical and Engineering Sciences* 376, no. 2121 (2018): 20170298.

Deacon, Robert T. "Public Good Provision Under Dictatorship and Democracy." *Public Choice* 139, nos. 1–2 (2009): 241–62.

Dechter, Aimée, and Glen H. Elder Jr. "World War II Mobilization in Men's Work Lives: Continuity or Disruption for the Middle Class?" *American Journal of Sociology* 110, no. 3 (2004): 761–93.

Delacote, Philippe, Tara L'Horty, Andreas Kontoleon, Thales A. P. West, Anna Creti, Ben Filewod, Gwenole LeVelly, Alejandro Guizar-Coutiño, Ben Groom, and Micah Elias. "Strong Transparency Required for Carbon Credit Mechanisms." *Nature Sustainability* 7, no. 6 (2024): 706–13.

Deleidi, Matteo, Mariana Mazzucato, and Gregor Semieniuk. "Neither Crowding In nor Out: Public Direct Investment Mobilising Private Investment into Renewable Electricity Projects." *Energy Policy* 140 (2020): 111195.

Dellepiane-Avellaneda, Sebastian. "Review Article: Good Governance, Institutions and Economic Development: Beyond the Conventional Wisdom." *British Journal of Political Science* 40, no. 1 (2010): 195–224.

Deloitte. *The Turning Point: A Global Summary*. Deloitte, 2022.

DePillis, Lydia. "Polluting Industries Say the Cost of Cleaner Air Is Too High." *The New York Times*, November 13, 2023. https://nytimes.com/2023/11/13/business/economy/smog-rules-economics.html.

Desai, Uday. *Ecological Policy and Politics in Developing Countries: Economic Growth, Democracy, and Environment*. Albany: State University of New York Press, 1998.

Devitt, Conor, and Richard S. J. Tol. "Civil War, Climate Change, and Development: A Scenario Study for Sub-Saharan Africa." *Journal of Peace Research* 49, no. 1 (2012): 129–45.

Diaz-Infante, Nadine, Michael Lazar, Samvitha Ram, and Austin Ray. "Demand for Online Education Is Growing. Are Providers Ready?" *McKinsey & Company*, 2022. https://mckinsey.com/industries/education/our-insights/demand-for-online-education-is-growing-are-providers-ready.

Dicker, Sophie, Sam Unsworth, Rebecca Byrnes, and Bob Ward. *Saving Lives and Livelihoods: The Benefits of Investments in Climate Change Adaptation and Resilience.* London: Grantham Research Institute on Climate Change and the Environment and Centre for Climate Change Economics and Policy, London School of Economics and Political Science, 2021.

Ditlevsen, Peter, and Susanne Ditlevsen. "Warning of a Forthcoming Collapse of the Atlantic Meridional Overturning Circulation." *Nature Communications* 14 (2023): 4254.

Dizik, Alina. "How the Great Recession Changed U.S. Shopping Habits." *Chicago Booth Review*, September 24, 2015. https://chicagobooth.edu/review/how-the-great-recession-changed-us-shopping-habits.

Dollar, David. "Is Globalization Good for Your Health?" *Bulletin of the World Health Organization* 79, no. 9 (2001): 827–33.

Dolšak, Nives, and Aseem Prakash. "The Politics of Climate Change Adaptation." *Annual Review of Environment and Resources* 43 (2018): 317–41.

Dreher, Axel, Valentin F. Lang, and Katharina Richert. "The Political Economy of International Finance Corporation Lending." *Journal of Development Economics* 140 (2019): 242–54.

Drezner, Daniel. "Bottom Feeders." *Foreign Policy* 121 (2000): 64–70.

Dryzek, John S. *Rational Ecology: Environment and Political Economy.* Oxford: Basil Blackwell, 1987.

Duan, Yuwan, and Xuemei Jiang. "Pollution Haven or Pollution Halo? A Re-Evaluation on the Role of Multinational Enterprises in Global CO_2 Emissions." *Energy Economics* 97 (2021): 105181.

Duanmu, Jing-Lin. "A Race to Lower Standards? Labor Standards and Location Choice of Outward FDI from the BRIC Countries." *International Business Review* 23, no. 3 (2014): 620–34.

Dubash, Navroz K., Markus Hagemann, Niklas Höhne, and Prabhat Upadhyaya. "Developments in National Climate Change Mitigation Legislation and Strategy." *Climate Policy* 13, no. 6 (2013): 649–64.

Dunlap, Riley E., and Robert J. Brulle. "Sources and Amplifiers of Climate Change Denial." In *Research Handbook on Communicating Climate Change*, edited by David C. Holmes and Lucy M. Richardson, 49–61. Cheltenham, UK: Edward Elgar, 2020.

Eang, Monida, Amelia Clarke, and Eduardo Ordonez-Ponce. "The Roles of Multinational Enterprises in Implementing the United Nations Sustainable Development Goals at the Local Level." *BRQ Business Research Quarterly* 26, no. 1 (2023): 79–97.

Easterly, William. "Was Development Assistance a Mistake?" *American Economic Review* 97, no. 2 (2007): 328–32.

Eaton, Collin. "Exxon Buys Pipeline Operator, Making Big Bet on Carbon." *The Wall Street Journal*, October 11, 2023. https://wsj.com/articles/exxon-buys-pipeline-operator-making-big-bet-on-carbon-a1d0e347.

Eaton, Collin, and Paul Kiernan. "Exxon Sues Two ESG Investors." *The Wall Street Journal*, January 22, 2024. https://wsj.com/business/energy-oil/exxon-sues-two-esg-investors-2057e696.

Eaton, Sarah, and Genia Kostka. "Authoritarian Environmentalism Undermined? Local Leaders' Time Horizons and Environmental Policy Implementation in China." *The China Quarterly* 218 (2014): 359–80.

Ebadian, Mohmood, Susan van Dyk, James D. McMillan, and Jack Saddler. "Biofuel Policies That Have Encouraged Their Production and Use: An International Perspective." *Energy Policy* 147 (2020): 111906.

Eckstein, David, Vera Künzel, and Laura Schäfer. *Global Climate Risk Index 2021*. Bonn: Germanwatch, 2021.

Economist Intelligence Unit, and World Wide Fund for Nature. *An Eco-Wakening: Measuring Global Awareness, Engagement and Action for Nature*. Gland: WWF, 2021.

El Dahan, Maha. "Davos 2023: Big Oil in Sights of Climate Activist Protests." *Reuters*, January 16, 2023. https://reuters.com/world/davos-2023-climate-activists-protest-over-big-oil-hijacking-debate-2023-01-15/

El Ghoul, Sadok, Omrane Guedhami, Huan Kuang, and Ying Zheng. "Does Climate Change Exposure Matter to Stakeholders? Evidence from the Costs of High Leverage." *Review of Corporate Finance* 4, nos. 1–2 (2024): 47–87.

Elkington, John. *Cannibals with Forks: The Triple Bottom Line of Twenty-First Century Business*. Gabriola Island, BC: New Society Publishers, 1998.

Elliott, Rebecca F. "Why Oil Companies Are Walking Back from Green Energy." *The New York Times*, November 18, 2024. https://nytimes.com/2024/11/18/business/energy-environment/cop-oil-gas-green-energy.html.

Ellsworth-Krebs, Katherine, Carolynne Lord, and Torik Holmes. "Hybrid Working Is Fueling Demand for More Tech and Bigger Homes – Both Are Bad News for the Planet." *The Conversation*, September 15, 2021. https://theconversation.com/hybrid-working-is-fuelling-demand-for-more-tech-and-bigger-homes-both-are-bad-news-for-the-planet-166385.
(Corrected author list with missing "and"; corrected capitalization: Is/Are)

Euklidiadas, M. Martínez. "Fujisawa Sustainable Smart Town: Planning for the Next 100 Years." *Tomorrow City*, 2024. https://tomorrow.city/fujisawa-sustainable-smart-town.

Evan, Tomáš, and Vladimír Holý. "Cultural Diversity and Its Impact on Governance." *Socio-Economic Planning Sciences* 89 (2023): 101681.

Ewing, Jack, and Ben Dooley. "Toyota, a Hybrid Pioneer, Struggles to Master Electric Vehicles." *The New York Times*, September 7, 2023.

https://nytimes.com/2023/09/07/business/toyota-hybrid-electric-vehicles.html.

Eze, Uchenna Cyril, and Nelson Oly Ndubisi. "Green Buyer Behavior: Evidence from Asia Consumers." *Journal of Asian and African Studies* 48, no. 4 (2013): 413–26.

Fails, Matthew D. "What Types of Political Regimes Subsidize Fuel Consumption?" *The Extractive Industries and Society* 9 (2022): 101037.

Falkner, Robert. "The Paris Agreement and the New Logic of International Climate Politics." *International Affairs* 92, no. 5 (2016): 1107–25.

Fankhauser, Sam. "Adaptation to Climate Change." *Annual Review of Resource Economics* 9 (2017): 209–30.

Fankhauser, Samuel, and Thomas K. M. McDermott. "Understanding the Adaptation Deficit: Why Are Poor Countries More Vulnerable to Climate Events than Rich Countries?" *Global Environmental Change* 27 (2014): 9–18.

Farzin, Y. Hossein, and Craig A. Bond. "Democracy and Environmental Quality." *Journal of Development Economics* 81, no. 1 (2006): 213–35.

Ferro, Esteban, and John S. Wilson. *Foreign Aid and Business Bottlenecks: A Study of Aid Effectiveness*. World Bank Policy Research Working Paper No. 5546, 2011.

Fisher, Dana R., and Sohana Nasrin. "Climate Activism and Its Effects." *Wiley Interdisciplinary Reviews: Climate Change* 12, no. 1 (2021): e683.

Flagg, Julia A., and Thomas K. Rudel. "Uneven Ambitions: Explaining National Differences in Proposed Emissions Reductions." *Human Ecology Review* 27, no. 1 (2021): 23–46.

Flavelle, Christopher, Jill Cowan, and Ivan Penn. "Climate Shocks Are Making Parts of America Uninsurable. It Just Got Worse." *The New York Times*, May 31, 2023. https://nytimes.com/2023/05/31/climate/climate-change-insurance-wildfires-california.html.

Flouris, Andreas, Manal Azzi, Halshka Graczyk, Balint Nafradi, and Natasha Scott, eds. *Heat at Work: Implications for Safety and Health. A Global Review of the Science, Policy, and Practice*. Geneva: International Labour Organization, 2024.

Flynn, Cassie, Silvia Tovar Jardon, Stephen Fisher, Matthew Blayney, Albert Ward, Hunter Smith, Paula Struthoff, and Zoë Fillingham. *The People's Climate Vote Report*. New York: United Nations Development Programme and Oxford University, 2024.

Fong, Clara. "Understanding the Global Push for Climate Finance." Council on Foreign Relations, 2024. https://cfr.org/backgrounder/understanding-global-push-climate-finance.

Fonjong, Lotsmart, Frank Matose, and David A. Sonnenfeld. "Climate Change in Africa: Impacts, Adaptation, and Policy Responses." *Global Environmental Change* 89 (2024): 102912.

Fonseca, Ryan. "Trump Could Make It Tougher to Afford Electric Cars. Why Elon Musk Doesn't Mind." *Los Angeles Times*, November 18, 2024. https://latimes.com/california/newsletter/2024-11-18/trump-may-kill-ev-tax-credit-musk-doesnt-mind-essential-california.

Forsythe, Michael, and Walt Bogdanich. "At McKinsey, Widespread Furor Over Work With Planet's Biggest Polluters." *The New York Times*, October 27, 2021. https://nytimes.com/2021/10/27/business/mckinsey-climate-change.html.

Franczak, Michael. "Who Pays for Climate Action?" *Foreign Policy*, June 3, 2024. https://foreignpolicy.com/2024/06/03/climate-finance-small-island-states-taxes-adaptation.

Frangoul, Anmar. "Orsted and BP Look to Develop Major Renewable Hydrogen Project in Germany." *CNBC*, November 10, 2020. https://cnbc.com/2020/11/10/orsted-and-bp-to-develop-major-renewable-hydrogen-project-in-germany-.html.

Frankel, Jeffrey A., and Andrew K. Rose. "Is Trade Good or Bad for the Environment? Sorting Out the Causality." *The Review of Economics and Statistics* 87, no. 1 (2005): 85–91.

Franta, Benjamin. "Weaponizing Economics: Big Oil, Economic Consultants, and Climate Policy Delay." *Environmental Politics* 31, no. 4 (2022): 555–75.

Franzó, Simone, and Alessio Nasca. "The Environmental Impact of Electric Vehicles: A Novel Life Cycle–Based Evaluation Framework and Its Applications to Multi-Country Scenarios." *Journal of Cleaner Production* 315 (2021): 128005.

Freedman, Andrew. "The Corporate Climate Migration Has Begun." *Axios*, December 10, 2021. https://axios.com/2021/12/10/corporate-climate-change-migration-extreme-weather.

Frenkel, Michael, and Benedikt Walter. "Do Bilateral Investment Treaties Attract Foreign Direct Investment? The Role of International Dispute Settlement Provisions." *The World Economy* 42, no. 5 (2019): 1316–42.

Friedman, Lisa. "Saudi Arabia Is a 'Wrecking Ball' in Global Climate Talks." *The New York Times*, November 18, 2024. https://nytimes.com/2024/11/18/climate/saudi-arabia-obstruction-fossil-fuels.html.

Füssel, Hans-Martin. "How Inequitable Is the Global Distribution of Responsibility, Capability, and Vulnerability to Climate Change: A Comprehensive Indicator-Based Assessment." *Global Environmental Change* 20, no. 4 (2010): 597–611.

Gabbatiss, Josh. "Analysis: Nearly a Tenth of Global Climate Finance Threatened by Trump Aid Cuts." *CarbonBrief*, January 8, 2025. https://carbonbrief.org/analysis-nearly-a-tenth-of-global-climate-finance-threatened-by-trump-aid-cuts.

Gabbatiss, Josh, and Tom Pearson. "Analysis: How Some of the World's Largest Companies Rely on Carbon Offsets to 'Reach Net-Zero.'" *CarbonBrief*, May 23, 2023. https://interactive.carbonbrief.org/carbon-offsets-2023/companies.html.

Gamso, Jonas. "Trade Partnerships and Environmental Performance in Developing Countries." *Journal of Environment and Development* 26, no. 4 (2017): 375–399.

"Environmental Policy Impacts of Trade with China and the Moderating Effect of Governance." *Environmental Policy and Governance* 28, no. 6 (2018): 395–405.

"Debt-for-Climate Swaps Can Save the Planet. Why Aren't They?" *Stanford Social Innovation Review*, 2023. https://ssir.org/articles/entry/debt_for_climate_swaps_can_save_the_planet_why_arent_they#

"Does Climate Aid Reduce Perceived Climate Risks to Foreign Direct Investors?" *Climate and Development*, 17, no. 9 (2025a): 857–867.

"Foreign Aid and Strategic Foreign Policy." In *The Oxford Handbook of Geoeconomics and Statecraft*, edited by Vinod K. Aggarwal and Tai Ming Cheung, 219–36. Oxford: Oxford University Press, 2025b.

Gamso, Jonas, Andrew Inkpen, and Kannan Ramaswamy. "Managing Geopolitical Risks: The Global Oil and Gas Industry Plays a Winning Game." *Journal of Business Strategy* 45, no. 3 (2024): 190–98.

Gamso, Jonas, and Anna Dimitrova. "Rewarding a Friend: Does the World Bank Direct Non-Commercial Risk Insurance to Countries That Support US Foreign Policy Interests?" *New Political Economy* 29, no. 1 (2024): 159–72.

Gamso, Jonas, and Robert Grosse. "Trade Agreement Depth, Foreign Direct Investment, and the Moderating Role of Property Rights." *Journal of International Business Policy* 4, no. 2 (2021): 308–25.

Gamso, Jonas, and Roy C. Nelson. "Does Partnering with the World Bank Shield Investors from Political Risks in Less Developed Countries?" *Journal of World Business* 54, no. 5 (2019): 100997.

Ganguly, Geetanjali, Joana Setzer, and Veerle Heyvaert. "If at First You Don't Succeed: Suing Corporations for Climate Change." *Oxford Journal of Legal Studies* 38, no. 4 (2018): 841–68.

Gao, Fei, and Gilvan C. Souza. "Carbon Offsetting with Eco-Conscious Consumers." *Management Science* 68, no. 11 (2022): 7879–97.

Garcia, Maria Cristina. *State of Disaster: The Failure of U.S. Migration Policy in an Age of Climate Change*. Chapel Hill: University of North Carolina Press, 2022.

Garrett, Kyla P., Ryan A. McManamay, and Christopher R. DeRolph. "When Energy Doesn't Add Up: Use of an Energyshed Framework in Assessing Progress Towards Renewable Energy Transitions." *Environmental Research: Infrastructure and Sustainability* 4, no. 1 (2024): 015004.

Gasparro, Kate, Vedran Zerjav, Efrosyni Konstantinou, and Carter B. Casady. "Vanguard Projects as Intermediation Spaces for Sustainability Transitions." *Project Management Journal* 53, no. 2 (2022): 196–210.

Geisler, Charles, and Ben Currens. "Impediments to Inland Resettlement under Conditions of Accelerated Sea Level Rise." *Land Use Policy* 66 (2017): 322–30.

Gelles, David. "A Sudden Rush to Make Sustainable Aviation Fuel Mainstream." *The New York Times*, February 21, 2023. https://nytimes.com/2023/02/21/climate/united-sustainable-aviation-fuel.html.

Gelles, David, and Christopher Flavelle. "The New Climate Gold Rush: Scrubbing Carbon from the Sky." *The New York Times*, December 22, 2024. https://nytimes.com/2024/12/22/climate/carbon-capture-global-warming.html.

Gelles, David, and Manuela Andreoni. "How Extreme Heat Affects Workers and the Economy." *The New York Times*, July 20, 2023. https://nytimes.com/2023/07/20/climate/how-extreme-heat-affects-workers-and-the-economy.html.

Geng, Duanyang, Junjun Liu, and Qinghua Zhu. "Motivating Sustainable Consumption Among Chinese Adolescents: An Empirical Examination." *Journal of Cleaner Production* 141 (2017): 315–22.

Georgieva, Kristalina, Vitor Gaspar, and Ceyla Pazarbasioglu. "Poor and Vulnerable Countries Need Support to Adapt to Climate Change." *IMF Blog*, March 23, 2022. https://imf.org/en/Blogs/Articles/2022/03/23/blog032322-poor-and-vulnerable-countries-need-support-to-adapt-to-climate-change.

Ghemawat, Pankaj. "Semiglobalization and International Business Strategy." *Journal of International Business Studies* 34, no. 2 (2003): 138–52.

"Globalization in the Age of Trump." *Harvard Business Review* (July–August 2017): 112–23.

Giambona, Erasmo, John R. Graham, and Campbell R. Harvey. "The Management of Political Risk." *Journal of International Business Studies* 48, no. 4 (2017): 523–33.

Gibbs, David, and Pauline Deutz. "Implementing Industrial Ecology? Planning for Eco-Industrial Parks in the USA." *Geoforum* 36, no. 4 (2005): 452–64.

Giffard, Hermione. *Making Jet Engines in World War II: Britain, Germany, and the United States*. Chicago: University of Chicago Press, 2016.

Gilley, Bruce. "Authoritarian Environmentalism and China's Response to Climate Change." *Environmental Politics* 21, no. 2 (2012): 287–307.

Giuli, Alberta Di, and Leonard Kostovetsky. "Are Red or Blue Companies More Likely to Go Green? Politics and Corporate Social Responsibility." *Journal of Financial Economics* 111, no. 1 (2014): 158–80.

Gleditsch, Nils Petter, Peter Wallensteen, Mikael Eriksson, Margareta Sollenberg, and Håvard Strand. "Armed Conflict 1946–2001: A New Dataset." *Journal of Peace Research* 39, no. 5 (2002): 615–37.

Goeteyn, Nils, and Frank Maes. "Environmental Agreements: An Effective Way to Improve Compliance?" *Chinese Journal of International Law* 10, no. 4 (2011): 791–826.

Goldberg, Matthew H., Jennifer R. Marlon, Xinran Wang, Sander van der Linden, and Anthony Leiserowitz. "Oil and Gas Companies Invest in Legislators that Vote Against the Environment." *Proceedings of the National Academy of Sciences of the United States of America* 117, no. 10 (2020): 5111–12.

Gonenc, Halit, and Aleksandra Poleska. "Multinationals, Research and Development, and Carbon Emissions: International Evidence." *Climate Policy* 23, no. 8 (2023): 959–74.

Gonzalez, Marco, Kristen N. Taddonio, and Nancy J. Sherman. "The Montreal Protocol: How Today's Successes Offer a Pathway to the Future." *Journal of Environmental Studies and Sciences* 5, no. 2 (2015): 122–29.

Gopalan, Sasidaran, and Ramkishen S. Rajan. "Has Foreign Aid Been Effective in the Water Supply and Sanitation Sector? Evidence from Panel Data." *World Development* 85 (2016): 84–104.

Gordon, Deborah. *Understanding Climate Engineering*. Washington, DC: Carnegie Endowment for International Peace, 2017.

Graham, Benjamin A. T., and Jacob R. Tucker. "The International Political Economy Data Resource." *Review of International Organizations* 14, no. 1 (2019): 149–61.

Graham, Benjamin A. T., Raymond Hicks, Helen Milner, and Lori D. Bougher. *World Economics and Politics Dataverse*. 2018. https://ncgg.princeton.edu/wep/dataverse.html.

Grant, Emily, and Jennifer D. Runkle. "Long-Term Health Effects of Wildfire Exposure: A Scoping Review." *The Journal of Climate Change and Health* 6 (2022): 100110.

Grasso, Marco. "Oily Politics: A Critical Assessment of the Oil and Gas Industry's Contribution to Climate Change." *Energy Research & Social Science* 50 (2019): 106–15.

Green, Jessica Fischer. *Rethinking Private Authority: Agents and Entrepreneurs in Global Environmental Governance*. Princeton, NJ: Princeton University Press, 2014.

Green, Jessica, Jennifer Hadden, Thomas Hale, and Paasha Mahdavi. "Transition, Hedge, or Resist? Understanding Political and Economic Behavior toward Decarbonization in the Oil and Gas Industry." *Review of International Political Economy* 29, no. 6 (2022): 2036–63.

Greenfield, Patrick. "COP29's New Carbon Market Rules Offer Hope After Scandal and Deadlock." *The Guardian*, November 24, 2024. https://theguardian.com/environment/2024/nov/24/cop29s-new-carbon-market-rules-offer-hope-after-scandal-and-deadlock.

Greenstone, Michael. "The Impacts of Environmental Regulations on Industrial Activity: Evidence from the 1970 and 1977 Clean Air Act Amendments and the Census of Manufactures." *Journal of Political Economy* 110, no. 6 (2002): 1175–1219.

Griffin, Paul. CDP Carbon Majors Report 2017. CDP Worldwide, 2017.

Grimaldi, Antonio, Kia Javanmardian, Dickon Pinner, Hamid Samandari, and Kurt Strovink. "Climate Change and P&C Insurance: A Threat and Opportunity." *McKinsey & Company*, November 2020. https://mckinsey.com/industries/financial-services/our-insights/climate-change-and-p-and-c-insurance-the-threat-and-opportunity.

Gross, Samantha. "The United States Can Take Climate Change Seriously while Leading the World in Oil and Gas Production." *Brookings*, January 2020. https://brookings.edu/articles/the-united-states-can-take-climate-change-seriously-while-leading-the-world-in-oil-and-gas-production.

Grosse, Robert, Jonas Gamso, and Roy C. Nelson. "China's Rise, World Order, and the Implications for International Business." *Management International Review* 61, no. 1 (2021): 1–26.

"De-Globalization is a Myth." *AIB Insights* 22, no. 2 (2022): 1–6.

Grunstein, Miriam. "Some Like It Hot: Mexico's Ambivalent Policy toward Climate Change." *Baker Institute for Public Policy*, May 2023. https://bakerinstitute.org/research/some-it-hot-mexicos-ambivalent-policy-toward-climate-change.

Gu, Grace Weishi, and Galina Hale. "Climate Risks and FDI." *Journal of International Economics* 146 (2023): 103731.

Gunay, Samet, and Bekir Emre Kurtulmuş. "COVID-19 Social Distancing and the US Service Sector: What Do We Learn?" *Research in International Business and Finance* 56 (2021): 101361.

Gustafsson, Maria-Therese, Jorge E. Rodriguez-Morales, and Lisa M. Dellmuth. "Private Adaptation to Climate Risks: Evidence from the World's Largest Mining Companies." *Climate Risk Management* 35 (2022): 100386.

Gutowski, Timothy G., Julian M. Allwood, Christoph Herrmann, and Sahil Sahni. "A Global Assessment of Manufacturing: Economic Development, Energy Use, Carbon Emissions, and the Potential for Energy Efficiency and Materials Recycling." *Annual Review of Environment and Resources* 38 (2013): 81–106.

Gutstein, Donald. *The Big Stall: How Big Oil and Think Tanks Are Blocking Action on Climate Change in Canada*. Toronto: James Lorimer & Company, 2018.

Habibi, Mohammad Reza, and Chiranjeev S. Kohli. "The Sharing Economy: A Hedge Against Recession Setbacks." *Journal of Business Strategy* 43, no. 4 (2022): 239–46.

Hagen, Achim, and Mark Schopf. "Political Influence on International Climate Agreements with Border Carbon Adjustment." *Journal of Environmental Economics and Management* 125 (2024): 102979.

Haines, A., R. S. Kovats, D. Campbell-Lendrum, and C. Corvalan. "Climate Change and Human Health: Impacts, Vulnerability and Public Health." *Public Health* 120, no. 7 (2006): 585–96.

Halliday, Simon, Jonathan Ilan, and Colin Scott. "The Public Management of Liability Risks." *Oxford Journal of Legal Studies* 31, no. 3 (2011): 527–50.

Halttunen, Krista, Raphael Slade, and Iain Staffell. "Diversify or Die: Strategy Options for Oil Majors in the Sustainable Energy Transition." *Energy Research & Social Science* 104 (2023): 103253.

Ham, Suyun Paul. "Stuck Bridges, Buckling Roads – Extreme Heat Is Wreaking Havoc on America's Aging Infrastructure." *The Conversation*, July 18, 2024. https://theconversation.com/stuck-bridges-buckling-roads-extreme-heat-is-wreaking-havoc-on-americas-aging-infrastructure-235851.

Hao, Feng, and Wanyun Shao. "What Really Drives the Deployment of Renewable Energy? A Global Assessment of 118 Countries." *Energy Research & Social Science* 72 (2021): 101880.

Haraguchi, Masahiko, and Upmanu Lall. "Flood Risks and Impacts: A Case Study of Thailand's Floods in 2011 and Research Questions for Supply Chain Decision Making." *International Journal of Disaster Risk Reduction* 14, no. 3 (2015): 256–72.

Harring, Niklas, and Sverker C. Jagers. "Why Do People Accept Environmental Policies? The Prospects of Higher Education and Changes in Norms, Beliefs and Policy Preferences." *Environmental Education Research* 24, no. 6 (2018): 791–806.

Hart, Jordan. "Bill Gates Is Optimistic About the Future of Fake Meat and Plant-Based Foods." *Business Insider*, January 2023. https://businessinsider.com/bill-gates-optimistic-future-fake-meats-plant-based-foods-2023-1.

Hart, Stuart L., and Mark B. Milstein. "Creating Sustainable Value." *Academy of Management Perspectives* 17, no. 2 (2003): 56–69.

Harvey, Fiona. "Rich Countries Hit $100bn Climate Finance Goal Two Years Late, Data Shows." *The Guardian*, November 16, 2023. https://theguardian.com/global-development/2023/nov/16/rich-countries-hit-climate-finance-goal-two-years-late-data.

"COP29: Which Climate Finance Ideas Are Most Likely to Work?" *The Guardian*, November 11, 2024. https://theguardian.com/environment/2024/nov/11/cop29-which-climate-finance-ideas-are-most-likely-to-work.

Hashai, Niron. "Within-Industry Diversification and Firm Performance – An S-Shaped Hypothesis." *Strategic Management Journal* 36, no. 9 (2015): 1378–1400.

Heath, Ryan. "The World Is on Fire and Our Leaders Are Failing, Poll Finds." *Politico*, February 8, 2022. https://politico.com/news/2022/02/08/citizens-politicians-combat-climate-change-00004590.

Hegerl, Gabriele C., and Susan Solomon. "Risks of Climate Engineering." *Science* 325, no. 5943 (2009): 955–56.

Heid, Bernd, Martin Linder, Sebastian Mayer, Anna Orthofer, and Mark Patel. "What Would It Take to Scale Critical Climate Technologies?" *McKinsey & Company*, 2023. https://mckinsey.com/capabilities/sustainability/our-insights/what-would-it-take-to-scale-critical-climate-technologies.

Heidenreich, Martin. "The Social Embeddedness of Multinational Companies: A Literature Review." *Socio-Economic Review* 10, no. 3 (2012): 549–79.

Henisz, Witold J., Edward D. Mansfield, and Mary Ann Von Glinow. "Conflict, Security, and Political Risk: International Business in Challenging Times." *Journal of International Business Studies* 41, no. 5 (2010): 759–64.

Hennessy, Jack, Duncan Mortimer, Rohan Sweeney, and Maame Esi Woode. "Donor Versus Recipient Preferences for Aid Allocation: A Systematic Review of Stated-Preference Studies." *Social Science & Medicine* 334 (2023): 116184.

Hewlett, Richard G. "Beginnings of Development in Nuclear Technology." *Technology and Culture* 17, no. 3 (1976): 465–78.

Hicks, Robert L., Bradley C. Parks, J. Timmons Roberts, and Michael J. Tierney. *Greening Aid? Understanding the Environmental Impact of Development Assistance*. Oxford: Oxford University Press, 2008.

Hill, Alice C., and Tess Turner. "Burning Threats: How Wildfires Undermine U.S. National Security." *Just Security*, August 2023. https://justsecurity.org/87265/burning-threats-how-wildfires-undermine-u-s-national-security.

Hillman, Amy J., Gerald D. Keim, and Douglas Schuler. "Corporate Political Activity: A Review and Research Agenda." *Journal of Management* 30, no. 6 (2004): 837–57.

Hillman, Amy J., Michael C. Witheres, and Brian J. Collins. "Resource Dependence Theory: A Review." *Journal of Management* 35, no. 6 (2009): 1404–27.

Hoffmann, Matthew. *Climate Governance at the Crossroads: Experimenting with a Global Response After Kyoto*. Oxford: Oxford University Press, 2011.

Hommel, Damian, and Alexander B. Murphy. "Rethinking Geopolitics in an Era of Climate Change." *GeoJournal* 78, no. 3 (2013): 507–24.

Hoppe, Janna, Ben Hinder, Ryan Rafaty, Anthony Patt, and Michael Grubb. "Three Decades of Climate Mitigation Policy: What Has It Delivered?" *Annual Review of Environment and Resources* 48 (2023): 615–50.

Hornsey, Matthew J., Cassandra M. Chapman, and Jacquelyn E. Humphrey. "Climate Skepticism Decreases When the Planet Gets Hotter and Conservation Support Wanes." *Global Environmental Change* 74 (2022): 102492.

Hornum, S. T., S. Bolwig, and S. L. M. Trærup. "Enabling Drip Irrigation Technology Diffusion and Adoption Among African Smallholders: A Document Analysis of Climate Action Plans and Donor Projects." *Climate and Development* 16, no. 5 (2024): 378–94.

Horton, Helena, Lucy Swan, Ana Lucía González Paz, and Harvey Symons. "The Climate Crisis in Charts: How 2024 Has Set Unwanted New Records." *The Guardian*, November 20, 2024. https://theguardian.com/environment/2024/nov/20/the-climate-crisis-in-charts-how-2024-has-set-unwanted-new-records.

Hovi, Jon, Detlef F. Sprinz, and Guri Bang. "Why the United States Did Not Become a Party to the Kyoto Protocol: German, Norwegian, and US Perspectives." *European Journal of International Relations* 18, no. 1 (2012): 129–50.

Hsueh, Lily. "Exxon, Apple and Other Corporate Giants Will Have to Disclose All Their Emissions Under California's New Climate Laws – That Will Have a Global Impact." *The Conversation*, October 9, 2023. https://theconversation.com/exxon-apple-and-other-corporate-giants-will-have-to-disclose-all-their-emissions-under-californias-new-climate-laws-that-will-have-a-global-impact-214630.

Corporations at Climate Crossroads: Multilevel Governance, Public Policy, and Global Climate Action. Cambridge, MA: MIT Press, 2025.

Hsiang, Solomon, Robert Kopp, Amir Jina, James Rising, Michael Delgado, Shashank Mohan, D. J. Rasmussen, Robert Muir-Wood, Paul Wilson, Michael Oppenheimer, Kate Larson, and Trevor Houser. "Estimating Economic Damage from Climate Change in the United States." *Science* 356, no. 6345 (2017): 1362–69.

Huang, Xiaoqi, Wei Liu, and Zhi Cao. "Environmental Courts and Foreign Direct Investments: Evidence from China." *Environmental Science and Pollution Research* 29, no. 21 (2022): 31400–12.

Hubbard, Graham. "Measuring Organizational Performance: Beyond the Triple Bottom Line." *Business Strategy and the Environment* 18, no. 3 (2009): 177–91.

Hundertmark, Thomas, Ken Lueck, and Brent Packer. "Water: A Human and Business Priority." *McKinsey Quarterly*, March 9, 2020. https://mckinsey.com/capabilities/sustainability/our-insights/water-a-human-and-business-priority.

Hunter, Trevor, and Pratima Bansal. "How Standard Is Standardized MNC Global Environmental Communication?" *Journal of Business Ethics* 71, no. 2 (2007): 135–47.

Hyde, Charles K. *Arsenal of Democracy: The American Automobile Industry in World War II*. Detroit: Wayne State University Press, 2013.

Iacobuţă, Gabriela Ileana, Clara Brandi, Adis Dzebo, and Sofia Donaji Elizalde Duron. "Aligning Climate and Sustainable Development Finance Through an SDG Lens: The Role of Development Assistance in Implementing the Paris Agreement." *Global Environmental Change* 74 (2022): 102509.

Iankova, Elena, and Jan Katz. "Strategies for Political Risk Mediation by International Firms in Transition Economies: The Case of Bulgaria." *Journal of World Business* 38, no. 3 (2003): 182–203.

Ikenberry, G. John. "The End of the Liberal International Order?" *International Affairs* 94, no. 1 (2018): 7–23.

International Bank for Reconstruction and Development/The World Bank. *Indonesia Economic Prospects: Trade and Growth for Economic Transformation*. Washington, DC: World Bank, 2022.

Ioannou, Ioannis, George Kassinis, and Giorgos Papagiannakis. "The Impact of Perceived Greenwashing on Customer Satisfaction and the Contingent Role of Capability Reputation." *Journal of Business Ethics* 185, no. 2 (2023): 333–47.

Irfan, Umair. "The Air Conditioning Paradox." *Vox*, May 2022. https://vox.com/science-and-health/23067049/heat-wave-air-conditioning-cooling-india-climate-change.

Irvine, Peter, Kerry Emanuel, Jie He, Larry W. Horowitz, Gabriel Vecchi, and David Keith. "Halving Warming with Idealized Solar Geoengineering

Moderates Key Climate Hazards." *Nature Climate Change* 9, no. 4 (2019): 295–99.

Ivashina, Victoria, and David Scharfstein. "Bank Lending During the Financial Crisis of 2008." *Journal of Financial Economics* 97, no. 3 (2010): 319–38.

Iwai, Nobuyuki, and Stanley R. Thompson. "Foreign Direct Investment and Labor Quality in Developing Countries." *Review of Development Economics* 16, no. 2 (2012): 276–90.

James, Harold. "Deglobalization: The Rise of Disembedded Unilateralism." *Annual Review of Financial Economics* 10 (2018): 219–37.

Jandhyala, Srividya, and Anupama Phene. "The Role of Intergovernmental Organizations in Cross-border Knowledge Transfer and Innovation." *Administrative Science Quarterly* 60, no. 4 (2015): 712–43.

Jandhyala, Srividya, and Robert J. Weiner. "Institutions Sans Frontières: International Agreements and Foreign Investment." *Journal of International Business Studies* 45, no. 6 (2014): 649–69.

Jandhyala, Srividya, Witold J. Henisz, and Edward D. Mansfield. "Three Waves of BITs: The Global Diffusion of Foreign Investment Policy." *Journal of Conflict Resolution* 55, no. 6 (2011): 1047–73.

Jaramillo, Juanita Álvarez, Jhon Wilder Zartha Sossa, and Gina Lía Orozco Mendoza. "Barriers to Sustainability for Small and Medium Enterprises in the Framework of Sustainable Development – Literature Review." *Business Strategy and the Environment* 28, no. 4 (2019): 512–24.

Jaworski, Taylor. "World War II and the Industrialization of the American South." *The Journal of Economic History* 77, no. 4 (2017): 1048–82.

Jensen, Nathan. "Political Risks, Democratic Institutions, and Foreign Direct Investment." *Journal of Politics* 70, no. 4 (2008): 1040–52.

Jensen, Nathan, and Noel P. Johnston. "Political Risk, Reputation, and the Resource Curse." *Comparative Political Studies* 44, no. 6 (2011): 662–88.

Jernnäs, Maria, and Eva Lövbrand. "Accelerating Climate Action: The Politics of Nonstate Actor Engagement in the Paris Regime." *Global Environmental Politics* 22, no. 3 (2022): 38–58.

Jevrejeva, S., L. P. Jackson, Aslak Grinsted, Daniel Linke, and B. Marzeion. "Flood Damage Costs under the Sea Level Rise with Warming of 1.5 °C and 2 °C." *Environmental Research Letters* 13, no. 7 (2018): 074014.

Jiang, Han, Yadong Luo, Jun Xia, Michael Hitt, and Jia Shen. "Resource Dependence Theory in International Business: Progress and Prospects." *Global Strategy Journal* 13, no. 1 (2023): 3–57.

Jiang, Yangxueqing, Norbert Schwarz, Katherine J. Reynolds, and Eryn J. Newman. "Repetition Increases Belief in Climate-Skeptical Claims, Even for Climate Science Endorsers." *PLoS One* 19, no. 8 (2024): e0307294.

Joyner, Christopher C. *International Law in the Twenty-First Century: Rules for Global Governance*. Lanham, MD: Rowman and Littlefield, 2005.

Kahn, Matthew E. "Why the Cost of Climate Change Can't Be Boiled Down to One Right Number, Despite Some Economists' Best Attempts." *The Conversation*, January 19, 2022. https://theconversation.com/why-the-cost-of-climate-change-cant-be-boiled-down-to-one-right-number-despite-some-economists-best-attempts-176432.

Kalinowski, Thomas. "The Green Climate Fund and Private Sector Climate Finance in the Global South." *Climate Policy* 24, no. 3 (2024): 281–96.

Kang, Wei, and Qingfang Wang. "The Impact of COVID-19 on Small Businesses in the US: A Longitudinal Study from a Regional Perspective." *International Regional Science Review* 46, no. 3 (2023): 235–64.

Katitas, Aycan, and Sonal Pandya. "Investment Incentives Attract Foreign Direct Investment: Evidence from the Great Recession." *Public Choice* 200, nos. 1–2 (2024): 323–45.

Kawai, Norifumi, Roger Strange, and Antonella Zucchella. "Stakeholder Pressures, EMS Implementation, and Green Innovation in MNC Overseas Subsidiaries." *International Business Review* 27, no. 5 (2018): 933–46.

Keith, David. *A Case for Climate Engineering*. Cambridge, MA: MIT Press, 2013.

Kenner, Dario, and Richard Heede. "White Knights, or Horsemen of the Apocalypse? Prospects for Big Oil to Align Emissions with a 1.5°C Pathway." *Energy Research & Social Science* 79 (2021): 102049.

Keohane, Robert O., and David G. Victor. "Cooperation and Discord in Global Climate Policy." *Nature Climate Change* 6, no. 6 (2016): 570–75.

Kerber, Ross, and Arunima Kumar. "Top Exxon Directors Cruise to Re-Election Despite Activist Opposition." *Reuters*, May 29, 2024. https://reuters.com/markets/commodities/exxon-shareholders-re-elect-two-directors-targeted-by-activists-2024-05-29.

Kerin, Roger A., P. Rajan Varadarajan, and Robert A. Peterson. "First-Mover Advantage: A Synthesis, Conceptual Framework, and Research Propositions." *Journal of Marketing* 56, no. 4 (1992): 33–52.

Kim, Nahyun, Jon J. Moon, and Haitao Yin. "Environmental Pressure and the Performance of Foreign Firms in an Emerging Economy." *Journal of Business Ethics* 137, no. 3 (2016): 475–90.

"Do Foreign Firms Help Make Local Firms Greener? Evidence of Environmental Spillovers in China." *Journal of International Business Studies* 53, no. 7 (2022): 1370–93.

Kim, W. Chan, and Renée Mauborgne. *Blue Ocean Strategy*. Boston, MA: Harvard Business School Press, 2005.

Kimball, Spencer. "The Covid Pandemic Drives Pfizer's 2022 Revenue to a Record $100 Billion." *CNBC*, January 31, 2023. https://cnbc.com/2023/01/31/the-covid-pandemic-drives-pfizers-2022-revenue-to-a-record-100-billion.html.

"Saudi Aramco CEO Says Energy Transition Is Failing, World Should Abandon 'Fantasy' of Phasing Out Oil." *CNBC*, March 18, 2024. https://cnbc.com/2024/03/18/saudi-aramco-ceo-says-energy-transition-is-failing-give-up-fantasy-of-phasing-out-oil.html.

Kirk, Ashley. "Visualised: How All of G20 Is Missing Climate Goals – but Some Nations Are Closer than Others." *The Guardian*, December 7, 2023. https://theguardian.com/environment/2023/dec/07/visualised-how-all-of-g20-is-missing-climate-goals-but-some-nations-are-closer-than-others.

Klein, Maury. *A Call to Arms: Mobilizing America for World War II*. New York: Bloomsbury Press, 2013.

Konisky, David M. "Regulator Attitudes and the Environmental Race to the Bottom Argument." *Journal of Public Administration Research and Theory* 18, no. 2 (2008): 321–44.

Kono, Daniel Yuichi, and Gabriella R. Montinola. "Foreign Aid and Climate Change Policy: What Can('t) the Data Tell Us?" *Politics and Governance* 7, no. 2 (2019): 68–92.

Köppel, Martin, and Detlef F. Sprinz. "Do Binding Beat Nonbinding Agreements? Regulating International Water Quality." *Journal of Conflict Resolution* 63, no. 8 (2019): 1860–88.

Korbin, Stephen J. *Managing Political Risk Assessment: Strategic Response to Environmental Change*. Berkeley: University of California Press, 2022.

Kornprobst, Markus, and T. V. Paul. "Globalization, Deglobalization and the Liberal International Order." *International Affairs* 97, no. 5 (2021): 1305–16.

Kostova, Tatiana, Kendall Roth, and M. Tina Dacin. "Institutional Theory in the Study of Multinational Corporations: A Critique and New Directions." *The Academy of Management Review* 33, no. 4 (2008): 994–1006.

Kou, Mingting, Lin Zhang, Hongxia Wang, Yufei Wang, and Zitong Shan. "The Heterogeneous Impact of Green Public Procurement on Corporate Green Innovation." *Resources, Conservation and Recycling* 203 (2024): 107441.

Koubi, Vally. "Climate Change and Conflict." *Annual Review of Political Science* 22 (2019): 343–60.

Kouloukoui, Daniel, Marcia Mara de Oliviera Marinho, Sônia Maria da Silva Gomes, Asher Kiperstok, and Ednildo Andrade Torres. "Corporate

Climate Risk Management and the Implementation of Climate Projects by the World's Largest Emitters." *Journal of Cleaner Production* 238 (2019): 117935.

Kountouris, Yiannis, and Eleri Williams. "Do Protests Influence Environmental Attitudes? Evidence from Extinction Rebellion." *Environmental Research Communications* 5, no. 1 (2023): 011003.

Krauss, Clifford. "Exxon Aims to Cut Methane Leaks, a Culprit in Global Warming." *The New York Times*, September 25, 2017. https://nytimes.com/2017/09/25/business/energy-environment/exxon-methane-leaks.html.

Kravitz, Ben, and Tyler Felgenhauer. "Climate Engineering Carries Serious National Security Risks – Countries Facing Extreme Heat May Try It Anyway, and the World Needs to Be Prepared." *The Conversation*, February 29, 2024. https://theconversation.com/climate-engineering-carries-serious-national-security-risks-countries-facing-extreme-heat-may-try-it-anyway-and-the-world-needs-to-be-prepared-222120.

Kreibich, Nicolas, and Lukas Hermwille. "Caught in Between: Credibility and Feasibility of the Voluntary Carbon Market Post-2020." *Climate Policy* 21, no. 7 (2021): 939–57.

Krpec, Oldrich, and Vladan Hodulak. "War and International Trade: Impact of Trade Disruption on International Trade Patterns and Economic Development." *Brazilian Journal of Political Economy, Center of Political Economy* 39, no. 1 (2019): 152–72.

Kupzok, Nils, and Jonas Nahm. "The Decarbonization Bargain: How the Decarbonizable Sector Shapes Climate Politics." *Perspectives on Politics* 22, no. 4 (2024): 1203–23.

Kuyper, Jonathan W., Björn-Ola Linnér, and Heike Schroeder. "Non-State Actors in Hybrid Global Climate Governance: Justice, Legitimacy, and Effectiveness in a Post-Paris Era." *WIREs Climate Change* 9, no. 1 (2018): e497.

Kuzma, Samantha, Liz Saccoccia, and Marlena Chertock. "25 Countries, Housing One-quarter of the Population, Face Extremely High Water Stress." *World Resources Institute*, August 16, 2023. https://wri.org/insights/highest-water-stressed-countries.

Lah, T. J., Yeoul Park, and Yoon Jik Cho. "The Four Major Rivers Restoration Project of South Korea: An Assessment of Its Process, Program, and Political Dimensions." *The Journal of Environment & Development* 24, no. 4 (2015): 375–94.

Lamb, William F., Giulio Mattioli, Sebastian Levi, J. Timmons Roberts, Stuart Capstick, Felix Creutzig, Jan C. Minx, Fin Müller-Hansen, Trevor Culhane, and Julia K. Steinberger. "Discourses of Climate Delay." *Global Sustainability* 2 (2020): e17.

Lamboll, Robin D., Zebedee R. J. Nicholls, Christopher J. Smith, Jarmo S. Kikstra, Edward Byers, and Joeri Rogelj. "Assessing the Size and Uncertainty of Remaining Carbon Budgets." *Nature Climate Change* 13, no. 12 (2023): 1360–67.

LaMonaca, Sarah, and Lisa Ryan. "The State of Play in Electric Vehicle Charging Services – A Review of Infrastructure Provision, Players, and Policies." *Renewable and Sustainable Energy Reviews* 154 (2022): 111733.

Langbroek, Joram H. M., Joel P. Franklin, and Yusak O. Susilo. "The Effect of Policy Initiatives on Electric Vehicle Adoption." *Energy Policy* 94 (2016): 94–103.

Lange, Andreas, Carsten Vogt, and Andreas Ziegler. "On the Importance of Equity in International Climate Policy: An Empirical Analysis." *Energy Economics* 29, no. 3 (2007): 545–62.

Lantushenko, Viktoriya, and Carolin Schellhorn. "The Rising Risks of Fossil Fuel Lobbying." *Global Finance Journal* 56 (2023): 100829.

Lawrence, Peter, and Daryl Wong. "Soft Law in the Paris Climate Agreement: Strength or Weakness?" *Review of European, Comparative & International Environmental Law* 26, no. 3 (2017): 276–86.

Lea, Emma, and Anthony Worsley. "Australian Consumers' Food-Related Environmental Beliefs and Behaviors." *Appetite* 50, nos. 2–3 (2008): 207–14.

Ledger, Ellen, and Carola Klöck. "Climate Justice through Climate Finance? Australia's Approach to Climate Finance in the Pacific." *npj Climate Action* 2 (2023): Article Number 19.

Lee, Hyun-hoon, and Donghyun Park. *Post-Covid Asia: Deglobalization, Fourth Industrial Revolution, and Sustainable Development*. Singapore: World Scientific Publishing Company, 2020.

Lee, Jin, Michael Ehst, Xue Zheng, and Martin Theuri. *The Kenya Climate Innovation Center: How It Operates and Lessons for Clean Technology Incubation*. Climate Technology Program Brief no. 2. Washington, DC: World Bank Group, 2016.

Lee, Leemen, and Li-Fei Chen. "Boosting Employee Retention Through CSR: A Configurational Analysis." *Corporate Social Responsibility and Environmental Management* 25, no. 5 (2018): 948–60.

Lee, Tien Ming, Ezra M. Markowitz, Peter D. Howe, Chia-Ying Ko, and Anthony A. Leiserowitz. "Predictors of Public Climate Change Awareness and Risk Perception around the World." *Nature Climate Change* 5, no. 11 (2015): 1014–20.

Lehmann, Martin. "Government-Business Relationships through Partnerships for Sustainable Development: The Green Network in Denmark." *Journal of Environmental Policy & Planning* 8, no. 3 (2006): 235–57.

Lejano, Raul P., and Shondel J. Nero. *The Power of Narrative: Climate Skepticism and the Deconstruction of Science*. Cambridge: Cambridge University Press, 2020.

Lesińska, Magdalena. "The European Backlash Against Immigration and Multiculturalism." *Journal of Sociology* 50, no. 1 (2014): 37–50.

Lewis, Joanna I. *Green Innovation in China: China's Wind Power Industry and the Global Transition to a Low-Carbon Economy*. New York: Columbia University Press, 2013.

Li, Mei, Gregory Trencher, and Jusen Asuka. "The Clean Energy Claims of BP, Chevron, ExxonMobil and Shell: A Mismatch between Discourse, Actions and Investments." *PLoS One* 17, no. 2 (2022): e0263596.

Li, Quan, and Rafael Reuveny. "Democracy and Environmental Degradation." *International Studies Quarterly* 50, no. 4 (2006): 935–56.

Li, Shuping, Jing Meng, Klaus Hubacek, Shaikh M. S. U. Eskander, Yuan Li, Peipei Chen, and Dabo Guan. "Revisiting Copenhagen Climate Mitigation Targets." *Nature Climate Change* 14, no. 5 (2024): 468–75.

Li, Yifei, and Judith Shapiro. *China Goes Green: Coercive Environmentalism for a Troubled Planet*. Cambridge, UK: Polity Press, 2020.

Li, Yina, Fei Ye, Chwen Sheu, and Qian Yang. "Linking Green Market Orientation and Performance: Antecedents and Processes." *Journal of Cleaner Production* 192 (2018): 924–31.

Liang, Xinyu, Shaojun Zhang, Ye Wu, Jia Xing, Xiaoyi He, K. Max Zhang, Shuxiao Wang, and Jiming Hao. "Air Quality and Health Benefits from Fleet Electrification in China." *Nature Sustainability* 2, no. 10 (2019): 962–71.

Lien, Lasse, and Bram Timmermans. "Crisis-Induced Innovation and Crisis-Induced Innovators." *Industry and Innovation* 31, no. 2 (2024): 183–217.

Lienert, Paul, and Joseph White. "Tesla's Rivals Scrap for Thin Slices of US EV Sales." *Reuters*, September 27, 2023. https://reuters.com/business/autos-transportation/teslas-rivals-scrap-thin-slices-us-ev-sales-2023-09-27.

Lin, Chieh-Yu, and Yi-Hui Ho. "Determinants of Green Practice Adoption for Logistics Companies in China." *Journal of Business Ethics* 98, no. 1 (2011): 67–83.

Lin, H. "Government–Business Partnerships for Radical Eco-Innovation." *Business & Society* 58, no. 3 (2019): 533–73.

Lin, Jing, Xiyang Cao, Xiaoqi Dong, and Yunbi An. "Environmental Regulations, Supply Chain Relationships, and Green Technological Innovation." *Journal of Corporate Finance* 88 (2024): 102645.

Lin, K.-C. "Protecting the Petroleum Industry: Renewed Government Aid to Fossil Fuel Producers." *Business and Politics* 16, no. 4 (2014): 549–78.

Lindsey, Rebecca, and Luann Dahlman. "Climate Change: Global Temperature." *National Oceanic and Atmospheric Administration*, January 12, 2024. https://climate.gov/news-features/understanding-climate/climate-change-global-temperature.

Link, Sharon, and Eitan Naveh. "Standardization and Discretion: Does the Environmental Standard ISO 14001 Lead to Performance Benefits?" *IEEE Transactions on Engineering Management* 35, no. 4 (2006): 508–19.

Liu, Yan, Xian Cheng, Stephen Shaoyi Liao, and Feng Yang. "The Impact of COVID-19 on the Tourism and Hospitality Industry: Evidence from International Stock Markets." *The North American Journal of Economics and Finance* 64 (2023): 101875.

Liu, Yipeng, Jong Min Lee, and Celia Lee. "The Challenges and Opportunities of a Global Health Crisis: The Management and Business Implications of COVID-19 from an Asian Perspective." *Asian Business & Management* 19, no. 3 (2020): 277–97.

Lockwood, Ben, and Matthew Lockwood. "How Do Right-Wing Populist Parties Influence Climate and Renewable Energy Policies? Evidence from OECD Countries." *Global Environmental Politics* 22, no. 3 (2022): 12–37.

Löfstedt, Ragnar E., and David Vogel. "The Changing Character of Regulation: A Comparison of Europe and the United States." *Risk Analysis* 21, no. 3 (2001): 399–416.

Long, Zoe, John Axsen, Inger Miller, and Christine Kormos. "What Does Tesla Mean for Car Buyers? Exploring the Role of Automotive Brand in Perceptions of Battery Electric Vehicles." *Transportation Research Part A: Policy and Practice* 125 (2019): 185–204.

Lopéz, Luis-Antonio, María-Ángeles Cadarso, Jorge Zafrilla, and Guadalupe Arce. "The Carbon Footprint of the U.S. Multinationals' Foreign Affiliates." *Nature Communications* 10 (2019): 1672.

López, Ramón, and Siddhartha Mitra. "Corruption, Pollution, and the Kuznets Environment Curve." *Journal of Environmental Economics and Management* 40, no. 2 (2000): 137–50.

Ma, Ting, and Yue Wang. "Globalization and Environment: Effects of International Trade on Emission Intensity Reduction of Pollutants Causing Global and Local Concerns." *Journal of Environmental Management* 297 (2021): 113249.

Maamoun, Nada. "The Kyoto Protocol: Empirical Evidence of a Hidden Success." *Journal of Environmental Economics and Management* 95 (2019): 227–56.

Macdonald, Kate. "The Socially Embedded Corporation." In *The Handbook of Global Companies*, edited by John Mikler, 371–87. Chichester, UK: John Wiley and Sons, 2013.

Macellari, Margherita, Alexander Yuriev, Francesco Testa, and Olivier Boiral. "Exploring Bluewashing Practices of Alleged Sustainability Leaders through a Counter-Accounting Analysis." *Environmental Impact Assessment Review* 86 (2021): 106489.

Madhok, Anoop. "Globalization, De-Globalization, and Re-Globalization: Some Historical Context and the Impact of the COVID Pandemic." *BRQ Business Research Quarterly* 24, no. 3 (2021): 199–203.

Madsen, Peter M. "Does Corporate Investment Drive a 'Race to the Bottom' in Environmental Protection? A Reexamination of the Effect of Environmental Regulation on Investment." *Academy of Management Journal* 52, no. 6 (2009): 1297–1318.

Magbool, Mohamad Abu Huzaifah bin, Azlan Amran, Mehran Nejati, and Krishnaswamy Jayaraman. "Corporate Sustainable Business Practices and Talent Attraction." *Sustainability Accounting, Management and Policy Journal* 7, no. 4 (2016): 539–59.

Mahdavi, Paasha, Cesar B. Martinez-Alvarez, and Michael L. Ross. "Why Do Governments Tax or Subsidize Fossil Fuels?" *The Journal of Politics* 84, no. 4 (2022): 2123–39.

Maibach, Edward, Teresa Myers, and Anthony Leiserowitz. "Climate Scientists Need to Set the Record Straight: There Is a Scientific Consensus That Human-Caused Climate Change Is Happening." *Earth's Future* 2, no. 5 (2014): 295–98.

Maizland, Lindsay. "Global Climate Agreements: Successes and Failures." *Council on Foreign Relations*, 2023. https://cfr.org/backgrounder/paris-global-climate-change-agreements.

Malcolm, Jay R., Canran Liu, Ronald P. Neilson, Lara Hansen, and Lee Hannah. "Global Warming and Extinctions of Endemic Species from Biodiversity Hotspots." *Conservation Biology* 20, no. 2 (2006): 538–48.

Malpede, Maurizio, and Marco Percoco. "Climate, Desertification, and Local Human Development: Evidence from 1564 Regions around the World." *The Annals of Regional Science* 72, no. 2 (2024): 377–405.

Mannion, Peter, Emma Parry, Mark Patel, Erik Ringvold, and Jonathan Scott. "Carbon Removals: How to Scale a New Gigaton Industry." *McKinsey & Company*, 2023. https://mckinsey.com/capabilities/sustainability/our-insights/carbon-removals-how-to-scale-a-new-gigaton-industry.

Marchiori, Carmen, Simon Dietz, and Alessandro Tavoni. "Domestic Politics and the Formation of International Environmental Agreements." *Journal of Environmental Economics and Management* 81 (2017): 115–31.

Marchiori, Luca, and Igmar Schumacher. "When Nature Rebels: International Migration, Climate Change, and Inequality." *Journal of Population Economics* 24, no. 2 (2011): 569–600.

Mares, Dennis. "Climate Change and Crime: Monthly Temperature and Precipitation Anomalies and Crime Rates in St. Louis, MO, 1990–2009." *Crime, Law and Social Change* 59, no. 2 (2013): 185–208.

Mares, Dennis, and Kenneth W. Moffett. "Climate Change and Interpersonal Violence: A 'Global' Estimate and Regional Inequalities." *Climatic Change* 135, no. 2 (2016): 297–310.

Marglin, Stephen A., and Juliet B. Schor, eds. *The Golden Age of Capitalism: Reinterpreting the Postwar Experience*. Oxford: Oxford University Press, 1992.

Marks, Danny. "China's Climate Change Policy Process: Improved but Still Weak and Fragmented." *Journal of Contemporary China* 19, no. 67 (2010): 971–86.

Marsh, Alastair, and Will Mathis. "Europe's Biggest Oil Company Quietly Shelves a Radical Plan to Shrink Its Carbon Footprint." *Bloomberg*, August 31, 2023. https://bloomberg.com/news/features/2023-08-31/shell-silently-abandoned-its-100-million-a-year-plan-to-offset-co2-emissions.

Marshall, Monty G., and Ted Robert Gurr. *POLITY™ IV Project: Political Regime Characteristics and Transitions, 1800–2018 Dataset Users' Manual*. 1st ed. Vienna: Centre for Systemic Peace, 2020.

Martin, Jamie. "The Global Crisis of Commodity Glut during the Second World War." *The International History Review* 43, no. 6 (2021): 1273–90.

Martin, Matthew, and Anthony Di Paola. "Aramco Plans to Produce Synthetic Fuels by 2025 at Test Plants." *Bloomberg*, October 25, 2023. https://bloomberg.com/news/articles/2023-10-25/aramco-plans-to-produce-synthetic-fuels-by-2025-at-test-plants.

Matthews, Christopher M., and Collin Eaton. "Inside Exxon's Strategy to Downplay Climate Change." *The Wall Street Journal*, 2023. https://wsj.com/business/energy-oil/exxon-climate-change-documents-e2e9e6af.

McBeath, Jerry A. *Big Oil in the United States: Industry Influence on Institutions, Policy, and Politics*. New York: Bloomsbury Publishing USA, 2016.

McCulloch, Neil, Davide Natalini, Naomi Hossain, and Patricia Justino. "An Exploration of the Association between Fuel Subsidies and Fuel Riots." *World Development* 157 (2022): 105935.

McFarlane, Sarah. "One Oil Company's Rocky Path to Renewable Energy." *The Wall Street Journal*, June 21, 2021. https://wsj.com/articles/one-oil-companys-rocky-path-to-renewable-energy-orsted-11623170953.

McGillvray, Glenn. "The COVID-19 Pandemic Has Revealed That Global Supply Chains Are a Huge House of Cards." *The Conversation*, June 21, 2021. https://theconversation.com/the-covid-19-pandemic-has-revealed-that-global-supply-chains-are-a-huge-house-of-cards-164821.

McGreal, Chris. "Revealed: 60% of Americans Say Oil Firms Are to Blame for the Climate Crisis." *The Guardian*, October 26, 2021. https://theguardian.com/environment/2021/oct/26/climate-change-poll-oil-gas-companies-environment.

McGuire, William, Ellen Alexandra Holtmaat, and Aseem Prakash. "Penalties for Industrial Accidents: The Impact of the Deepwater Horizon Accident on BP's Reputation and Stock Market Returns." *PLoS One* 17, no. 6 (2022): e0268743.

McMichael, Anthony J., Rosalie E. Woodruff, and Simon Hales. "Climate Change and Human Health: Present and Future Risks." *The Lancet* 367, no. 9513 (2006): 11–17.

Mendelsohn, Robert, Ariel Dinar, and Larry Williams. "The Distributional Impact of Climate Change on Rich and Poor Countries." *Environment and Development Economics* 11, no. 2 (2006): 159–78.

Mengel, Matthias, Anders Levermann, Katja Frieler, Alexander Robinson, Ben Marzeion, and Ricarda Winkelmann. "Future Sea Level Rise Constrained by Observations and Long-Term Commitment." *Proceedings of the National Academy of Sciences of the United States of America* 113, no. 10 (2016): 2597–2606.

Mertz, Ole, Kristen Halsnæs, Jørgen E. Olesen, and Kjeld Rasmussen. "Adaptation to Climate Change in Developing Countries." *Environmental Management* 43, no. 5 (2009): 743–52.

Midlarsky, Manus I. "Democracy and the Environment: An Empirical Assessment." *Journal of Peace Research* 35, no. 3 (1998): 341–61.

Miller, Kenneth P. *Texas vs. California: A History of Their Struggle for the Future of America*. Oxford: Oxford University Press, 2020.

Milman, Oliver. "'No Safe Place': Kiribati Seeks Donors to Raise Islands from Encroaching Seas." *The Guardian*, November 18, 2022. https://theguardian.com/environment/2022/nov/18/cop27-kiribati-donors-raise-islands-sea-level-rise.

Milman, Oliver, Andrew Witherspoon, Rita Liu, and Alvin Chang. "The Climate Disaster Is Here." *The Guardian*, October 14, 2021. https://theguardian.com/environment/ng-interactive/2021/oct/14/climate-change-happening-now-stats-graphs-maps-cop26.

Milner, Helen V. "The Political Economy of International Trade." *Annual Review of Political Science* 2 (1999): 91–114.

Minas, Stephen. "The Paris Agreement's Technology Framework and the Need for 'Transformational Change.'" *Carbon & Climate Law Review* 14, no. 4 (2020): 241–54.

Mitchell, Ronald B., Liliana B. Andonova, Mark Axelrod, Jörg Balsiger, Thomas Bernauer, Jessica F. Green, James Hollway, Rakhyun E. Kim, and Jean-Frédéric Morin. "What We Know (and Could Know) About International Environmental Agreements." *Global Environmental Politics* 20, no. 1 (2020): 103–21.

Monbiot, George. "Carbon Offsetting Is Not Warding Off Environmental Collapse – It's Accelerating It." *The Guardian*, January 26, 2022. https://theguardian.com/commentisfree/2022/jan/26/carbon-offsetting-environmental-collapse-carbon-land-grab.

Muñoz, John, Susan Olzak, and Sarah A. Soule. "Going Green: Environmental Protest, Policy, and CO_2 Emissions in U.S. States, 1990–2007." *Sociological Forum* 33, no. 2 (2018): 403–21.

Mortimer, Gary. "Climate Explained: Are Consumers Willing to Pay More for Climate-Friendly Products?" *The Conversation*, September 14, 2020. https://theconversation.com/climate-explained-are-consumers-willing-to-pay-more-for-climate-friendly-products-146757.

Moses, Elizabeth, Beatriz Cardenas, and Jessica Seddon. "The Most Successful Air Pollution Treaty You've Never Heard Of." *World Resources Institute*, September 16, 2020. https://wri.org/insights/most-successful-air-pollution-treaty-youve-never-heard.

Moullier, Thomas, and Keiko Sakoda. Building Regulation for Resilience: Converting Disaster Experience into a Safer Built Environment – The Case of Japan. World Bank Group Working Paper, 2018.

Moyo, Dambisa. *Dead Aid: Why Aid Is Not Working and How There Is a Better Way for Africa*. London: Penguin Books, 2009.

"Are Businesses Ready for Deglobalization?" *Harvard Business Review*, December 2019. https://hbr.org/2019/12/are-businesses-ready-for-deglobalization.

Msiska, Moses, Alex Ng, and Randall K. Kimmel. "Doing Well by Doing Good with the Performance of United Nations Global Compact Climate Change Champions." *Humanities and Social Sciences Communications* 8 (2021): 321.

Mundaca, Luis, Diana Ürge-Vorsatz, and Charlie Wilson. "Demand-Side Approaches for Limiting Global Warming to 1.5 °C." *Energy Efficiency* 12, no. 2 (2019): 343–62.

Mutambatsere, Emelly, and Philip Schellekens. The Why and How of Blended Finance. International Finance Corporation Discussion Paper, 2020.

Myslikova, Zdenka, and Kelly Sims Gallagher. "Mission Innovation Is Mission Critical." *Nature Energy* 5, no. 10 (2020): 732–34.

Nachmany, Michal, and Joana Setzer. *Global Trends in Climate Change Legislation and Litigation: 2018 Snapshot*. London: London School of Economics and Political Science, Grantham Research Institute on Climate Change and the Environment, 2018. https://lse.ac.uk/granthaminstitute/publication/global-trends-in-climate-change-legislation-and-litigation-2018-snapshot.

Nachmany, Michal, Rebecca Byrnes, and Swenja Surminski. *National Laws and Policies on Climate Change Adaptation: A Global Review*. London: Grantham Research Institute on Climate Change and the Environment and Centre for Climate Change Economics and Policy, 2019.

Najibi, Nasser, and Naresh Devineni. "Recent Trends in the Frequency and Duration of Global Floods." *Earth System Dynamics* 9, no. 2 (2018): 757–83.

National Research Council, Division on Earth and Life Studies, Board on Atmospheric Sciences and Climate, Ocean Studies Board, and Committee on Geoengineering Climate: Technical Evaluation and Discussion of Impacts. *Climate Intervention: Reflecting Sunlight to Cool Earth*. Washington, DC: The National Academies Press, 2015.

Nébié, Elisabeth Kago Ilboudo, Diaba Ba, and Alessandra Giannini. "Food Security and Climate Shocks in Senegal: Who and Where Are the Most Vulnerable Households?" *Global Food Security* 29 (2021): 100513.

Nelson, Eshe. "Big Banks Quit Climate Change Groups Ahead of Trump's Term." *The New York Times*, January 20, 2025. https://nytimes.com/2025/01/20/business/trump-climate-action-banks.html.

Neumayer, Eric, and Laura Spess. "Do Bilateral Investment Treaties Increase Foreign Direct Investment to Developing Countries?" *World Development* 33, no. 10 (2005): 1567–85.

Newman, Rebecca, and Ilan Noy. "The Global Costs of Extreme Weather That Are Attributable to Climate Change." *Nature Communications* 14 (2023): Article 6103.

Ngobo, Paul Valentin, and Maurice Fouda. "Is 'Good' Governance Good for Business? A Cross-National Analysis of Firms in African Countries." *Journal of World Business* 47, no. 3 (2012): 435–49.

Nichols, Mary. "Governors Are Leading the Fight against Climate Change and Deforestation around the World, Filling a Void Left by Presidents." *The Conversation*, January 22, 2025. https://theconversation.com/governors-are-leading-the-fight-against-climate-change-and-deforestation-around-the-world-filling-a-void-left-by-presidents-256988.

Nichols, Will, and Rory Clisby. "40% of Oil and Gas Reserves Threatened by Climate Change." *Verisk Maplecroft*, May 13, 2021. https://maplecroft.com/insights/analysis/40-of-oil-and-gas-reserves-threatened-by-climate-change.

Nieman, Mark David, and Cameron G. Thies. "Property Rights Regimes, Technological Innovation, and Foreign Direct Investment." *Political Science Research and Methods* 7, no. 3 (2019): 451–469.

Ning, Lutao, and Fan Wang. "Does FDI Bring Environmental Knowledge Spillovers to Developing Countries? The Role of the Local Industrial Structure." *Environmental and Resource Economics* 71, no. 2 (2018): 381–405.

Niranjan, Ajit. "Revealed: US Airlines Lobbied EU Over Its Plan to Monitor Plane Emissions." *The Guardian*, August 28, 2024a. https://theguardian.com/environment/article/2024/aug/28/revealed-us-airlines-lobbied-eu-over-its-plan-to-monitor-plane-emissions.

"Climate Hero or Villain? Fossil Fuel Frenzy Challenges Norway's Green Image." *The Guardian*, July 26, 2024b. https://theguardian.com/environment/article/2024/jul/26/climate-hero-villain-fossil-fuel-frenzy-challenges-norway-green-image.

Noor, Dharna. "Over 1,700 Coal, Oil and Gas Lobbyists Granted Access to COP29, Says Report." *The Guardian*, November 15, 2024. https://theguardian.com/environment/2024/nov/15/coal-oil-and-gas-lobbyists-granted-access-to-cop29-says-report.

Noor, Dharna, and Damian Carrington. "COP29 Climate Finance Deal Criticized as 'Travesty of Justice' and 'Stage-Managed.'" *The Guardian*, November 24, 2024. https://theguardian.com/environment/2024/nov/24/cop29-climate-finance-deal-criticised-travesty-justice-stage-managed.

Norman, Wayne, and Chris MacDonald. "Getting to the Bottom of 'Triple Bottom Line.'" *Business Ethics Quarterly* 14, no. 2 (2004): 243–62.

Nuhu, Steven Kuba, Zainuddin Abdul Manan, Sharifah Rafidah Wan Alwi, and Mohd Nadzri Md Reba. "Roles of Geospatial Technology in Eco-Industrial Park Site Selection: State-of-the-Art Review." *Journal of Cleaner Production* 309 (2021): 127361.

Nunnenkamp, Peter, and Julius Spatz. "Intellectual Property Rights and Foreign Direct Investment: A Disaggregated Analysis." *Review of World Economics* 140, no. 3 (2004): 393–414.

Oberhaus, Daniel. "Amazon, Google, Microsoft: Here's Who Has the Greenest Cloud." *Wired*, September 17, 2019. https://wired.com/story/amazon-google-microsoft-green-clouds-and-hyperscale-data-centers.

Oberthür, Sebastian, and Claire Dupont. "The European Union's International Climate Leadership: Towards a Grand Climate Strategy?" *Journal of European Public Policy* 28, no. 7 (2021): 1095–1114.

Oberthür, Sebastian, and Claire Roche Kelly. "EU Leadership in International Climate Policy: Achievements and Challenges." *The International Spectator* 43, no. 3 (2008): 35–50.

Oh, Chaewoon, and Shunji Matsuoka. "The Genesis and End of Institutional Fragmentation in Global Governance on Climate Change from a Constructivist Perspective." *International Environmental Agreements: Politics, Law and Economics* 17, no. 2 (2017): 143–59.

Ojea, Sabela. "Aramco to Acquire 50% Stake in Air Products' Blue Hydrogen Industrial Gases." *MarketWatch*, April 29, 2024. https://marketwatch.com/story/aramco-to-acquire-50-stake-in-air-products-blue-hydrogen-industrial-gases-68e8f717.

Okafor, Luke Emeka, M. Kabir Hassan, Mamunur Rashid, Darniya Prabu, and Ahmad Sabit. "Risk Dimensions, Risk Clusters, and Foreign Direct Investments in Developing Countries." *International Review of Economics & Finance* 82 (2022): 636–49.

Olney, W. W. "A Race to the Bottom? Employment Protection and Foreign Direct Investment." *Journal of International Economics* 91, no. 2 (2013): 191–203.

Omelicheva, Mariya Y. "Natural Disasters: Triggers of Political Instability?" *International Interactions* 37, no. 4 (2011): 441–65.

Onoz, Ergun, and Claudio Giachetti. "Will Rivals Enter or Wait Outside When Faced with Litigation Risk? Patent Litigation in Complex Product Industries and International Market Entry." *Strategic Organization* 21, no. 2 (2023): 339–79.

Ordóñez, D. F., C. Ganzer, T. Halfdanarson, A. G. Garay, P. Patrizio, A. Bardow, G. Guillén-Gosálbez, N. Shah, and N. Mac Dowell. "Quantifying Global Costs of Reliable Green Hydrogen." *Energy Advances* 2, no. 12 (2023): 2042–54.

Orzes, Guido, Antonella Maria Moretto, Mattia Moro, Matteo Rossi, Marco Sartor, Federico Caniato, and Guido Nassimbeni. "The Impact of the United Nations Global Compact on Firm Performance: A Longitudinal Analysis." *International Journal of Production Economics* 227 (2020): 107664.

Otto, Friederike E. L. "Attribution of Extreme Events to Climate Change." *Annual Review of Environment and Resources* 48 (2023): 813–28.

Otto, Friederike E. L., Mariam Zachariah, Fahad Saeed, Ayesha Siddiqi, Kamil Shahzad, Haris Mushtaq, T. Arulalan, Krishna AchutaRao, S. T. Chaithra, Clair Barnes, Sjoukje Philip, Sarah Kew, Robert Vautard, Gerbrand Koren, Izidine Pinto, Piotr Wolski, Maja Vahlberg, Roop Singh, Julie Arrighi, Maarten van Aalst, Lisa Thalheimer, Emmanuel Raju, Sihan Li, Wenchang Yang, Luke J. Harrington, and Ben Clarke. *Climate Change Likely Increased Extreme Monsoon Rainfall, Flooding Highly Vulnerable Communities in Pakistan*. World Weather Attribution, 2022. https://worldweatherattribution.org/wp-content/uploads/Pakistan-floods-scientific-report.pdf.

Ourbak, Timothée, and Alexandre K. Magnan. "The Paris Agreement and Climate Change Negotiations: Small Islands, Big Players." *Regional Environmental Change* 18, no. 8 (2018): 2201–07.

Overfelt, Maggie. "As The North Face Battles Patagonia in Outdoors Market, It Bets Tackling Climate Change Will Pay Off." *CNBC*, August 14, 2020. https://cnbc.com/2020/08/14/as-north-face-battles-patagonia-it-bets-climate-change-will-pay-off.html.

Ozanne, Lucie K., Marcus Phipps, Todd Weaver, Michal Carrington, Michael Luchs, Jesse Catlin, Shirpa Gupta, Nicholas Santos, Kristin Scott, and Jerome Williams. "Managing the Tensions at the Intersection of the Triple Bottom Line: A Paradox Theory Approach to Sustainability Management." *Journal of Public Policy & Marketing* 35, no. 2 (2016): 249–61.

Pack, Howard, and Janet Rothenberg Pack. "Foreign Aid and the Question of Fungibility." *The Review of Economics and Statistics* 75, no. 2 (1993): 258–65.

Paglialunga, Elena, Andrea Coveri, and Antonello Zanfei. "Climate Change and Within-Country Inequality: New Evidence from a Global Perspective." *World Development* 159 (2022): 106030.

Pallanich, Jennifer. "Northern Lights Ready for First CO_2 in 2025." *Journal of Petroleum Technology*, February 21, 2024. https://jpt.spe.org/northern-lights-ready-for-first-co2-in-2025.

Pandve, Harshal T. "India's National Action Plan on Climate Change." *Indian Journal of Occupational & Environmental Medicine* 13, no. 1 (2009): 17–19.

Pandya, Sonal S. "Political Economy of Foreign Direct Investment: Globalized Production in the Twenty-First Century." *Annual Review of Political Science* 19 (2016): 455–75.

Park, Chan Young, Wooyong Jung, and Seung H. Han. "Risk Perception Gaps Between Construction Investors and Financial Investors of International Public–Private Partnership (PPP) Projects." *Sustainability* 12, no. 21 (2020): 9003.

Park, Hung-Suck, Eldon R. Rene, Soo-Mi Choi, and Anthony S. F. Chiu. "Strategies for Sustainable Development of Industrial Park in Ulsan, South Korea – From Spontaneous Evolution to Systematic Expansion of Industrial Symbiosis." *Journal of Environmental Management* 87, no. 1 (2008): 1–13.

Park, Susan. "Environmental Great Powers and Multilateral Environmental Agreements." In *Great Powers, Climate Change, and Global Environmental Responsibilities*, edited by Robert Falkner and Barry Buzan, 227–48. Oxford: Oxford University Press, 2022.

Parker, Charles F., Christer Karlsson, and Mattias Hjerpe. "Assessing the European Union's Global Climate Change Leadership: From

Copenhagen to the Paris Agreement." *Journal of European Integration* 39, no. 2 (2017): 239–52.

Pascual, Unai, Eneko Garmendia, Jacob Phelps, and Elena Ojea. "Opportunities and Conditions for Successful Foreign Aid to the Forestry Sector." In *Aid Effectiveness for Environmental Sustainability*, edited by Yongfu Huang and Unai Pascual, 257–305. Singapore: Palgrave Macmillan, 2018.

Pasztor, Janos, Cynthia Scharf, and Kai-Uwe Barani Schmidt. "Solar Geoengineering Is Coming. It's Time to Regulate It." *Foreign Policy*, May 23, 2023. https://foreignpolicy.com/2023/05/23/solar-geoengineering-radiation-modification-srm-regulation-climate-change.

Paul, Harpreet Kaur. "Climate Finance: Rich Countries Aren't Meeting Aid Targets – Could Legal Action Force Them?" *The Conversation*, October 26, 2021. https://theconversation.com/climate-finance-rich-countries-arent-meeting-aid-targets-could-legal-action-force-them-169069.

Patz, Jonathan A., Diarmid Campbell-Lendrum, Tracey Holloway, and Jonathan A. Foley. "Impact of Regional Climate Change on Human Health." *Nature* 438, no. 7066 (2005): 310–17.

Pepermans, Guido. "European Energy Market Liberalization: Experiences and Challenges." *International Journal of Economic Policy Studies* 13, no. 3 (2019): 3–26.

Perkins, Richard, and Eric Neumayer. "Implementing Multilateral Environmental Agreements: An Analysis of EU Directives." *Global Environmental Politics* 7, no. 3 (2007): 13–41.

"Does the 'California Effect' Operate Across Borders? Trading- and Investing-Up in Automobile Emission Standards." *Journal of European Public Policy* 19, no. 2 (2012): 217–37.

Pfeffer, Jeffrey, and Gerald R. Salancik. *The External Control of Organizations: A Resource Dependence Perspective*. New York: Harper and Row, 1978.

The External Control of Organizations: A Resource Dependence Perspective. 2nd ed. Stanford: Stanford Business Books, 2003.

Pianezzi, Daniela, Yuji Mori, and Shahzad Uddin. "Public-Private Partnerships in a Smart City: A Curious Case in Japan." *International Review of Administrative Sciences* 89, no. 3 (2023): 632–47.

Pinkse, Jonatan, and Ans Kolk. "Multinational Enterprises and Climate Change: Exploring Institutional Failures and Embeddedness." *Journal of International Business Studies* 43, no. 3 (2012): 332–41.

Pokhrel, Yadu, Farshid Felfelani, Yusuke Satoh, Julien Boulange, Peter Burek, Anne Gädeke, Dieter Gerten, Simon N. Gosling, Manolis Grillakis, Lukas Gudmundsson, Naota Hanasaki, Hyungjun Kim,

Aristeidis Koutroulis, Junguo Liu, Lamprini Papadimitriou, Jacob Schewe, Hannes Müller Schmied, Tobias Stacke, Camelia-Eliza Telteu, Wim Thiery, Ted Veldkamp, Fang Zhao, and Yoshihide Wada. "Global Terrestrial Water Storage and Drought Severity Under Climate Change." *Nature Climate Change* 11, no. 3 (2021): 226–33.

Porter, Gareth. "Trade Competition and Pollution Standards: 'Race to the Bottom' or 'Stuck at the Bottom'?" *The Journal of Environment & Development* 8, no. 2 (1999): 133–51.

Potoski, Matthew, and Aseem Prakash. "Green Clubs and Voluntary Governance: ISO 14001 and Firms' Regulatory Compliance." *American Journal of Political Science* 49, no. 2 (2005): 235–48.

Povitkina, Marina. Democracy, Bureaucratic Capacity and Environmental Performance. Quality of Government Institute Working Paper, 2015.

Powis, Carter M., David Byrne, Zachary Zobel, Kelly N. Gassert, A. C. Lute, and Christopher R. Schwalm. "Observational and Model Evidence Together Support Widespread Exposure to Noncompensable Heat under Continued Global Warming." *Science Advances* 9, no. 36 (2023): eadg9297.

Prakash, Aseem, and Matthew Potoski. "Racing to the Bottom? Trade, Environmental Governance, and ISO 14001." *American Journal of Political Science* 50, no. 2 (2006): 350–64.

"Investing Up: FDI and the Cross-Country Diffusion of ISO 14001 Management Systems." *International Studies Quarterly* 51, no. 3 (2007): 723–44.

"The EU Effect: Does Trade with the EU Reduce CO_2 Emissions in the Developing World?" *Environmental Politics* 26, no. 1 (2017): 27–48.

Prakash, Prarthana. "Danish Wind Giant Ørsted Replaces CEO with Shares Down 85% and Trump Pressures Looming." *Fortune*, January 31, 2025. https://fortune.com/europe/2025/01/31/wind-energy-orsted-replaces-ceo-donald-trump.

Preston, Brian J. "The Influence of the Paris Agreement on Climate Litigation: Causation, Corporate Governance and Catalyst (Part II)." *Journal of Environmental Law* 33, no. 2 (2021): 227–56.

Promchote, Parichart, S.-Y. Simon Wang, and Paul G. Johnson. "The 2011 Great Flood in Thailand: Climate Diagnostics and Implications from Climate Change." *Journal of Climate* 29, no. 1 (2016): 367–79.

Puller, Steven L. "The Strategic Use of Innovation to Influence Regulatory Standards." *Journal of Environmental Economics and Management* 52, no. 3 (2006): 690–706.

Qian, Nancy. "Making Progress on Foreign Aid." *Annual Review of Economics* 7 (2015): 277–308.

Quell, Molly. "Landmark Climate Change Case Opens at Top U.N. Court as Island Nations Fear Rising Seas." *Los Angeles Times*, December 2,

2024. https://latimes.com/world-nation/story/2024-12-02/landmark-climate-change-case-opens-at-the-top-un-court-as-island-nations-fear-rising-seas.

Quinson, Tim, and Kevin Crowley. "Exxon Feels the Heat as More Investors Assail Climate Conduct." *Bloomberg*, May 15, 2024. https://bloomberg.com/news/articles/2024-05-15/exxon-feels-the-heat-as-more-investors-assail-its-climate-conduct.

Rainforest Action Network, BankTrack, Indigenous Environmental Network, Oil Change International, Reclaim Finance, and Sierra Club. *Banking on Climate Change: Fossil Fuel Finance Report 2020*. 2020.

Raiser, Kilian, Henriette Naims, and Thomas Bruhn. "Corporatization of the Climate? Innovation, Intellectual Property Rights, and Patents for Climate Change Mitigation." *Energy Research & Social Science* 27 (2017): 1–8.

Ram, Rati, and Kevin Honglin Zhang. "Foreign Direct Investment and Economic Growth: Evidence from Cross-Country Data for the 1990s." *Economic Development and Cultural Change* 51, no. 1 (2002): 205–15.

Ran, Ran. "Perverse Incentive Structure and Policy Implementation Gap in China's Local Environmental Politics." *Journal of Environmental Policy & Planning* 15, no. 1 (2013): 17–39.

Rasul, Mohammad, M. A. Hazrat, Md Abdus Sattar, and M. I. Jahirul. "The Future of Hydrogen: Challenges on Production, Storage and Applications." *Energy Conversion and Management* 272, no. 3 (2022): 116326.

Rattalino, Francesco. "Circular Advantage Anyone? Sustainability-Driven Innovation and Circularity at Patagonia, Inc." *Thunderbird International Business Review* 60, no. 5 (2018): 747–55.

Razaei, Sajjad, Khaled Alsamri, Elio Simeoni, Jacquelin Hyunh, and Jack Brouwer. "Techno-Economic and Environmental Analysis of Clean Hydrogen Deployment: A Case Study of Los Angeles International Airport." *Energy Conversion and Management* 340, no. 15 (2025): 119946.

Reed, J. R. "A Rising Number of U.S. Companies Are Flagging Wildfire Risk as Suppression Costs Climb." *CNBC*, November 10, 2019. https://cnbc.com/2019/11/10/more-companies-are-flagging-wildfire-risk-as-suppression-costs-climb.html.

Reed, Stanley. "Saudi Arabia Eyes a Future Beyond Oil." *The New York Times*, May 29, 2024. https://nytimes.com/2024/05/29/business/saudi-arabia-renewable-energy-solar-wind.html.

Regan, Helen. "Indonesia Is Putting Business Before the Environment and That Could Be Disastrous for Its Rainforests." *CNN*, October 12, 2020.

https://cnn.com/2020/10/12/asia/indonesia-omnibus-law-environment-intl-hnk/index.html.

Reichheld, Ashley, John Peto, and Cory Ritthaler. "Research: Consumers' Sustainability Demands Are Rising." *Harvard Business Review*, September 7, 2023. https://hbr.org/2023/09/research-consumers-sustainability-demands-are-rising.

Rendtorff, Jacob Dahl. "Sustainable Solutions to the Global Climate Problem: The Case of the Renewable and Green Energy Company Ørsted." In *Value Creation for a Sustainable World: Innovating for Ecological Regeneration and Human Flourishing*, edited by Laszlo Zsolnai, Thomas Walker, and Paul Shrivastava, 63–80. Cham: Palgrave Macmillan, 2023.

Richard, Brice, and James Lambert. *The Global Green Economy: Capturing the Opportunity*. Singapore: ARUP and Oxford Economics, 2023.

Richardson, Doug, Jarrod Kath, Vivekananda M. Byrareddy, Didier P. Monselesan, James S. Risbey, Dougal T. Squire, and Carly R. Tozer. "Synchronous Climate Hazards Pose an Increasing Challenge to Global Coffee Production." *PLOS Climate* 2, no. 3 (2023): e0000134.

Richert, Claire, Abbie Rogers, and Michael Burton. "Measuring the Extent of a Social License to Operate: The Influence of Marine Biodiversity Offsets in the Oil and Gas Sector in Western Australia." *Resources Policy* 43 (2015): 121–29.

Rivera, Jorge, and Chang Hoon Oh. "Environmental Regulations and Multinational Corporations' Foreign Market Entry Investments." *Policy Studies Journal* 41, no. 2 (2013): 243–72.

Rivera, Jorge E., Chang Hoon Oh, Jennifer Oetzel, and Viviane Clement. *Business Adaptation to Climate Change*. Cambridge: Cambridge University Press, 2022.

Robinson, William T., Gurumurthy Kalyanaram, and Glen L. Urban. "First-Mover Advantages from Pioneering New Markets: A Survey of Empirical Evidence." *Review of Industrial Organization* 9, no. 1 (1994): 1–23.

Rode, David C., Jeffrey J. Anderson, Haibo Zhai, and Paul S. Fischbeck. "Six Principles to Guide Large-Scale Carbon Capture and Storage Development." *Energy Research & Social Science* 103 (2023): 103214.

Rogers, Adam. "The Real Reason Tesla Is Letting Rival Car Companies Use Its EV Charging Stations." *Business Insider*, July 5, 2023. https://businessinsider.com/tesla-ford-gm-volvo-supercharger-electric-cars-charger-network-data-2023-7.

Rogers, Everett M. *Diffusion of Innovations*. New York: Free Press, 1962.

Roller, Edeltraud. *The Performance of Democracies: Political Institutions and Public Policy*. Oxford: Oxford University Press, 2005.

Román-Palacios, Christian, and John J. Wiens. "Recent Responses to Climate Change Reveal the Drivers of Species Extinction and Survival." *Proceedings of the National Academy of Sciences of the United States of America* 117, no. 8 (2020): 4211–17.

Rosenbloom, Stephanie. "Retail Sales Are Weakest in 35 Years." *The New York Times*, December 5, 2008. https://nytimes.com/2008/12/05/business/economy/05shop.html.

"Don't Ask. You Can Afford It." *The New York Times*, May 2, 2009. https://nytimes.com/2009/05/02/business/02dollar.html.

Roy, Diana. "What's Causing the Panama Canal Logjam." Council on Foreign Relations, August 23, 2023. https://cfr.org/in-brief/whats-causing-panama-canal-logjam.

"How the Caribbean Is Building Climate Resilience." Council on Foreign Relations, February 8, 2024. https://cfr.org/backgrounder/how-caribbean-building-climate-resilience.

Rudra, Nita. "Globalization and the Strengthening of Democracy in the Developing World." *American Journal of Political Science* 49, no. 4 (2005): 704–30.

Sabherwal, Anandita, Matthew T. Ballew, Sander van der Linden, Abel Gustafson, Matthew H. Goldberg, Edward W. Maibach, John E. Kotcher, Janet K. Swim, Seth A. Rosenthal, and Anthony Leiserowitz. "The Greta Thunberg Effect: Familiarity with Greta Thunberg Predicts Intentions to Engage in Climate Activism in the United States." *Journal of Applied Social Psychology* 51, no. 4 (2021): 321–33.

Sabir, Samina, Anum Rafique, and Kamran Abbas. "Institutions and FDI: Evidence from Developed and Developing Countries." *Financial Innovation* 5, no. 1 (2019): Article 8.

Sachs, Jeffrey D. "Globalization and Patterns of Economic Development." *Review of World Economics* 136, no. 4 (2000): 579–600.

Saikawa, Eri. "Policy Diffusion of Emission Standards: Is There a Race to the Top?" *World Politics* 65, no. 1 (2013): 1–33.

Sakhel, Alice. "Corporate Climate Risk Management: Are European Companies Prepared?" *Journal of Cleaner Production* 165 (2017): 103–18.

Salehyan, Idean, and Cullen S. Hendrix. "Climate Shocks and Political Violence." *Global Environmental Change* 28 (2014): 239–50.

Santos, Ana, and Rosa Forte. "Environmental Regulation and FDI Attraction: A Bibliometric Analysis of the Literature." *Environmental Science and Pollution Research* 28, no. 7 (2021): 8873–88.

Sato, Misato, Glen Gastlow, Catherine Higham, Joana Setzer, and Frank Venmans. *Impacts of Climate Litigation on Firm Value*. Centre for Climate Change Economics and Policy Working Paper 421/Grantham

Research Institute on Climate Change and the Environment Working Paper 397. London: London School of Economics and Political Science, 2023.

Sattorova, Mavluda. "Investor Responsibilities from a Host State Perspective: Qualitative Data and Proposals for Treaty Reform." *American Journal of International Law* 113 (2019): 22–27.

Schäfer, Laura, Koko Warner, and Sönke Kreft. "Exploring and Managing Adaptation Frontiers with Climate Risk Insurance." In *Loss and Damage from Climate Change: Concepts, Methods and Policy Options*, edited by Reinhard Mechler, Laurens M. Bouwer, Thomas Schinko, Swenja Surminski, and JoAnne Linnerooth-Bayer, 317–41. Cham: Springer, 2018.

Schäferhoff, Marco, Sabine Campe, and Christopher Kaan. "Transnational Public-Private Partnerships in International Relations: Making Sense of Concepts, Research Frameworks, and Results." *International Studies Review* 11, no. 3 (2009): 451–74.

Schreurs, Miranda A. "The Paris Climate Agreement and the Three Largest Emitters: China, the United States, and the European Union." *Politics and Governance* 4, no. 3 (2016): 219–23.

Schulz, Steven A., and Rod L. Flanigan. "Developing Competitive Advantage Using the Triple Bottom Line: A Conceptual Framework." *Journal of Business & Industrial Marketing* 31, no. 4 (2016): 449–58.

Scott, Matthew. *Climate Change, Disasters, and the Refugee Convention.* Cambridge: Cambridge University Press, 2020.

Scruggs, Lyle, and Salil Benegal. "Declining Public Concern About Climate Change: Can We Blame the Great Recession?" *Global Environmental Change* 22, no. 2 (2012): 505–15.

Sengupta, Somini. "The Rich World's Promise of $100 Billion in Climate Aid Inches Forward." *The New York Times*, October 25, 2021. https://nytimes.com/2021/10/25/climate/100-billion-climate-aid-cop26.html.

Sethi, S. Prakash, and Donald H. Schepers. "United Nations Global Compact: The Promise–Performance Gap." *Journal of Business Ethics* 122, no. 2 (2014): 193–208.

Setzer, Joana. "Why Are Climate Action Cases Rising?" *London School of Economics and Political Science*, 2024. https://lse.ac.uk/research/research-for-the-world/sustainability/climate-legislation-and-litigation.

Setzer, Joana, and Catherine Higham. *Global Trends in Climate Change Litigation: 2022 Snapshot.* London: Grantham Research Institute on Climate Change and the Environment and Centre for Climate Change Economics and Policy, London School of Economics and Political Science, 2022.

Shain, Emily. "Ørsted, WWF Partner to Address Biodiversity Impact of Offshore Wind Deployment." *ESG Today*, July 14, 2022. https://esgtoday.com/orsted-wwf-partner-to-address-biodiversity-impact-of-offshore-wind-deployment.

Shankman, Sabrina. "Welcome to the Climate Apocalypse. (It Will Get Worse.)" *The Boston Globe*, July 24, 2021. https://bostonglobe.com/2021/07/24/science/welcome-climate-apocalypse-it-will-get-worse.

Shao, Yanmin, and Zhongfei Chen. "Can Government Subsidies Promote the Green Technology Innovation Transformation? Evidence from Chinese Listed Companies." *Economic Analysis and Policy* 74 (2022): 716–27.

Shapiro, Daniel M., Carlos Vecino, and Jing Li. "Exploring China's State-Led FDI Model: Evidence from the Extractive Sectors in Latin America." *Asia Pacific Journal of Management* 35, no. 1 (2018): 11–37.

Shaver, Julia. "The State of Telehealth Before and After the COVID-19 Pandemic." *Primary Care: Clinics in Office Practice* 49, no. 4 (2022): 517–30.

Shear, Falik, Badar Nadeem Ashraf, and Shazaib Butt. "Sensing the Heat: Climate Change Vulnerability and Foreign Direct Investment Inflows." *Research in International Business and Finance* 66 (2023): 102005.

Sherrington, Rachel. "Hundreds of Lobbyists for Industrial Farming Attend Cop29 Climate Summit." *The Guardian*, November 19, 2024. https://theguardian.com/environment/2024/nov/19/hundreds-of-lobbyists-for-industrial-farming-attend-cop29-climate-summit.

Shi, Hongyu, and Qun Zhou. "Government R&D Subsidies, Environmental Regulation and Corporate Green Innovation Performance." *Finance Research Letters* 69, Part B (2024): 106088.

Shichor, David, and John W. Heeren. "Reflecting on Corporate Crime and Control: The Wells Fargo Banking Saga." *Journal of White Collar and Corporate Crime* 2, no. 2 (2021): 97–108.

Shinkle, George A., Gerard P. Hodgkinson, and Michael Shayne Gary. "Government Policy Changes and Organizational Goal Setting: Extensions to the Behavior Theory of the Firm." *Journal of Business Research* 129 (2021): 406–17.

Shiogama, Hideo, Masahiro Watanabe, Yukiko Imada, Masato Mori, Masayoshi Ishii, and Masahide Kimoto. "An Event Attribution of the 2010 Drought in the South Amazon Region Using the MIROC5 Model." *Atmospheric Science Letters* 13, no. 3 (2013): 170–75.

Shu, Ei, and Arie Y. Lewin. "A Resource Dependence Perspective on Low-Power Actors Shaping Their Regulatory Environment: The Case of Honda." *Organization Studies* 38, no. 8 (2017): 1039–58.

Si, Yutong, Dipa Desai, Diana Bozhilova, Sheila Puffer, and Jennie C. Stephens. "Fossil Fuel Companies' Climate Communication Strategies: Industry Messaging on Renewables and Natural Gas." *Energy Research & Social Science* 98 (2023): 103028.

Simatupang, Renata, Akbar Dachlan, and Galuh Maharani. "Indonesia's Controversial Omnibus Law on Job Creation." DevTech, August 14, 2023. https://devtechsys.com/insights/2023/08/14/indonesias-controversial-omnibus-law-on-job-creation.

Simpliciano, Liv, Maeve Galvin, Clara Barry, Delphine Willox, Isabella Luglio, and Ysabi Marie Dobles. *What Fuels Fashion?* London: Fashion Revolution, 2024. https://fashionrevolution.org/transparency.

Singh, Sweta. "Consulting Firms See Gains from Economy's Woes." *Reuters*, May 29, 2008. https://reuters.com/article/us-usa-downturn-consulting firms/consulting-firms-see-gains-from-economys-woes-idUSBNG18024920080529.

Skjærseth, Jon Birger. "Major Oil Companies in Climate Policy: Strategies and Compliance." In *Implementing the Climate Regime: International Compliance*, edited by Jon Hovi and Geir Ulfstein, 187–208. London: Routledge, 2005.

Skovgaard, Jakob, and Harro van Asselt. "The Politics of Fossil Fuel Subsidies and Their Reform: Implications for Climate Change Mitigation." *WIREs Climate Change* 10, no. 4 (2019): e581.

Skovgaard, Jakob, Kevin M. Adams, Kendra Dupuy, Adis Dzebo, Mikkel Funder, Adam Moe Fejerskov, and Zoha Shawoo. "Global Environmental Politics." *Global Environmental Politics* 23, no. 2 (2023): 125–47.

Sloggy, Matthew R., Jordan F. Suter, Mani Rouhi Rad, Dale T. Manning, and Chris Goemans. "Changing Opinions on a Changing Climate: The Effects of Natural Disasters on Public Perceptions of Climate Change." *Climatic Change* 168, nos. 3–4 (2021): 25.

Smith, Mitchell P. *Environmental and Health Regulation in the United States and the European Union: Protecting Public and Planet*. New York: Palgrave Macmillan, 2012.

So, Kat. *Climate Deniers of the 118th Congress*. Washington D.C.: Center for American Progress, 2024. https://americanprogress.org/article/climate-deniers-of-the-118th-congress.

Sottilotta, Cecilia Emma. *Rethinking Political Risk: Concepts, Theories, Challenges*. London: Routledge, 2016.

Soumaré, Issouf. "Does FDI Improve Economic Development in North African Countries?" *Applied Economics* 47, no. 51 (2015): 5510–33.

Sovacool, Benjamin K., and Peter Enevoldsen. "One Style to Build Them All: Corporate Culture and Innovation in the Offshore Wind Industry." *Energy Policy* 86 (2015): 402–15.

Stampler, Laura. "Alexandria Ocasio-Cortez Calls Out Facebook, Google and Microsoft for 'Implicit Support' of Climate Change Denial." *Fortune*, January 28, 2019. https://fortune.com/2019/01/28/alexandria-ocasio-cortez-calls-out-facebook-google-microsoft-for-implicit-support-of-climate-change-denial.

Stankovic, Tatjana, Jon Hovi, and Tara Skodvin. "The Paris Agreement's Inherent Tension between Ambition and Compliance." *Humanities and Social Sciences Communications* 10 (2023): 550.

Stechemesser, Annika, Nicolas Koch, Ebba Mark, Elina Dilger, Patrick Klösel, Laura Menicacci, Daniel Nachtigall, Felix Pretis, Nolan Ritter, Moritz Schwarz, Helena Vossen, and Anna Wenzel. "Climate Policies That Achieved Major Emission Reductions: Global Evidence from Two Decades." *Science* 385, no. 6711 (2024): 884–92.

Steinebach, Yves. "Instrument Choice, Implementation Structures, and the Effectiveness of Environmental Policies: A Cross-National Analysis." *Regulation & Governance* 16, no. 1 (2022): 225–42.

Stokes, Leah Cardamore. *Short Circuiting Policy: Interest Groups and the Battle over Clean Energy and Climate Policy in the American States.* Oxford: Oxford University Press, 2020.

Storeng, Katerini Tagmatarchi, and Antoine de Bengy Puyvallée. "Civil Society Participation in Global Public Private Partnerships for Health." *Health Policy and Planning* 33, no. 8 (2018): 928–36.

Storrow, Benjamin. "How One Fossil Fuel Company Became a Green Giant." *E&E News*, September 9, 2020. https://subscriber.politicopro.com/article/eenews/2020/09/09/how-one-fossil-fuel-company-became-a-green-giant-011206.

Stott, Peter A., D. A. Stone, and M. R. Allen. "Human Contribution to the European Heatwave of 2003." *Nature* 432, no. 7017 (2004): 610–14.

Stroebel, Johannes, and Jeffrey Wurgler. "What Do You Think About Climate Finance?" *Journal of Financial Economics* 142, no. 2 (2021): 487–98.

Su, Hung-Chung, Suvrat Dhanorkar, and Kevin Linderman. "A Competitive Advantage from the Implementation Timing of ISO Management Standards." *Journal of Operations Management* 37, no. 1 (2015): 31–44.

Sundström, Aksel. "Covenants with Broken Swords: Corruption and Law Enforcement in Governance of the Commons." *Global Environmental Change* 31 (2015): 253–62.

Surminski, Swenja. "Disregard for Physical Climate Risks Is Locking Corporates into Dangerous Futures." *Grantham Research Institute on Climate Change and the Environment*, 2021. https://lse.ac.uk/granthaminstitute/news/disregard-for-physical-climate-risks-is-locking-corporates-into-dangerous-futures.

Surminski, Swenja, Laurens M. Bouwer, and Joanne Linnerooth-Bayer. "How Insurance Can Support Climate Resilience." *Nature Climate Change* 6, no. 4 (2016): 333–34.

Surminski, Swenja, Manuela Di Mauro, J. Alastair R. Bagglee, Richenda K. Connell, Joel Hankinson, Anna R. Hayworth, Bingunath Ingirige, and David Proverbs. "Assessing Climate Risks Across Different Business Sectors and Industries: An Investigation of Methodological Challenges at National Scale for the UK." *Philosophical Transactions A* 376, no. 2121 (2018): 20170307.

Swiss Re Institute. *The Economics of Climate Change: No Action Is Not an Option*. Zurich: Swiss Re Institute, 2021.

Tabuchi, Hiroko. "Toyota Led on Clean Cars. Now Critics Say It Works to Delay Them." *The New York Times*, July 25, 2021. https://nytimes.com/2021/07/25/climate/toyota-electric-hydrogen.html.

"Inside the Saudi Strategy to Keep the World Hooked on Oil." *The New York Times*, November 21, 2022. https://nytimes.com/2022/11/21/climate/saudi-arabia-aramco-oil-solar-climate.html.

Tabuchi, Hiroko, and Brad Plumer. "How Green Are Electric Vehicles?" *The New York Times*, March 2, 2021. https://nytimes.com/2021/03/02/climate/electric-vehicles-environment.html.

"How Green are Electric Vehicles?" *The New York Times*, 2023. https://nytimes.com/2021/03/02/climate/electric-vehicles-environment.html

Tabuchi, Hiroko, and Lisa Friedman. "Oil Executives Grilled Over Industry's Role in Climate Disinformation." *The New York Times*, October 28, 2021. https://nytimes.com/2021/10/28/climate/oil-executives-house-disinformation-testimony.html.

Tadadjeu, Sosson, Henri Njangang, and Andinet Woldemichael. "Are Resource-Rich Countries Less Responsive to Global Warming? Oil Wealth and Climate Change Policy." *Energy Policy* 182 (2023): 113774.

Tang, Chia-Hsien, Chih-Yu Chin, and Yen-Hsien Lee. "Coronavirus Disease Outbreak and Supply Chain Disruption: Evidence from Taiwanese Firms in China." *Research in International Business and Finance* 56 (2021): 101355.

Temple, James. "Carbon Removal Hype Is Becoming a Dangerous Distraction." *MIT Technology Review*, July 8, 2021. https://technologyreview.com/2021/07/08/1027908/carbon-removal-hype-is-a-dangerous-distraction-climate-change.

"Why Concerns Over the Sustainability of Carbon Removal Are Growing." *MIT Technology Review*, February 29, 2024. https://

technologyreview.com/2024/02/29/1089220/why-concerns-over-the-sustainability-of-carbon-removal-are-growing.

Thomas, Adelle, and Emily Theokritoff. "Climate-for-Debt Swaps for Small Islands." *Nature Climate Change* 11, no. 11 (2021): 889–91.

Thompson, Barney. "Political Risk Is Now a Growth Industry in Its Own Right." *Financial Times*, September 8, 2014. https://ft.com/content/c1b94922-3765-11e4-8472-00144feabdc0.

Thorpe, Lorna. "Coca-Cola – Replenishing Water in the Drinks Industry." *The Guardian*, July 21, 2011. https://theguardian.com/sustainable-business/coca-cola-water-stewardship.

Timperley, Jocelyn. "The Broken $100-Billion Promise of Climate Finance – and How to Fix It." *Nature*, October 25, 2021. https://nature.com/articles/d41586-021-02846-3.

Tingley, Dustin, and Michael Tomz. "International Commitments and Domestic Opinion: The Effect of the Paris Agreement on Public Support for Policies to Address Climate Change." *Environmental Politics* 29, no. 7 (2020): 1135–56.

Tobin, Jennifer L., and Susan Rose-Ackerman. "When BITs Have Some Bite: The Political-Economic Environment for Bilateral Investment Treaties." *Review of International Organizations* 6, no. 1 (2011): 1–32.

Toktay, L. Beril, Abhinav Shubham, Donghyun (Daniel) Choi, and Manpreet S. Hora. "Companies Are Still Committing to Net-Zero Emissions, Even If It's a Bumpy Road – Here's What the Data Show." *The Conversation*, June 6, 2024. https://theconversation.com/companies-are-still-committing-to-net-zero-emissions-even-if-its-a-bumpy-road-heres-what-the-data-show-239487.

Tooze, Adam. *Crashed: How a Decade of Financial Crises Changed the World*. London: Penguin, 2019.

Torrella, Kenny. "Were the Impossible and Beyond Burgers a Fad, or Is Plant-Based Meat Here to Stay?" *Vox*, April 17, 2023. https://vox.com/future-perfect/2023/4/17/23682232/impossible-beyond-plant-based-meat-sales.

Tran, Vinh Du, David S. Sibley, and Simon Wilkie. "Second Mover Advantage and Entry Timing." *Journal of Industrial Economics* 60, no. 3 (2012): 517–35.

Tsipiras, Katelyn, and Will J. Grant. "What Do We Mean When We Talk About the Moral Hazard of Geoengineering." *Environmental Law Review* 24, no. 1 (2022): 27–44.

Tsui, Joseph L.-H., Rosario Evans Pena, Monika Moir, Rhys P. D. Inward, Eduan Wilkinson, James Emmanuel San, Jenicca Poongavanan, Sumali

Bajaj, Bernardo Gutierrez, Abhishek Dasgupta, Tulio de Oliveira, Moritz U. G. Kraemer, Houriiyah Tegally, and Prathyush Sambaturu. "Impacts of Climate Change-Related Human Migration on Infectious Diseases." *Nature Climate Change* 14, no. 8 (2024): 793–802.

Twidale, Susanna. "Global Carbon Removal Market Could Reach $100 Billion/Yr from 2030–35, Report Says." *Reuters*, June 27, 2024. https://reuters.com/sustainability/climate-energy/global-carbon-removal-market-could-reach-100-billionyr-2030-35-report-says-2024-06-27.

United Nations. *COVID-19 and E-Commerce: A Global Review*. Geneva: United Nations, 2021.

United Nations Conference on Trade and Development. *World Investment Report 2022: International Tax Reforms and Sustainable Investment*. Geneva: UNCTAD, 2022.

United Nations Environment Programme. *Environmental Rule of Law: First Global Report*. Nairobi: UNEP, 2019.

United Nations Environment Programme. *Emissions Gap Report 2024: No More Hot Air ... Please!* Nairobi: UNEP, 2024.

United Nations Environment Programme, and GRID-Arendal. *Spreading Like Wildfire: The Rising Threat of Extraordinary Landscape Fires*. Nairobi: UNEP, 2022.

Urpelainen, Johannes, and Elisha George. "Reforming Global Fossil Fuel Subsidies: How the United States Can Restart International Cooperation." *Brookings*, July 14, 2021. https://brookings.edu/articles/reforming-global-fossil-fuel-subsidies-how-the-united-states-can-restart-international-cooperation.

Uteuova, Aliya. "Starbucks Develops Coffee Seeds That Can Withstand Climate Change Effects." *The Guardian*, October 4, 2023. https://theguardian.com/business/2023/oct/04/starbucks-arabica-coffee-seed-climate-change.

Utting, Peter, and Ann Zammit. "United Nations–Business Partnerships: Good Intentions and Contradictory Agendas." *Journal of Business Ethics* 90, no. 1 (2009): 39–56.

Van Aalst, Maarten K. "The Impacts of Climate Change on the Risk of Natural Disasters." *Disasters* 30, no. 1 (2006): 5–18.

van der Zwaan, Bob, and Koen Smekens. "CO_2 Capture and Storage with Leakage in an Energy-Climate Model." *Environmental Modeling & Assessment* 14, no. 2 (2009): 135–48.

van Stokkom, Hein T. C., Antonius J. M. Smits, and Rob S. E. W. Leuven. "Flood Defense in the Netherlands: A New Era, a New Approach." *Water International* 30, no. 1 (2005): 76–87.

Vecellio, Daniel J., Qinqin Kong, W. Larry Kenney, and Matthew Huber. "Greatly Enhanced Risk to Humans as a Consequence of Empirically Determined Lower Moist Heat Stress Tolerance." *Proceedings of the National Academy of Sciences of the United States of America* 120, no. 42 (2023): e2305427120.

Venghaus, Sandra, Meike Henseleit, and Maria Belka. "The Impact of Climate Change Awareness on Behavioral Changes in Germany: Changing Minds or Changing Behavior." *Energy, Sustainability and Society* 12, no. 1 (2022): Article 8.

Verweij, Stefan, Tim Busscher, and Margo van den Brink. "Effective Policy Instrument Mixes for Implementing Integrated Flood Risk Management: An Analysis of the 'Room for the River' Program." *Environmental Science & Policy* 116 (2021): 204–12.

Vesa, Juho, Antti Gronow, and Tuomas Ylä-Anttila. "The Quiet Opposition: How the Pro-Economy Lobby Influences Climate Policy." *Global Environmental Change* 63 (2020): 102117.

Veugelers, Reinhilde, Simone Tagliapietra, and Cecilia Trasi. "Green Industrial Policy in Europe: Past, Present, and Prospects." *Journal of Industry, Competition and Trade* 24, no. 1 (2024): 4.

Victor, David G. *Global Warming Gridlock: Creating More Effective Strategies for Protecting the Planet*. Cambridge: Cambridge University Press, 2011.

Voigt, Christina. "The Power of the Paris Agreement in International Climate Litigation." *Review of European, Comparative & International Environmental Law* 32, no. 2 (2023): 237–49.

Voldsgaard, Asker, and Mogens Rüdiger. "Innovative Enterprise, Industrial Ecosystems, and Sustainable Transition: The Case of Transforming DONG Energy to Ørsted." In *Handbook of Climate Change Mitigation and Adaptation*, edited by Maximilian Lackner, Baharak Sajjadi, and Wei-Yin Chen, 3633–84. Cham: Springer, 2022.

Vousdoukas, Michalis I., Panagiotis Athanasiou, Alessio Giardino, Lorenzo Mentaschi, Alessandro Stocchino, Robert E. Kopp, Pelayo Menéndez, Michael W. Beck, Roshanka Ranasinghe, and Luc Feyen. "Small Island Developing States under Threat by Rising Seas Even in a 1.5 °C Warming World." *Nature Sustainability* 6, no. 12 (2023): 1552–64.

Wallace-Wells, David. "Beyond Catastrophe: A New Climate Reality Is Coming into View." *The New York Times Magazine*, October 26, 2022. https://nytimes.com/interactive/2022/10/26/magazine/climate-change-warming-world.html.

Walt, Vivienne. "BYD Is Already Beating Tesla. Its New Europe Playbook Shows Why It's Poised to Dominate the EV Race." *Fortune*, July 29,

2025. https://fortune.com/2025/07/29/byd-china-electric-cars-europe-hungary-manufacturing.
Wang, Miao. "Manufacturing FDI and Economic Growth: Evidence from Asian Economies." *Applied Economics* 41, no. 8 (2009): 991–1002.
Wang, Mingrong, Xi Zhang, and Yi Hu. "The Green Spillover Effect of the Inward Foreign Direct Investment: Market Versus Innovation." *Journal of Cleaner Production* 328 (2021): 129501.
Wang, Zhijian. "Road to Human-Centric Smart City Governance in Japan: The Case of Fujisawa Sustainable Smart Town." *Global Policy* 15, suppl. 6 (2024): 84–91.
Wang, Zhongcheng, Xinyue Li, Xinhong Xue, and Yahuan Liu. "More Government Subsidies, More Green Innovation? The Evidence from Chinese New Energy Vehicle Enterprises." *Renewable Energy* 197 (2022): 11–21.
Watkiss, Paul, Magnus Benzie, and Richard J. T. Klein. "The Complementarity and Comparability of Climate Change Adaptation and Mitigation." *WIREs Climate Change* 6, no. 6 (2015): 541–57.
Watts, Jonathan. "Just 57 Companies Linked to 80% of Greenhouse Gas Emissions since 2016." *The Guardian*, April 4, 2024. https://theguardian.com/environment/2024/apr/04/just-57-companies-linked-to-80-of-greenhouse-gas-emissions-since-2016.
Weber, Elke U. "Experience-Based and Description-Based Perceptions of Long-Term Risk: Why Global Warming Does Not Scare Us (Yet)." *Climatic Change* 77, nos. 1–2 (2006): 103–20.
Wehner, Michael F., and James P. Kossin. "The Growing Inadequacy of an Open-Ended Saffir-Simpson Hurricane Wind Scale in a Warming World." *Proceedings of the National Academy of Sciences of the United States of America* 121, no. 7 (2024): e2308901121.
Weiler, Florian, Carola Klöck, and Matthew Dornan. "Vulnerability, Good Governance, or Donor Interests? The Allocation of Aid for Climate Change Adaptation." *World Development* 104 (2018): 65–77.
Weinhofer, Georg, and Timo Busch. "Corporate Strategies for Managing Climate Risks." *Business Strategy and the Environment* 22, no. 2 (2013): 121–44.
Weiss, Edith Brown, and Harold K. Jacobson. "Getting Countries to Comply with International Agreements." *Environment: Science and Policy for Sustainable Development* 41, no. 6 (1999): 16–20.
Wendt, Paul. "The Control of Rubber in World War II." *Southern Economic Journal* 13, no. 3 (1947): 203–27.
Wennersten, John R., and Denise Robbins. *Rising Tides: Climate Refugees in the Twenty-First Century*. Bloomington: Indiana University Press, 2017.

Wenzel, Matthias, Sarah Stanske, and Marvin B. Lieberman. "Strategic Responses to Crisis." *Strategic Management Journal* 42, no. 2 (2021): 016–27.

Westervelt, Amy. "Oil Companies Sold the Public on a Fake Climate Solution – and Swindled Taxpayers Out of Billions." *Vox*, March 7, 2024. https://vox.com/climate/363076/climate-change-solution-shell-exxon-mobil-carbon-capture.

Wettestad, Jørgen, Tor Håkon Jackson Inderberg, and Lars H. Gulbrandsen. "Exploring Paths and Innovation in Norwegian Carbon Capture and Storage Policy." *Environmental Policy and Governance* 34, no. 2 (2024): 125–36.

Wiegant, Daniel, Art Dewulf, and Josephine Van Zeben. "Alignment Mechanisms to Effectively Govern the Sustainable Development Goals." *World Development* 182 (2024): 106721.

Williams, A. Park, Benjamin I. Cook, and Jason E. Smerdon. "Rapid Intensification of the Emerging Southwestern North American Megadrought in 2020–2021." *Nature Climate Change* 12, no. 3 (2022): 232–34.

Williams, Oliver F. "The UN Global Compact: The Challenge and the Promise." *Business Ethics Quarterly* 14, no. 4 (2004): 755–74.

"The United Nations Global Compact: What Did It Promise?" *Journal of Business Ethics* 122, no. 2 (2014): 241–51.

Wischnath, Gerdis, and Halvard Buhaug. "On Climate Variability and Civil War in Asia." *Climatic Change* 122, no. 4 (2014): 709–21.

Witt, Michael A. "De-Globalization: Theories, Predictions, and Opportunities for International Business Research." *Journal of International Business Studies* 50, no. 7 (2019): 1053–77.

Witt, Michael A., Peter Ping Li, Liisa Välikangas, and Arie Y. Lewin. "De-Globalization and Decoupling: Game Changing Consequences?" *Management and Organizational Review* 17, no. 1 (2021): 6–15.

Woods, Neal D. "Interstate Competition and Environmental Regulation: A Test of the Race-to-the-Bottom Thesis." *Social Science Quarterly* 87, no. 1 (2006): 174–89.

World Bank Group. *Low-Carbon Zones: A Practitioner's Handbook*. Washington, DC: World Bank, 2014.

Wright, Christopher, and Daniel Nyberg. *Climate Change, Capitalism, and Corporations*. Cambridge: Cambridge University Press, 2015.

Wu, Guancen, Xian Xu, Xing Niu, and Li Tao. "How Does Government Policy Improve Green Technology Innovation: An Empirical Study in China." *Frontiers in Environmental Science* 9 (2022): 799794.

Wu, Jie, and Zhenzhong Ma. "Export Intensity and MNE Customers' Environmental Requirements: Effects on Local Chinese Suppliers'

Environment Strategies." *Journal of Business Ethics* 135, no. 2 (2016): 327–39.

Wu, Jing, Lichun Tang, Rayman Mohamed, Qianting Zhu, and Zheng Wang. "Modeling and Assessing International Climate Financing." *Frontiers of Earth Science* 10, no. 2 (2016): 253–63.

Wu, Lichao, Lili Wang, and Lan Lin. "Learn to Be Green: FDI Spillover Effects on Eco-Innovation in China." *Industrial and Corporate Change* 32, no. 5 (2023): 1192–1216.

Wu, Pei-Chin, Meng (Matt) Wei, and Steven D'Hondt. "From New York to Jakarta, Land in Many Coastal Cities Is Sinking Faster than Sea Levels Are Rising." *The Conversation*, February 21, 2024. https://theconversation.com/from-new-york-to-jakarta-land-in-many-coastal-cities-is-sinking-faster-than-sea-levels-are-rising-220120.

Wu, Xiaoli, An Pan, and Qunzhi She. "Direct and Indirect Effects of Climate Aid on Carbon Emissions in Recipient Countries." *Journal of Cleaner Production* 290 (2021): 125204.

Wu, Yongchao, and Xinyu Gao. "Can the Establishment of Eco-Industrial Parks Promote Urban Green Innovation? Evidence from China." *Journal of Cleaner Production* 341 (2022): 130855.

Xie, Xuemei, Qiwei Zhu, and Ruoyi Wang. "Turning Green Subsidies into Sustainability: How Green Process Innovation Improves Firms' Green Image." *Business Strategy and the Environment* 28, no. 7 (2019): 1416–33.

Xing, Yuquing, and Charles D. Kolstad. "Do Lax Environmental Regulations Attract Foreign Investment?" *Environmental and Resource Economics* 21, no. 1 (2002): 1–22.

Xu, Han. "Does Government Support Affect Private Partners' Profitability in Public-Private Partnerships? Evidence from China." *Humanities and Social Sciences Communications* 10 (2023): Article no. 223.

Xu, Zhenci, Yingjie Li, Sophia N. Chau, Thomas Dietz, Canbing Li, Luwen Wan, Jindong Zhang, Liwei Zhang, Yunkai Li, Min Gon Chung, and Jianguo Liu. "Impacts of International Trade on Global Sustainable Development." *Nature Sustainability* 3, no. 11 (2020): 964–71.

Yang, Wu-E, Pei-Wen Lai, Zhi-Qiu Han, and Zheng-Peng Tang. "Do Government Policies Drive Institutional Preferences on Green Investment? Evidence from China." *Environmental Science and Pollution Research* 30, no. 3 (2023): 8297–8316.

Yang, Zhi, Heng Chen, Cheng Peng, and Xiaolei Liu. "Exploring the Role of Environmental Regulations in the Production and Diffusion of Electric Vehicles." *Computers & Industrial Engineering* 173 (2022): 108675.

Yeo, Han-Koo, and Gokhan Akinci. "Low-Carbon, Green Special Economic Zones." In *Special Economic Zones: Progress, Emerging Challenges, and Future Directions*, edited by Thomas Farole and Gokhan Akinci, 283–306. Washington, DC: World Bank Publications, 2011.

Yimere, Abay. "Africa's Top Climate Change Challenges: A Fairer Deal on Phasing Out Fossil Fuels and Mobilising Funds." *The Conversation Africa*, August 18, 2025. https://theconversation.com/africas-top-climate-change-challenges-a-fairer-deal-on-phasing-out-fossil-fuels-and-mobilising-funds-262077.

Yohe, Gary W. "I'm an Economist. Here's Why I'm Worried the California Insurance Crisis Could Trigger Broader Financial Instability." *The Conversation*, January 21, 2025. https://theconversation.com/im-an-economist-heres-why-im-worried-the-california-insurance-crisis-could-trigger-broader-financial-instability-247620.

Yuan, Jingbo, Muhammad Faisal Shahzad, Abdul Waheed, and Wenyue Wang. "Sustainable Development and Brand Loyalty: Exploring the Dynamics of Corporate Social Responsibility, Customer Attitudes, and Emotional Contagion." *Corporate Social Responsibility and Environmental Management* 31, no. 2 (2024): 1042–51.

Zachariah, Mariam, Sjoukje Philip, Izidine Pinto, Maja Vahlbertg, Roop Singh, and Friederike E. L. Otto. *Extreme Heat in North America, Europe and China in July 2023 Made Much More Likely by Climate Change*. London: Grantham Institute for Climate Change, 2023.

Zahavi, Talli, and Dovev Lavie. "Intra-Industry Diversification and Firm Performance." *Strategic Management Journal* 34, no. 8 (2013): 978–98.

Zaloga, Steven J. "Soviet Air Defense Radar in the Second World War." *The Journal of Soviet Military Studies* 2, no. 1 (1989): 104–16.

Zeihan, Peter. *The End of the World Is Just the Beginning: Mapping the Collapse of Globalization*. New York: Harper Collins, 2022.

Zeng, Ka, and Joshua Eastin. "Do Developing Countries Invest Up? The Environmental Effects of Foreign Direct Investment from Less-Developed Countries." *World Development* 40, no. 11 (2012): 2221–33.

Zeppetello, Lucas R. Vargas, Adrian E. Raftery, and David S. Battisti. "Probabilistic Projections of Increased Heat Stress Driven by Climate Change." *Communications Earth & Environment* 3 (2022): Article no. 183.

Zhang, Zengkai, Dabo Guan, Ran Wang, Jing Meng, Heran Zheng, Kunfu Zhu, and Huibin Du. "Embodied Carbon Emissions in the Supply Chains of Multinational Enterprises." *Nature Climate Change* 10, no. 12 (2020): 1096–101.

Zhang, Zhihe, Yufei Hou, Zixuan Li, and Mulin Li. "From Symbolic to Substantive Green Innovation: How Does ESG Ratings Optimize

Corporate Green Innovation Structure." *Finance Research Letters* 63 (2024): 105401.

Zhao, Qi, Yuming Guo, Tingting Ye, Antonio Gasparrini, Shilu Tong, Ala Overcenco, Aleš Urban, Alexandra Schneider, Alireza Entezari, Ana Maria Vicedo-Cabrera, Antonella Zanobetti, Antonis Analitis, Ariana Zeka, Aurelio Tobias, Baltazar Nunes, Barrak Alahmad, Ben Armstrong, Bertil Forsberg, Shih-Chun Pan, Carmen Íñiguez, Caroline Ameling, César De la Cruz Valencia, Christofer Åström, Danny Houthuijs, Do Van Dung, Dominic Royé, Ene Indermitte, Eric Lavigne, Fatemeh Mayvaneh, Fiorella Acquaotta, Francesca de'Donato, Francesco Di Ruscio, Francesco Sera, Gabriel Carrasco-Escobar, Haidong Kan, Hans Orru, Ho Kim, Iulian-Horia Holobaca, Jan Kyselý, Joana Madureira, Joel Schwartz, Jouni J. K. Jaakkola, Klea Katsouyanni, Magali Hurtado Diaz, Martina S. Ragettli, Masahiro Hashizume, Mathilde Pascal, Micheline de Sousa Zanotti Stagliorio Coélho, Nicolás Valdés Ortega, Niilo Ryti, Noah Scovronick, Paola Michelozzi, Patricia Matus Correa, Patrick Goodman, Paulo Hilario Nascimento Saldiva, Rosana Abrutzky, Samuel Osorio, Shilpa Rao, Simona Fratianni, Tran Ngoc Dang, Valentina Colistro, Veronika Huber, Whanhee Lee, Xerxes Seposo, Yasushi Honda, Yue Leon Guo, Michelle L. Bell, and Shanshan Li. "Global, Regional, and National Burden of Mortality Associated with Non-Optimal Ambient Temperatures from 2000 to 2019: A Three-Stage Modelling Study." *The Lancet Planetary Health* 5, no. 7 (2021): e415–25.

Zheng, Yu. "Credibility and Flexibility: Political Institutions, Governance, and Foreign Direct Investment." *International Interactions* 37, no. 3 (2011): 293–319.

Zhou, Peng, Frank M. Song, and Xiaoqi Huang. "Environmental Regulations and Firms' Green Innovations: Transforming Pressure into Incentives." *International Review of Financial Analysis* 86 (2023): 102504.

Zhu, Yixiang, Cheng He, Michelle Bell, Yuqiang Zhang, Zafar Fatmi, Ying Zhang, Maryam Zaid, Jovine Bachwendkizi, Cong Liu, Lu Zhou, Renjie Chen, and Haidong Kan. "Association of Ambient Temperature with the Prevalence of Intimate Partner Violence Among Partnered Women in Low- and Middle-Income South Asian Countries." *JAMA Psychiatry* 80, no. 9 (2023): 952–61.

Zraick, Karen. "Tyson Faces Lawsuit Over Labeling of 'Climate-Smart' Beef." *The New York Times*, September 18, 2024. https://nytimes.com/2024/09/18/climate/tyson-beef-climate-lawsuit.html.

Zürn, Michael, and Stefan Schäfer. "The Paradox of Climate Engineering." *Global Policy* 4, no. 3 (2013): 266–77.

Index

Printed in the United Kingdom by TJ Clays Ltd.